Rimba

RIMBAUD

WALLACE FOWLIE

Phoenix Books
THE UNIVERSITY OF CHICAGO PRESS
Chicago & London

ACKNOWLEDGMENTS

This present study is a rewriting of two earlier books. The first, *Rimbaud: The Myth of Childhood*, required a total revision in the light of recent discoveries concerning Rimbaud's life. The second, *Rimbaud's Illuminations*, more purely literary criticism, has been altered very little. I am grateful to James Laughlin, of New Directions, and Barney Rosset, of Grove Press, for their permission to publish this revised study. The frontispiece is a portrait of Rimbaud after a drawing by Marcoussis.

WALLACE FOWLIE

This book is also available in a clothbound edition from
THE UNIVERSITY OF CHICAGO PRESS

London; Grove Press, New York. The present edition © 1965 by The University of Chicago. All rights reserved. Published 1965. First Phoenix Edition 1967. Second Impression 1967. Printed in the United States of America

To Henry Miller

Contents

Part I

Biography

Seven-Year-Old Poets
1854–1869

CHARLEVILLE, named after its founder Charles de Gonzague, duke of Mantua, is a peaceful provincial town, through which flows the Meuse River. Its seventeenth-century houses have a quiet dignity. At its center the large square (*la place ducale*) with its cobblestones and fountain and graceful arcades is early seventeenth century. Its population is bourgeois: merchants and industrialists; and the working class. Its twin city, Mézières, is older and prouder, more aristocratic with its citadel and ramparts, and hence was more vulnerable to the two invasions of 1870 and 1914. These two cities of the Ardennes, by their strategic position, close to Belgium, are at the head of the invasion roads into France.

In the middle of the nineteenth century, the Forty-seventh Regiment was garrisoned at Mézières. One evening every week the band gave a concert in the square in Charleville, referred to today as *le square de la gare*. It was the principal entertainment of the week for all ages of the population. One summer in 1852, Captain Frédéric Rimbaud, of the Forty-seventh Regiment, met, at the band concert, Vitalie Cuif. They were married on February 8, 1853.

Captain Rimbaud was thirty-eight when he first met Vitalie Cuif. He was born in the province of La Franche–Comté and had followed a military career from an early age. He loved the adventures the army afforded him. His regiment had participated in the conquest of Algeria. In Algeria, at Sebdou, he served in the administrative part of the army because of his skill in writing and the clarity of his reports. Writing was a passion for him. It is known he left several works in manuscript that have never been found. He returned to France in 1847, and his regiment was assigned to the Ardennes.

Prior to her marriage with this captain, Vitalie Cuif had led a difficult life. Her mother had died when she was five. Her father had a small farm in Roche, near Attigny. As she grew into young womanhood, she had to assume responsibility of running the house and farm. Her brothers, lazy by nature and given to heavy drinking, were additional charges for her. It is not to be wondered that with such a background she developed a love for work, a habit of thrift, devout religious habits, and a tendency toward authoritarianism. In 1852, Vitalie was living with her father in the center of Charleville, at 14, Rue Thiers, in a small apartment over a bookstore.

Captain Rimbaud lived with his wife only intermittently when on leave from his regiment. Their first child, Frédéric, was born in November, 1853. The following year, on October 20, at six in the morning, Arthur was born. He was baptized on November 20 in the church of Notre-Dame de Charleville. A third child, a girl, died three months after her birth in 1857. A second daughter, Vitalie, was born in 1858. The last of the five children, Isabelle, was born in 1860. With her four children, Mme Rimbaud moved to a more densely populated neighborhood, at 73, Rue Bourbon. Captain Rimbaud made a few attempts to live with his family, but quarrels between him and Vitalie were frequent. In August, 1860, the captain joined his regiment in Cambrai, and from that time on nothing further was heard from him by the family. Mme Rimbaud suffered from this desertion, but resolutely devoted her life to the education and the training of her children.

During the two years when the family lived on the Rue Bourbon, the two young boys Frédéric and Arthur, in their efforts to play with other small boys of the neighborhood, instituted a family drama which is the theme of one of Rimbaud's most brilliant poems, *Les Poètes de sept ans*. Mme Rimbaud is presented as the stern mother forbidding her sons from playing with other boys. Outwardly Arthur is the obedient child:

> *Tout le jour il suait d'obéissance*

but this hypocrisy encouraged the most serious of inner disobediences. The poem is especially harsh toward the mother whose severity and whose demands were responsible for the soul of her son given over to hate.

> *L'âme de son enfant livrée aux répugnances.*

Arthur tried to escape from her by hiding in the latrine, but she called him back. He tried to escape by playing with other children in the garden, but she sent them away. The boy learned to escape maternal domination only in his thoughts, only in his mind. The final image of the poem about this seven-year-old poet, recalled so lucidly by the real poet of fifteen years, is the image of the boy alone in his room stretching himself out on pieces of canvas. His physical contact with the canvas could evoke the sails of great ships and prophesy to a child's imagination the real departures of free men:

> couché sur des pièces de toile
> Ecrue, et pressentant violemment la voile!

This poem (which Izambard affirms was written in Douai in September or October, 1870, just when Rimbaud was turning sixteen) is clearly autobiographical. It is, moreover, the first of the major poems. In it he evokes his solitude at the age of seven, the awakening of his sexual instinct, and the awakening of his poet's imagination. The Mother, capitalized in the opening line (*Et la Mère*), summarizes all the forces controlling the boy. She has caused him to turn away from God (*Il n'aimait pas Dieu*) and to prefer workmen, dressed in their heavy jackets. Arthur's childhood was a revolt against a single enemy: his mother. He had to learn all forms of violence in order to resist her and play adequately the role of bad boy which she had imposed upon him. Like most children, Arthur had a purity and tenderness which he tried vainly to offer. He had to learn how to improvise and enact impurity and to cultivate his hate. He had to forge a mask that would conceal all his unused tenderness. He condemned and cursed the affectionate part of his nature in a voluntary exercise of schizophrenia.

Some of the meaning of Rimbaud's work is in the prevaricating mask he had to wear at the age of seven. The effort that Rimbaud was to make somewhat later toward the creation of a language was similar to the effort he made at the age of seven toward the creation of a being that was not he. At the age of seven, a boy does not create poetry, but he may create a life which is as symbolic and as meta-phorical as true poetry. Children often invent misdemean-ors to commit in order to legitimatize the title that adults have given them of punishable children.

The modern story of Rimbaud resembles in some ways the mythical story of Achilles, raised by women and forced even to wear a girl's dress, who did not fail later to ac-complish his destiny of warrior. The boy from Charleville, not having known the affection of woman during his first years, exploited during the three years of his poet's life the richness of a tender, sensitive heart. The Greek boy, having known only feminine sweetness during his first years, ex-ploited during his years of a soldier the heroism of a soul born for the most ferocious combat. The femininity of Achilles is similar to the feigned fury of young Rimbaud.

The seven-year-old poet, lying on the pieces of canvas in his bare room with drawn blinds, experienced the most exotic sea voyages and thus performed a rite of the imagi-nation. Nijinsky, at the end of *L'Après-Midi d'un faune,* performed the same gesture as he lay down on the veil of the last nymph to escape. The faun did not know whether he had dreamed the nymphs or not. Rimbaud, when he became a visionary and a poet, did not know whether he had been the unhappy child of his poem, *Les Poètes de sept ans.* This poem tells us how vainly young Arthur had loved small urchins of his own age, how ideally he had loved the laborers he watched returning home at nightfall, how sensuously he had fought with a young girl. These are the child memories of love that Rimbaud described. They are ephemeral and grotesque.

In 1862, Mme Rimbaud moved to an apartment on the Cours d'Orléans, No. 13, a principal street connecting Charleville with Mézières. About this time she began informing people that she was a widow. For three years, 1862–65, Arthur attended the Institution Rossat in Charleville, and began studying at the Collège de Charleville in the spring of 1865. In October, he entered *la sixième classe* where his good performance as a pupil began to attract the attention of his teachers. Arthur and his brother made their first communion in 1866, in the new parish church. The famous photograph, taken on this occasion, shows Frédéric standing and Arthur seated with a thoughtful and yet slightly surly expression on his face. Before the end of the year, the family again moved, this time to 20, Rue Forest in the neighborhood where the railroad station was to be built.

In October, 1867, on the recommendation of the collège principal, Arthur skipped *la cinquième* and entered *la quatrième classe*. M. Pérette was the teacher. He was elderly, strict, and given to fits of anger. He recognized Arthur's intelligence but predicted a bad ending. The principal was convinced he had some kind of genius in his school, either evil or good. *Rien de banal,* he once said, *ne germera dans cette tête, ce sera le génie du Mal ou celui du Bien.* This was the most pious moment in Rimbaud's life and so markedly that he was called by other pupils "a dirty bigot" (*sale petit cagot*). Louis Pierquin, who had been one of the pupils, evokes in his *Souvenirs* the picture, so often described, of the Rimbaud family going to eleven o'clock mass on Sunday. Leading the way, the two girls, Vitalie and Isabelle, hand in hand; in the second line, Frédéric and Arthur, also hand in hand, and each holding a blue cotton umbrella; closing the march, Mme Rimbaud, at the correct regimental distance.

Ernest Delahaye, who many years later will write three books on Rimbaud, was a pupil from Mézières attending the Collège de Charleville in 1867. He first knew Frédéric and then became a friend of Arthur during *la classe de troisième* (1867–68). Delahaye was the one close friend of Rimbaud during his school years. Arthur was already writing poems. To celebrate the first communion of the son of Napoleon III, he wrote an ode in Latin and sent it to the imperial prince. This was the first of a series of literary gestures by which Rimbaud tried to call attention to himself and to his talent as a poet.

He was reading all the poetry he could find, and especially *Le Parnasse contemporain,* a monthly publication which had begun in 1866, and in which he read the poems of Hérédia, Coppée, Gautier, Banville, Verlaine. In the *classe de seconde* (1868–69), the teacher was a young *licencié,* Duprez, a man of considerable finesse and sensibility whom Rimbaud was determined to captivate. The class that year was difficult to manage because of the presence of a group of seminarians, somewhat older than the others. The regular students and the future priests fell into two opposing factions, and Rimbaud, because of the success of his French and Latin compositions, four of which were published in the *Moniteur de l'enseignement secondaire,* easily became the leader of the lay group. The end of the school year (*la distribution des prix* in August, 1869) brought to Rimbaud a scholastic triumph that had never been known, when he was awarded nine first prizes!

Rimbaud turned fifteen in October, 1869. Until that time he seems to have been a docile boy, a pious and studious child. But his mother, a proud woman of limited intelligence, had closed her son off from the universe and isolated him in feelings of rebellion and hate. At other times Rimbaud wore the mask of rebel whose scatological images blasphemed. He was a boy of two countenances.

2

The First Escapes (Mémoire) 1870

IN JANUARY, 1870, Georges Izambard, a *licencié*, aged twenty-two, was appointed to teach Rimbaud's *classe de rhétorique* at the Collège de Charleville. He came from Douai, in northern France, where he had been brought up by three elderly maiden ladies, the Gindre sisters, distant relatives of his family. He was a poet in his own right. Rimbaud was determined to impress the young teacher by class performance and worked harder than ever on his writing. Izambard was amazed by the gifts and the accomplishments of his pupil. An intimate friendship soon developed between them. After class they took long walks together and carried on conversations on poets and poetry. The experience was new for Rimbaud. He felt himself considered a poet by a man who believed in poetry, and who lent him copies of Lucretius, Hugo, and Banville.

Respect, gratitude, and affection were all parts of the sentiment which the young pupil felt for the young teacher. St. Augustine noted in his *Confessions* a similar experience when, in Milan, he met Ambrose and began to love him (*Et eum amare coepi.* V. 13, 23). And Dante also, in *The Divine Comedy,* named his master, Brunetto Latini, for whom he had a profound affection. In that section of hell where he recognized his former teacher (*Siete voi, qui, ser Brunetto? Inf.* XV, 30), he pays homage to the Florentine: *Mi insegnavate come l'uom s'eterna.* There is in this short phrase, "You have taught me how man makes himself eternal," a key to the sentiment Rimbaud probably felt for Izambard: the prestige of letters. This prestige was a form of love to which he was to confide his heart and his innocence.

The first teacher to influence the life of a young artist replaces the father. Rimbaud had not known his real father and he sought, unconsciously perhaps, in the features of Izambard what James Joyce calls "the ghost of the unquiet father." In a brilliant passage in *Ulysses,* where Stephen Dedalus discusses his search for a father by evoking Hamlet, Joyce tells us that the Church is really founded on the Father and not on the Madonna.

Each month during the spring of 1870, Rimbaud read the poems of the Paris poets in *Le Parnasse contemporain.* In May he sent his first letter to Théodore de Banville and enclosed a long poem, *Credo in unam,* and two short poems, *Ophélie* and *Sensation.* Banville was the leading Parnassian. Some of the excitement of writing poetry for Rimbaud was the excitement over thoughts of having it published. He pleads with Banville to find a place for his poems in *Le Parnasse contemporain* so that he will appear in company with the acknowledged poets of the day. Most poets at the beginning of their career write such a letter: frank and servile in tone, a letter which is both homage to an older poet and claim for recognition. He ends his letter with the words: *Ambition! ô Folle!*

Banville replied that the remaining issues of the series were filled.

In addition to Delahaye and Izambard, Rimbaud had annexed a third friend during the spring of 1870: Auguste Bretagne, a bachelor, aged thirty-five, employed by a sugar factory in Charleville. He was a large man, gruff in outward manner, but sensitive to poetry and to Rimbaud's interest in it. He was a scoffer, a rebel against all forces of authority: parents, priests, teachers, administrators. In Bretagne, whom he met in cafés, Rimbaud found a jovial confirmation for attitudes that had already developed in him. Outwardly, at home and in school, Rimbaud was still, at the end of the school year, in July, submissive and well behaved. But it might be presumed that inwardly he was ready to sever all bonds.

On the 18th of July, Izambard informed Rimbaud that he had won first prize in Latin poetry at the Concours Académique—an event obscured on the following day when France declared war on Prussia. Charleville and Mézières were soon filled with soldiers, and the thoughts of everyone were on the preparations for war.

The Prussian invasion began, and Izambard left for Douai on July 24 to join the army. This separation—Rimbaud stood alone on the platform as the train pulled out—was a first experience of grief and loss. The early French victory of Sarrebrück, on August 2, raised the hopes of everyone. Frédéric and other boys left home to follow the army. On August 6, graduation day, Rimbaud was awarded seven first prizes, but this recognition of his merits hardly affected him. The summer stretched before him, empty without the companionship of Izambard.

In a letter to Izambard, written on the 25th of August, many elements of Rimbaud's relationship with his teacher are revealed. Rimbaud's life in Charleville had been made possible by the loan of Izambard's books, by the man's friendliness, and by his presence. Now, with his departure, the drabness of the provincial town was more apparent than ever. The bourgeois habits Rimbaud had grown to hate were exaggerated by the pompous military parades performed by men who were far from heroic. "It's a terrible picture," Rimbaud wrote, "to see retired grocers putting on their uniforms again" (*C'est effrayant, les épiciers retraités qui revêtent l'uniforme*). His summer was consumed by alternating attacks of depression and fury. The postal service, because of the war, had stopped sending books to the bookstores. Gradually, the boy was stagnating in what he felt to be an exile: *on est exilé dans sa patrie.* His favorite retreat was Izambard's room in Charleville, to which he had the key. He read all the books in the teacher's small library. By the end of August one escape remained: a real escape.

Four days after writing the letter to Izambard, on the 29th of August, Rimbaud boarded the train for Givet in Belgium. His plan was to change at Charleroi and there take the Brussels-Paris express. His plan worked, but his limited resources prevented his buying a through ticket to Paris. He was seized at the Gare du Nord and put in the prison of Mazas, on the Boulevard Diderot. From there he wrote to his mother, to the chief of police in Charleville, and to Izambard. The tone of the last letter is a command (*je vous l'ordonne*) and almost a cajolery as well. He wrote that he has loved Izambard as a brother and now is ready to love him as a father. Immediately Izambard wrote to the governor of the prison and begged for the boy's release.

He enclosed money for the return train fare. Rimbaud
chose to return home by way of Douai where he stayed
with Izambard and the Gindre sisters between approximately the 8th and 28th of September. In his poem, *Les
Chercheuses de poux,* the "two charming sisters" who de-
loused the child are doubtless a memory of the maternal
care given to Rimbaud in Douai by les demoiselles Gindre.
Izambard has written an account of the days Rimbaud
spent with him in Douai, of the seriousness with which the
adolescent poet copied his poems to show them to Paul
Demeny, a friend of Izambard in Douai, who was a poet
and just a few years older than Izambard. This was probably the moment when Rimbaud wrote *Les Poètes de sept
ans.*

At the insistence of Rimbaud, Izambard brought the
boy home at the end of September. She welcomed her son
with a slap and called Izambard an accomplice to the
boy's unseemly behavior.

To offset the boredom of Charleville, Rimbaud renewed
his friendship with Ernest Delahaye in Mézières. He felt
at ease with Delahaye, whose mother, proprietress of a
grocery store, welcomed young Rimbaud. The poet's second flight from Charleville took place on October 7 when
he again took the train in the direction of Givet. He
stopped at various places on the way to Charleroi, where
he asked the director of the newspaper, *Journal de Charleroi,* for an editorial position. Rimbaud reached Brussels
on this trip, where he was welcomed and lodged by a
friend of Izambard. On his way home, he stopped for the
second time at Douai. This was the last time Izambard
saw Rimbaud. Mme Rimbaud had written and insisted
that the boy be sent home by the police.

From Charleville, Rimbaud wrote to Izambard at Douai. His letter of November 2 speaks of his unrest and boredom: *Je meurs, je me décompose dans la platitude.* His two escapes of 1870, the first to Paris and Douai, and the second to Brussels and Douai, testified to all he loathed in Charleville. In his letter he speaks of his affection for Izambard and his desire to make something of himself in order better to merit this friendship. Working hard at his verse and becoming a poet would be one way of expressing his gratitude. He realizes this determination involves some naïve egoism, and he justifiably signs his letter, *ce sans cœur de Rimbaud.*

In this pupil-teacher relationship, Rimbaud gave some expression to docility and gratitude. For approximately nine months Georges Izambard strongly influenced Rimbaud's life. During the same months deep dissatisfactions with bourgeois security were growing in the boy. In his poem *A la musique,* where he describes the military band playing in the park of Charleville and the public of obese, retired dignitaries, he captures something of the placid, dull atmosphere against which he was revolting. During the same months, the insistency of sexual desire was beginning to be felt. His poem *Roman* described the familiar stalking of girls under the linden trees and the lust aroused in him by the spectacle of bare flesh. Delahaye, one of his most intimate friends of this period, claims there was no trace whatsoever of homosexual interests in Rimbaud's speech and behavior. Izambard had been able to channel the boy's attention toward poetic activity and literary ambition. Rimbaud's relationship with Izambard, as long as it lasted, was honorable. It was an even compound of affection and admiration that filled a few months in his life.

He repudiated his mother's discipline and accepted the fraternal advice of his teacher, until the moment when, in 1871, he turned toward the lurid horizon and literary attractions of Paris.

Mémoire

This controversial poem describes, according to Paterne Berrichon, the poet's brother-in-law, Rimbaud's first flight to Paris on the 29th of August, 1870. This biographical interpretation has been accepted by the critics Rolland de Renéville and Ruchon. Marcel Coulon believes the poem describes the departure of Rimbaud's father in August, 1864. The woman in the poem would be then Mme Rimbaud. Etiemble and Gauclère disapprove of adhering to any one biographical explanation. Delahaye, in pointing out the river as feminine, calls attention to the importance of the element of water. The Meuse River is the starting point in *Mémoire,* and the poem is on the theme of flight. The scene may well be the *prairie* separating Charleville from Mézières. The Meuse crosses this *prairie,* and perpendicular to it, the railroad tracks stretch out in the direction of Paris. *Mémoire* is essentially a poem of sensations and of episodes that are suggestively recalled and remembered. Each sensation evokes another, and the poem grows, as a river does, by accumulating reflections: flashes of light and objects, some of which are real and some of which grow out of unusual juxtapositions.

Mémoire is composed of five sections. Each section, of eight lines, is a rapidly sketched picture of the *prairie* and the river. The opening words of the first section, *L'eau claire,* designate the protagonist. The river water, as bitter as the salt tears of a child, seem first to be dominated by the white bodies of the women bathing in it in the sunlight. They resemble white angels as they play in the water, their clothes on the bank. The picture is like a canvas of Cézanne where the bathers are no more important than the river or the sky or the green fields. The image is interrupted by the poet with a negative exclamation: *non!* The river, *Elle, sombre,* dominates the scene and pulls down from the surrounding hills shadows for curtains. The river in its bed, like the persistent symbol of woman, expels the real and fleshly women, and recaptures the center of the picture.

In the second section, a series of words: *couches, robes, foi conjugale,* precede and announce the new protagonist: the wife, *l'Epouse.* She dominates the sun scene. It is noon, when the sun warms the earth. The spouse is like the river reflecting perfectly the rosy sphere of the sun. Everything in the two stanzas designates the roundness of woman's sex: the golden louis, the warm eyelid, the mirror, and the rosy sphere that is the reflection of the sun on the water as well as the sun itself. Woman as spouse is the second character in *Mémoire,* the waiting fidelity, round and warm in her flesh, as the river Meuse is the mirror of the sun. The river flower, *le souci d'eau,* is a marsh marigold, although Delahaye looks upon it as a *nénufar* (waterlily).

The third section is more dramatically concerned with a protagonist-mother. This is the *prairie* scene where the mother (*Madame*), too erect, crushes the flowers as she walks, and where the children, too obedient to her will, read, as they sit on the grass, their leather-bound prize books. Even in the freedom of the fields, the family severity is not lessened. Suddenly one of the group, either a boy or a man, either son or husband, containing in himself the whiteness of a thousand angels—all the purity visible in the white bodies of women bathing and workmen in the fields—leaves and goes off beyond the mountain, beyond the scene of false freedom. The mother (or wife), black and cold as the river, rushes after the one who is fleeing. It is a silent scene, where, as in a dance, only the actions count, only the movements of rushing off, in order to escape or retrieve. Woman here is matriarch, black in her dress against the flowers and the grass of the *prairie,* black in her chase after the white angel, as the river is black against the earth's body.

By contrast with the violent third movement, the fourth reflects a nostalgic mood. The woman who has now been abandoned would seem to be no longer the mother but the mistress. Her memories are sensual: the arms that held her, the April moonlight on her bed, the germination of August nights. She is alone to weep and listen to the wind in the poplar trees and watch the labors of an old boatman in his motionless boat. The *chantiers* alluded to did once exist in Charleville, where the river sand was sifted. The image of the boatman is the most fully developed in the poem. It closes this section and fills the fifth.

After evoking the picture of a man dredging the river bed for sand, the poet, in the final tableau, speaks directly for the first time. He is a second character because in the fifth episode the protagonist seems to be the boat immobilized on the water by its chain. The boy is in the boat, and he is presented as being frustrated in each of his desires. The boat is too firmly attached, and his arms are too short for him to pull from the water either flower which tempts him—the yellow or blue. The roses (or the flower) of the water reeds were devoured long ago (possibly by the descent of night), and the chain of the boat is buried in the mud of the river bed. Delahaye believes this episode is a reminiscence of a boat on the Meuse in which Arthur and his brother played as boys. In *Mémoire* the boy is defeated in his efforts to retrieve some color of life and some symbol of freedom. The boat also is immobilized. But under the boat flows the freedom of the "clear water," an eye that sees limitlessly. Here the river, as in the opening stanza, is the protagonist and the boy is presented as trying to reach the river and plunge into the recesses of the eye that is watching him.

The five characters of *Mémoire,* each of whom dominates one section: the water (*L'eau claire*), the spouse (*l'Epouse*), the mother (*Madame*), the mistress (*Qu'elle pleure*) and the river's eye (*cet œil d'eau*) are the same; and the poet, in each scene, is trying to understand his relation with nature: which is woman, which is everything that is not he, everything that is outside of him.

L'eau claire is the familiar recreation of his childhood landscapes. This is his contemplation of woman during which no desire destroys his love.

L'Epouse is the vision of the spouse jealous of the male who is so endowed with infidelity that she must possess him and hold within herself his maleness.

Madame is transcribed as a whirlwind of maternal tyranny, dark as a storm mustering its power in one corner of the world to rush after the white angel escaping. Either son or husband, it is the male escaping from the fleshly bondage of the female toward the lost innocence of his spirit.

"The abandoned mistress" (*Qu'elle pleure à présent*) recalls moments of passion and ecstasy. It would seem to be the memory of young womanhood submitting herself to the act of love and then being abandoned to the solitude of other nights.

Cet œil d'eau is the flowing life of the river, the continuing principle of life that man is unable to seize or arrest or comprehend.

No one element in this poem is explained or taught or emphasized. The poem is both primitive and extremely sophisticated in its acceptance of fate and physical frustration, religious in its awareness of mysteries that decide the drama of man at a terrifying distance from his physical body. In each of the scenes, it is possible to see a confusion of two dramas: Rimbaud's personal drama concerning his relationship with his mother; and the more universal drama of man's relationship with woman.

But *Mémoire* is no one experience at any one moment. It is the dream of the poet Rimbaud where in cinematographic procession all the characters of his life are merged into one—or into one eidolon of changing proportions but always of recognizable traits. A mother can play all kinds of roles for a child: a playmate, a teacher, an idol, a tyrant, the source of stories, of kisses, of warmth, of hostility. The variety of these roles dictates the fluid texture of *Mémoire* and the series of scenes, each one of which disappears as soon as it is formed.

The recapture of innocence is one of man's spiritual quests. *Mémoire* is a sequence of scenes in Rimbaud's remembrance of this quest where, always on the verge of reaching the realm of purity, he is at the final moment impeded by the principle of the material world, symbolized in its various aspects of river, of wife, of matriarch. The color of blackness and the sensation of frigidity are attributes of this character, and they are in opposition to man's search for his earliest simplicity. Every major poem by Rimbaud is the microcosm of his complete story. No moral, no commentary, no key can in any absolute sense be exhumed from the verses. It is the poem of flight where the boy is a solitary white angel of the spirit fleeing before all the black angels of the earth and the river.

3

Poetic Ambitions (*Le Bateau ivre*) 1871

Aᴄᴛᴇʀ ʙᴏᴍʙɪɴɢ Mézières the last day of 1870, the German army took possession of Charleville and Mézières in January, 1871. While the buildings of the *collège* were transformed into a military hospital, the municipal theatre in Charleville was used for classes, but Rimbaud, despite constant quarrels with his mother, refused to attend. By selling his silver watch, he was able to purchase a train ticket for Paris and left Charleville on February 25. It was a brief and painful visit to the capital. Most of the literary personalities he had hoped to see had left Paris. The German army paraded on the Champs-Elysées on March 1. A bookseller gave Rimbaud the address of the artist André Gill—89, Rue d'Enfer—but when he called, the studio was empty. When Gill returned, he found Rimbaud asleep on a couch. Irritated by the intrusion and Rimbaud's manner, the artist sent him off with a small sum of money. A few days after this, in early March, when he was penni-

less and suffering from both loneliness and hunger, the boy
made his way back to Charleville on foot. To imitate the
Parnassians, he let his hair grow long and brazened it out
with the youngsters of Charleville, who openly made fun
of him. There is a drawing of Ernest Delahaye showing
Rimbaud in Parnassian hair style.

The Paris Commune was proclaimed on the 18th of
March, and when the news reached Charleville a day or
two later, Rimbaud's elation, shared by Delahaye, was
based on the conviction that they were witnessing a turning point in the history of their country, that the masses
were rising up in order to insure freedom and justice. In
company with Delahaye, he carried on readings and literary conversations, and resolutely refused to return to
school when classes reopened in early April.

Exact details concerning Rimbaud's life during the rest
of April are difficult to ascertain. Two fairly reliable
sources, Delahaye and Fernand Gregh, relate that he went
to Paris, and lived for a while in one of the Paris barracks
(*la caserne de Babylone*). A fellow of his own age, Forain,
destined to become an excellent artist, was a companion
for Rimbaud during the days of the Commune. His life
in the barracks was an initiation to the toughness of the
soldiers and their obscenity. Rimbaud's poem *Le Cœur
volé*, first called *Le Cœur supplicié* and then *Le Cœur
du pitre*, is related, in the boldness of its imagery, to this
experience. The heart "stolen," the heart "tortured," and
the heart "of a clown," are the heart of a sixteen-year-old
boy subjected to scenes of extreme coarseness and possibly
of pederasty in the barracks. The poem, written in the
form of a triolet, of three stanzas, refers to the soldiers'
jokes, to obscene wall drawings, and to a violent physical
revulsion on the part of the poet.

May, 1871, was one of the most fertile months in Rimbaud's life when he probably wrote *Le Cœur volé*. It was also the month in which he wrote his two celebrated letters, one to Izambard (May 13) and the other to his friend Demeny (May 15), on the function of the poet. In these *Lettres du voyant*, he formulated a poetic credo of which *Le Bateau ivre* was to be the first successful illustration. In the letter to Izambard, it is obvious that the boy's feelings about his teacher were changing. The opening of the letter is an attack on the teaching profession, on the security of that vocation and on its sterility. The tone of the letter is distinctly disagreeable: *Vous revoilà professeur . . . vous finirez toujours comme un satisfait.*

In the second letter, two days later, to Paul Demeny, Rimbaud explains what he means by a *voyant* and proceeds to outline a manifesto or a program that will be followed by the major poets during the next sixty or seventy years. The activities he describes belong equally to aesthetics and to psychological behavior, and Rimbaud will be the first to carry out the program in his writings and in his life. The language of the letter, in its brilliance and in its boldness, is almost that of a deranged person. Both his mother and Ernest Delahaye believed that Rimbaud at this time was close to being subjected to a form of madness. He had become stridently antireligious. *Les Premières communions,* a poem written on the occasion of his sister Isabelle's first communion, testifies to the violence of his attacks on the Church. He was a nuisance for the venerable city librarian. In *Les Assis,* where he describes the library and the readers, he develops the tone of grotesquerie almost as if he were lashing back at his enemies.

Delahaye was a constant companion for Rimbaud throughout the summer when almost every scene in the streets of Charleville aroused his anger. The few sous given him by his mother to pay for his seat at Mass were not enough for his pipe tobacco, and he depended on the generosity of Delahaye and Bretagne. He was in debt for books bought on credit. On the 15th of August, he sent a long poem to Théodore de Banville, *Ce qu'on dit au poète à propos de fleurs,* which he signed Alcide Bava, and which was a satire on aspects of Banville's poetry. The Ardennes poet insinuates that the flowers, familiar to Banville's readers, are not worth more than a sea-bird's excrement.

Bretagne, on listening to Rimbaud's discouragement and disgruntledness at the end of the summer, suggested that the poet Paul Verlaine, whom he had once known, might be able to help. Eagerly Rimbaud accepted the suggestion, and had Delahaye copy out a few poems to accompany a long letter in which he expressed some of his literary ideals and several of his dissatisfactions with life in Charleville. When, after a few days of impatient waiting, no answer from Verlaine was received, Rimbaud composed a second letter of urgent supplication and enclosed in it further poems.

Before Verlaine's answer came, on the 9th of September, Rimbaud had begun the writing of *Le Bateau ivre,* destined to become his most famous poem. Verlaine's letter was cordial and enthusiastic. He asked for time to prepare Rimbaud's visit to Paris. The definitive invitation came soon after the middle of the month, with the fervent words: *Venez, chère grande âme, on vous appelle, on vous attend.* Included in the note was a money order to cover the expenses of the journey. The money had been collected from several poets. Before leaving Charleville, Rimbaud read *Le Bateau ivre* to Delahaye, and said goodbye to Bretagne and the others who had encouraged him with the assurance that he was going to dazzle the Paris literary world.

Rimbaud's first evening in Paris with Verlaine, who was twenty-six years old, was painful for all concerned. Verlaine and his wife Mathilde, who was to give birth to a son the following month, were living at 14, Rue Nicolet, in Montmartre, in the house of Mathilde's parents. M. Théodore Mauté was not in Paris that evening. Mme Mauté and her daughter, and another guest, Charles Cros, a poet and friend of Verlaine, made useless efforts to engage Rimbaud in conversation. The boy had grown tall and demonstrated the awkwardness of a suddenly increased stature. His hands were large and red. His face was tanned by the summer sun. His light brown hair was thick and unruly. An ironic smile distorted his sensuous lips. Everything marked Rimbaud as the provincial adolescent: his accent of the Ardennes, the insolence of his expression, his stubbornness in refusing to answer questions.

He was playing the role of an ill-mannered boy, and even of a *voyou,* in a home that had turned out to be much more bourgeois than he had expected. He had originally counted on some degree of spiritual intimacy and affection with Verlaine whose invitation would have been sufficient to inflame any ambitious boy-poet. The tone of Verlaine's sentence, *Venez, chère grande âme . . .* , must have still been in the boy's heart as he looked at the people around the dining table on that first evening: the pregnant wife, the mother-in-law, the doctor-poet Cros, and Verlaine himself who seemed subdued in the conventional atmosphere. Rimbaud's insolence and his silence came not only from his awkwardness and his provincial timidity. They were also a mask covering his disappointment at finding a poet he admired and whom he had wanted to seduce intellectually in a family setting he loathed because it was obviously the Paris equivalent of his family scenes in Charleville.

For a short time, the space of three or four weeks, Rimbaud became the center of interest of many Paris poets, of the Parnassians in particular, who gathered once a month at a banquet where they called themselves Les Vilains-Bonshommes (or Les Affreux-Bonshommes). Rimbaud was invited to the dinner at the beginning of October. After Verlaine introduced him, he read some of his poems, including *Le Bateau ivre*. A letter of Léon Valade, of October 5, gives a detailed account with personal impressions of this event. He calls Verlaine the inventor of Rimbaud and his John the Baptist on the Left Bank. He quotes another poet as describing the gathering by the phrase which will be used to establish one of the earliest "myths": "Jesus among the doctors." Valade tried to improve on this formula by changing it to "the devil among the doctors." At the end of the letter, the writer concludes that Rimbaud is a new genius: *c'est un génie qui se lève*. The majority of the Paris poets who saw Rimbaud during the last months of 1871 were less generous in their estimates. They were harsh in their criticism of his bad manners and convinced that the new direction he was giving French poetry was false. At best they granted him the brilliance of a momentary and passing star.

After a period of two to three weeks, Rimbaud left Verlaine's house. He accepted hospitality from others: from André Gill and Banville notably. By the middle of December, he was occupying a room which Verlaine had rented for him, on the Rue Campagne-Première, in Montparnasse.

Long before Rimbaud's arrival in September, matters had been going badly between Verlaine and his wife. The birth of a son on the 30th of October did not remedy the separation that was growing between them. Verlaine's habit of drinking had become excessive, and he had already experienced fits of delirium tremens during which he had struck his wife. The friendship between Verlaine and Rimbaud developed during the time they spent together in various cafés. From the beginning, Verlaine played the more sentimental, the more passive role in the relationship. The effect of Rimbaud's conversation was to incite Verlaine against all the stabilizing elements in his life.

In company with Forain, the eighteen-year-old artist he had met at the time of the Commune, Rimbaud visited the Louvre, but was bored with the display of famous paintings. The photographer Etienne Carjat, who was interested in poetry, made an excellent photograph of Rimbaud in October, just when the poet was turning seventeen.

One after the other, Rimbaud's possible friends and hosts turned against him. Only Verlaine was faithful in seeing him and helping him. When this became evident, insinuations and gossip about their relationship began to circulate. Verlaine's friend Edmond Lepelletier referred to it in a newspaper article in November, but neither Rimbaud nor Verlaine seemed affected.

A club of writers, called *Le Cercle Zutique,* was founded at the end of October, and held meetings in the Hôtel des Etrangers, on the Boulevard Saint-Michel. The musician Ernest Cabaner served as barman, and Rimbaud was assigned to him as a helper. A composite work, a collection of parodies and drawings, many of which are obscene, emerged from these jovial meetings: *Album dit Zutique.* The principal collaborators to the work, dated October

22–November 9, 1871, in addition to Rimbaud and Verlaine, are Germain Nouveau, Cros, André Gill, Jean Richepin, and Etienne Carjat. The songs about Rimbaud refer to him as the young genius from Charleville who is dying of hunger in Paris and who is advised to go home to his mother. In the poem, as was probably the case in real life, Rimbaud merely replies that he is waiting: *J'attends, j'attends, j'attends!* . . .

At the end of November, when Ernest Delahaye, on his first visit to Paris, looked up Rimbaud and found him at the Hôtel des Etrangers, he was surprised to find how much taller the boy had grown. In discussing his life with Delahaye, Rimbaud was scathing on the false intellectuality of Paris, on the stupidity and avariciousness he had come upon in the capital. The boy was changed and had grown bitterly disillusioned within a few months.

Le Bateau ivre

When Rimbaud wrote *Le Bateau ivre,* in Charleville, in August, 1871, he was sixteen. A poet's activity of a little over a year preceded the composition. He had written poems in Latin at the *collège,* and some of the phrases in the new poem echo a form of latinity that was part of the boy's linguistic background. In French he had written long and short poems that reveal Parnassian ancestry and imitation. In addition to the two major poems, *Le Cœur volé* and *Les Poètes de sept ans,* he had already written the two letters of May on the function of the poet. In these *Lettres du voyant,* he had advanced a poet's creed of which *Le Bateau ivre* was to be a significant illustration.

In Rimbaud's childhood experiences there was no large boat, no large river, and no ocean. There had been, however, a small boat on the Meuse. In the river, where it flowed near the *collège*, there was an island, and midway between the island and the shore floated a raft used by the workmen from the tanneries. A small boat for use of the tanners was attached to a spot near the shore by means of a long padlocked chain and iron stake. On the way home from school, Arthur and Frédéric often climbed into the boat, pushed it out into the river as far as the chain would permit, and, leaning first to the right and then to the left, would cause the boat to rock as in a storm. After this simulated violence, Arthur would lie down flat on his stomach and peer as far as he could into the depths of the river. To some imponderable degree, this often repeated scene on the Meuse plays its part in the storms and contemplative passages of *Le Bateau ivre*.

Rimbaud's experience as reader is also extremely important in the genesis of the long poem. No precise allusion to other works clutter *Le Bateau ivre*, but it does contain many literary reminiscences. Many of the images that find their way into his composition have recognizable literary sources, but they had been subjected to the boy's imagination and transformed by his personal experiences. *Le Bateau ivre* illustrates the creative process in art, which is inevitably a *re*-creation.

Chateaubriand and Victor Hugo, above all, seem to have stimulated the boy-poet. *Les Natchez* and *Atala* of Chateaubriand, with their scenes of torture perpetrated by Indians and their North American forest scenes, and the evocation of the sea in Hugo's *Travailleurs de la mer* are two sources of language and vision in the poem. James Fenimore Cooper's *La Prairie*, in its French translation, and Jules Verne's *Vingt Mille Lieues sous la mer*, were widely read by boys about 1870, and provided Rimbaud with images of prairies and of solitary figures sinking into the sea. Baudelaire's long poem *Le Voyage,* with its rich symbol of the sea, unquestionably left its mark on Rimbaud. The Latin phrase from Horace, *levior cortice (plus léger qu'un bouchon),* is not so important as biblical verses from Job, for example. Chapters 37 and 38 of Job abound in questions which the Hebrew visionary might have asked the poet of the Ardennes who had already defined his vocation as that of visionary: "Hast thou entered into the springs of the sea? or hast thou walked in the search of the depth?" And a few verses farther on: "Hast thou entered into the treasure of the snow? or hast thou seen the treasures of the hail?"

And yet the real introduction to *Le Bateau ivre* is Rimbaud's earlier poem, *Les Poètes de sept ans.* There we learn something of the mental activity and the psyche of the boy Rimbaud that finally are projected and crystallized in his art. There we learn something about his Bible readings, his dreary Sundays, and his revolt against maternal domination. But *Les Poètes de sept ans* especially concerns the successful adventures of Rimbaud's childhood, those of his imagination: the stories he invented about life (*les romans sur la vie*), the freedom seized from the world of the spirit (*la liberté ravie*), the litany of exotic lands (*forêts, soleils, rives, savanes*), the evocative power of pictures (*journaux illustrés*) and of fictional sailings (*couché sur des pièces de toiles*) that were able to convert prairies into sea billows (*la prairie amoureuse où des houles . . .*).

Le Bateau ivre is a complete intellectual and spiritual autobiography. All of Rimbaud's past is in it, as well as the general lines of his future. The genesis of the poem is quite literally the poet's life and the beginning of that activity of the human spirit where the temporal is found to be rooted in the eternal and when a day or a single dream is a lifetime.

The first five stanzas form the introduction and announce the major theme: liberation. The boat speaks and is obviously the symbol of the poet who in his drunkenness has discovered a release from the stable world of conventions. The first phase in the liberation is the disappearance of the haulers who were taken by Indians and nailed naked to colored stakes. This reference places the scene in North America, possibly on the Mississippi, where the natives crucify the foreign invaders. After losing its haulers, the boat loses its crew and its cargo. Henceforth it is able to follow its own will and feel the freedom of the river waters. It has a child's desire for the disorderly and the blatant, a desire that is a natural self-affirmation. There are no shore lights to direct its course through the domain of excitement and haste and fracas. The pure element of the water, limitless and powerful, penetrates the very being of the boat, and its taste is like that of hard apples to a child: the taste of danger and stolen booty. When a wave crashes over the deck, the last elements of direction and control are dispersed. Anchor and rudder are swept into the sea where they disappear. The liberation has been completed. The poem of the sea begins.

The second movement of the poem (stanzas 6–15) begins with the temporal statement: "From then on" (*Et dès lors*) and is a long listing of what the boat saw in its disordered, uncharted voyage. It resembles a litany, with the simple verbs introducing each stanza: *je sais, j'ai vu, j'ai rêvé, j'ai suivi, j'ai heurté, j'ai vu*. With the first verb (*je sais*) is affirmed the new knowledge of violence and peace, of the evening sky streaked with lightning and the dove-swarming sky of dawn. With the second verb (*j'ai vu*) is affirmed the vision of the setting sun when its rays stretch out across the water like long ceremonial figures of ancient actors. With the third verb (*j'ai rêvé*) is affirmed the dream of polar nights when light seems to mount from the snow as phosphorus rises from the ocean depths. With the fourth verb (*j'ai suivi*), the poet affirms the boat's quest for the unseizable power and the unseizable form of the ocean swell. The fifth and sixth verbs (*j'ai heurté*, *j'ai vu*) affirm the boat's collision with the mainland and the vision of sea monsters caught in the gulfs along the coastline. . . . This is the longest section of the poem, because it relates the boat's discovery of the universe: its splendor, its giganticism, its violence. Each experience leads to another in a search for sensation. The intoxication of the boat has transformed reality into a series of pictures more horrible and wondrous than those of ordinary dreams.

The third movement (stanzas 16–22) interrupts the violence and vision of the voyage, and serves as transition between the elaborateness of the second movement and the pathos of the concluding passage. Abruptly the boat becomes conscious of itself in the midst of its lurid experiences. In the midst of drunkenness there can be a pause for self-recognition and a feeling of horror. The limitless freedom of the boat has led it into an impasse. Freedom in excess may easily incarcerate a human spirit. At a high moment of its virile excitement, the boat instinctively draws within itself and feels itself to be a woman on her knees, quieted and humbled. This moment marks the beginning of a period of subjectivism and self-examination. In the presence of this woman, who is now a *bateau perdu*, drowned men sink silently into the sea, and the skies, rather than appearing as a ruddy goal to pierce, collapse over the boat. *Je regrette l'Europe* is the unexpected confession. The boat misses Europe and the land of its origins. Throughout the days and nights of the voyage, the vigor of the boat had been dormant. The visions had been imaginary and unreal. Behind the experiences of self-dispersal and indulgences, a boy had been quietly waiting for the excesses to spend themselves.

The final movement (stanzas 23–25) narrates the emergence from the tranquil source of the poet's being, of his real desire divested of his imagination. He evokes his return to the street puddle, known to him as a child, on which he once sailed a paper boat. This is the return to his origins and to his personal experiences. By means of the symbolic boat, he passed through the cosmic experience of drunkenness in order to will at the end a sinking into the sea of all his visions. The return to sobriety is in the simplicity and pathos of the mud puddle in a European street. *Le Bateau ivre* describes first the intoxication of the mind and the senses, and then it describes in the final image the intoxication of the heart which is always a knowledge of man's oneness with every part of his experience and the fervent awakening of his humility.

The literal meaning of the poem is thus concealed in the ornateness and preciosity of the symbol. The distance between the voyage of the drunken boat and the small boat at the end of a chain on the Meuse River in Charleville exemplifies the almost cosmic power of a symbol. In *Le Bateau ivre,* the experience of the poet seems to have no literal relation to the experience of the same man as citizen. Rimbaud's sentence in his letter to Izambard,

Je est un autre ("*I* is someone else"), corroborates this. The will to be a poet, a creative artist, is the real experience narrated in *Le Bateau ivre*.

The symbol of the boat is of such a nature that it suggests several interpretations or analogies. More than an allegory in the usual sense, *Le Bateau ivre* illustrates a transformation or a "derangement of the senses," when a river boat becomes a magical boat capable of the most excessive intoxications, as in his poem, *La Chevelure*, the hair of his mistress becomes for Baudelaire an ocean and a wilfully expanded universe. Even at the age of sixteen, Arthur Rimbaud seems to have known that the world is both man's fortune and his peril. To conquer the world inevitably involves a self-defeat. The forms which exaltation takes, the forms which imagination takes, are difficult to distinguish from pride. The voyage invented by the poet's imagination, if it were realized fully, would equate the experience of failure. This is possibly the moral meaning of *Le Bateau ivre* whose ultimate scene is not a triumphant vision but a humble and even bathetic scene of reality. The piercing beauty of the last image is that of humility. The quest is reached in the failure of an imaginary adventure and liberation.

In two passages, the word "love" is used in *Le Bateau ivre*. On both occasions it is associated with the sea, and the words used with it make the experience out to be a form of intoxication. The ocean is first seen to be that site where the bitter rednesses of love ferment: *Où / Fermentent les rousseurs amères de l'amour!* In the second passage, love is described as the bitter element that has caused the boat to swell with intoxicating torpor. *L'âcre amour m'a gonflé de torpeurs enivrantes.* The spiritual or anagogical meaning of *Le Bateau ivre* would seem to be in its prophetic quality, in the future destiny of the poet which seems to be implicit in the poem. The boy of sixteen sees himself already as the legendary character who, after traveling through distant countries, returns to the land of his race in order to die there. If love is the absolute experience for man, a poet's work, a poet's pretension are as incoherent as any other man's. A full knowledge of love implies an immobilization of the lover, far different from the restless motion of the drunken boat and the restlessness of the poet's subsequent voyages.

4

A Season in Hell
1872–1873

IN JANUARY, 1872, Fantin-Latour painted a group of
eight poets placed around a table. It was a large
painting called *Coin de Table* and commemorated one
of the gatherings of the Vilains-Bonshommes. Verlaine
and Rimbaud are included in the group. Earlier in the
month, in his studio on the Rues des Beaux-Arts, Fantin-
Latour had made a gouache study of Rimbaud's head.
The painting was exhibited in the May Salon and sold
to a young Englishman. Since 1911, it has belonged to the
collection of modern French painting in the Louvre.
During the past quarter of a century, the detail of Rimbaud's head has been widely reproduced as the typical
portrait of the youthful poet in the midst of the older
Paris poets.

During the month of January the marital situation of
Verlaine and Mathilde grew worse, and at the same time
irritation with Rimbaud's insolent behavior grew more

marked in the group of poets and artists he frequented. After a serious quarrel, Mathilde left Paris with her son for Périgueux, and Verlaine went to live with his mother. As a condition for her return the estranged wife demanded that Rimbaud be sent home. This was not done immediately, but by March the poet was back in Charleville. There he saw old friends, especially Delahaye, who observed in him more cynicism than ever, and an obvious desire to shock by relating, perhaps inventing the Paris vices he had known. It is highly possible that at this time in Charleville he began writing some of the prose poems which will eventually form the group of *Illuminations*. He received laconic letters from Forain and slangy, affectionate letters from Verlaine, letters which later were discovered and used by the Belgian police.

The reconciliation between Verlaine and Mathilde was temporary, and in May the quarrels between them were more violent than ever. Rimbaud returned to Paris in May and lived for a while in a garret on the Rue Monsieur-le-Prince. He renewed his friendship with Forain and with Jean Richepin who belonged to the Zutiste group. In June he was living in the Hôtel de Cluny, near the Sorbonne. In a letter written to Delahaye and dated Parmonde-Jumphe 72, he described his hatred of summer, his endless thirst, his memories of the rivers in the Ardennes and Belgium. He describes also the room he had occupied in Rue Monsieur-le-Prince and his habit of buying bread in the morning and eating it in his room. On the Rue Saint-Jacques, the shop of an absinthe distiller had become a meeting place for students, painters, poets, and street singers. Rimbaud was a habitué and by this time was a familiar figure to the students of the Latin Quarter. The theme of thirst and rivers is in the new poems of this

period: in *Comédie de la soif,* for example, and *Larme.*
The solitude of Rimbaud's life was more marked, and
his sense of hostility toward the world. Verlaine was working for an insurance company and could see Rimbaud only
in the evenings. Moreover, at this time, his life was rigor-
ously controlled by Mathilde and her father. By July,
Rimbaud, in a fit of boredom and despondency, told Verlaine that he was leaving and asked him to leave with him.

Together they set out for Brussels and made brief stops
on the way at Charleville and Charleroi. Once they had
settled in Brussels, Mathilde made an effort to join her
husband and bring him back with her to Paris. This effort in July failed. Verlaine's need for Rimbaud's companionship was too strong at this time, and he expressed
this need quite frankly in a letter to his wife. This marked
the beginning of the most dramatic year in the lives of
Verlaine and Rimbaud, a year that was to culminate on
the 10th of July, 1873, with the shooting scene in Brussels. It was a year of quarreling, of intellectual stimula-
tion, of spiritual unrest. Together the two poets found
excitement, but not peace. No pattern of harmony was
ever established between them because the world constantly intervened.

After exploring together parts of Belgium in August,
the two friends took the channel boat to Dover and the
train to London. This was in September. Verlaine called
on an old friend of his, Félix Régamey, the painter, who
did sketches of Verlaine and Rimbaud in London. Reminiscences of the English metropolis are in *Les Illuminations,* and in Verlaine's *Romances sans paroles.* The main
financial support came from Verlaine's mother. Meantime,
in Paris, divorce proceedings, instituted by Mathilde,
continued, and the dossier, as it formed, included accu-

sations concerning the nature of the friendship between the two men. This kind of accusation infuriated Rimbaud, who wrote to his mother about it. Mme Rimbaud went immediately to Paris to discuss the matter with Mathilde. No satisfaction resulted from this visit, and she was unable to recover the letters and manuscripts of her son which he claimed were in Verlaine's Paris house. These included *La Chasse spirituelle,* that had been destroyed, according to Verlaine, by Mathilde. Alarmed by the turn of events and by the failure of her mission, Mme Rimbaud insisted that her son return to Charleville. He did obey this time, but at the end of the year found his native town more depressing than ever, in comparison with the excitement of London.

In early January, 1873, a letter from Verlaine spoke of a persistent illness, of his loneliness in London, and of his need to see his friend. Unable to secure from his mother the necessary money for the trip, Rimbaud, through the intervention of Delahaye, received the means from Verlaine's mother. Both Rimbaud and Verlaine's mother, realizing the seriousness of Verlaine's illness, went to London and urged him to approach his wife and have the divorce proceedings canceled. In early April, Verlaine did leave for Paris with the intention of discussing this possibility with Mathilde and bringing about some form of reconciliation. But at the last minute he changed his mind and went to Belgium instead.

Meanwhile Rimbaud returned home. On Good Friday, April 11, 1873, he reached the farm at Roche where his mother and sisters and brother had been living for a few weeks. They were not expecting his arrival. Mme Rimbaud, profiting from the Easter vacation, was in Roche to supervise some repair work on the buildings of her farm

and to find a new man to run the farm for her. At first,
Rimbaud, who was not familiar with Roche, explored the
property and then isolated himself in the granary where
he worked seriously on a piece of writing that had been
on his mind for some time and on which he had possibly
worked already in London. It was a confessional kind of
writing, an effort to relate the drama of his childhood, to
explain his illusions by his distant Gallic ancestors, to
pierce the future with prophetic statements on his destiny,
to crystallize his research on the power of poetry, on the
alchemy of words. Without much doubt, it was at Roche,
in the *grenier* of his mother's farm, in April, 1873, that
Arthur Rimbaud wrote at least drafts of some of the important pages of *Une Saison en enfer.*

After the family returned to Charleville, Rimbaud
experienced the same constrictions as earlier, the same
difficulties he had always felt in cohabitation with his
mother. On Sundays, he met friends, Verlaine and
Delahaye in particular, in nearby towns, but during the
week he worked assiduously in the town library on the
new "stories," on *les petites histoires en prose,* as he
called them. In his letters dating from this period, he
complains of the drabness of Charleville and of his lack
of books. But he speaks of his need to finish the new
manuscript, the half dozen "terrible stories" (*histoires
atroces*) he still has to write.

At the end of May, Verlaine and Rimbaud again went
to London. Verlaine's health, at least temporarily, had
been restored, and his mother had returned to Arras. He
had decided to give up all attempts to stop the separation
proceedings. There seems to have been, at first, a com-
paratively peaceful moment in London in the relationship
between the two poets. Rimbaud continued to work on his

new writing, on what was to become *Une Saison en enfer*. Some of his time he spent reading in the British Museum. Both Verlaine and Rimbaud gave private lessons in French, as a means of self-support. Then gradually signs of irritability and quarrels began again. Rimbaud's attitude of insolence in public places was a source of embarrassment to Verlaine. Insinuations about their friendship grew more blatant and to such an extent that they were watched by the secret police.

A particularly violent quarrel between them took place on July 3. It is impossible to ascertain the real reason for the quarrel, but as a result of it, Verlaine left the house, followed by Rimbaud, and walked to St. Catherine's Docks where he embarked on a boat. Rimbaud was left alone and penniless in London. The next day he received a letter from Verlaine, written *en mer* announcing a definitive break, a determination never to see Rimbaud again. Rimbaud's answer derided his friend's decision. He analyzed pitilessly Verlaine's vacillatory temperament and made the strong point that he, Rimbaud, had been the leading factor in Verlaine's life.

Verlaine's letters from Brussels at this time, written to his friends, to his mother, and to Rimbaud's mother, all speak of his determination to end his life. He sent a similar message, both by letter and telegram to Mathilde. Once again, in this frantic moment of Verlaine's life, his mother rushed to him, to help him. On his decision to enlist and join the fighting in Spain, he sent a telegram to Rimbaud to come to the Hôtel Liégeois. Rimbaud did come to Brussels and reached the Hôtel Liégeois on the evening of July 9. After a day of discussion and controversy, Verlaine bought a revolver and fifty cartridges. When at one moment, Rimbaud declared he was leaving,

Verlaine, enraged, bolted the door of the room and shot twice at his friend. One bullet pierced the left wrist of Rimbaud and the other went into the wall.

Verlaine's mother was nearby, and she helped with the first bandaging. Then the three went to the Hôpital Saint-Jean where Rimbaud was cared for. Back at the hotel, the quarrel broke out again, at the end of which Verlaine finally consented to Rimbaud's leaving Brussels. But he insisted on accompanying Rimbaud to the station. While walking slightly ahead, Verlaine, emotionally over-wrought, suddenly turned about and again threatened his friend with the revolver. Rimbaud took to his heels and called out to a policeman for help. As a result of this street episode, the two men were taken to the police station. Rimbaud was soon released, in the company of Mme Verlaine. But Verlaine was confined to jail for violence and for the inflicting of the bullet wound.

As soon as the bullet was extracted from Rimbaud's wrist, July 17, he left the hospital. Immediately he filed with the judge a document withdrawing all complaint against Verlaine. But the investigations had gone too far for this document to be effective. Rimbaud rented a room over a *bureau de tabac,* probably on the Rue des Bouchers, and it was there that a twenty-year-old painter, Jef Ros-man, painted Rimbaud lying on his bed, covered with a red quilt. The painting, on which Rimbaud's suffering is quite visible, is a poignant document on the entire epi-sode and is today in the collection of the bibliophile Henri Matarasso. (The authenticity of this painting has been challenged; the subject may not be Rimbaud.)

On the 8th of August, Verlaine was condemned by the law court in Brussels to two years of prison and a fine of two hundred francs. The charge was attempted manslaughter. He remained in prison eighteen months. The beginning of his prison term coincided with Rimbaud's return to Roche where he resumed work on his writing. It was doubtless at this time that he changed the original titles of *Livre païen* or *Livre Nègre* to *Une Saison en enfer*. The Verlaine episode had undoubtedly furnished him with the subject matter of the chapter *La vierge folle et l'epoux infernal*. At the end of the work, Rimbaud inscribed the date: *avril-août 1873*.

A Brussels printer, Jacques Poot, whose address was 37, Rue aux Choux, agreed to print five hundred copies of *Une Saison en enfer*. The contract called for an advance payment and for the total cost when the copies would be ready. The advance payment was given by Mme Rimbaud when the manuscript was delivered to M. Poot, probably at the beginning of September. Verlaine had been transferred to the prison in Mons on the 25th of October, and it was approximately at that time that Rimbaud returned to Brussels to collect the author's copies of his work. He left at the prison office in Brussels Verlaine's copy, with the inscription: *A. P. Verlaine, A. Rimbaud*. (Verlaine was to bequeath the copy to his son.) The friendship between Rimbaud and Verlaine seems to have ended because of the strong emotional experience Verlaine underwent in Mons and because of his conversion to Catholicism.

Rimbaud gave a copy of the fifty-two-page booklet to Ernest Delahaye and sent some copies to Forain to be distributed among his friends in Paris. It is recorded in many books that Rimbaud burned the remaining copies of the edition, in a desire to make more complete his flight from literature. This incineration of *Une Saison* is a false legend. All the copies, except the few taken by Rimbaud himself, remained closeted at the printer's until

1901, when a Belgian bibliophile, Léon Losseau, discovered and purchased them. Rimbaud had been unable to pay the printing bill of the one book he had wanted to see published. Subsequently he may have forgotten about the existence of the copies in Belgium, but he did not attempt to destroy them.

When Rimbaud went to Paris in October, 1873, he was badly received by the poets and artists and blamed for the catastrophe of Verlaine's imprisonment. The scorn and coldness he felt in his former acquaintance in Paris, at a time when a few copies of *Une Saison en enfer* were circulating, disheartened Rimbaud and unquestionably impelled him to consider giving up literature. One meeting in Paris at this moment did count. At the Café Tabourey, Rimbaud was approached by a young poet from Provence, Germain Nouveau, who was twenty-two. They had already met at the Hôtel des Etrangers, at meetings of the Cercle Zutique, and had collaborated on the *Album,* and now their friendship must have developed swiftly because they were soon making plans to travel together around the world. What Rimbaud saw in late 1877 of the literary life in Paris disgusted him. He spent the winter in Roche where he destroyed the few copies he still had of *Une Saison* and various manuscripts. Copies of some of these were in the possession of Verlaine. This destructive gesture of Rimbaud was far more casual than Isabelle and Paterne Berrichon will one day interpret it as being.

It had been a momentous year. Neither Verlaine nor Rimbaud acknowledged the charge of homosexuality and vigorously repudiated the accusation. Verlaine's poem *Crimen amoris,* which will be published in *Jadis et Naguère* of 1884, is an image of his love for Rimbaud. The younger of the two adolescent demons described in the poem escapes from the festivity and cries out from the top of a tower: *Oh! je serai celui-là qui créera Dieu* ("I shall be the one to create God"). It is a spiritual portrait of Rimbaud by the man who knew him best: the portrait of a prodigy believing himself a creator in a divine sense. Briefly Rimbaud had become a godlike adolescent whose spirit was powerful enough to dominate men, and then leave them for other conquests.

Behind the quarrels, the scenes of drunkenness, the revolver shots, and the police trials, the meaning of Rimbaud's experience gradually emerges. He was seeking power and the use of power through the knowledge of immorality, of intoxication, and even of poetry. Rimbaud's portrait given by Verlaine in *Crimen amoris* is comparable to Lautréamont's *Maldoror* who makes of evil a way to knowledge. It is a Baudelairian pose, and one familiar to the romantic hero. Verlaine was at all times the man of velleities, uncertain of his sentiments and his projects for existence.

As a boy, Arthur Rimbaud's first escape had been to the wall of his mother's garden; his second, to the woods around Charleville; his third, to the roads leading north to Brussels and south to Paris; his fourth, to Paris itself. His escape to the cities, to Paris, Brussels, and London, was more complex. During the month of intermittent cohabitation with Verlaine, Rimbaud was possessed not so much by concupiscence as by the desire for knowledge and by poetic ambition. Whereas Verlaine was at all times ready for an unstable conversion to Catholicism, the kind which comes about from fear of immorality and from nostalgia for early pious devotions, Rimbaud showed himself to be of another temperament. He was resentful for not knowing the unknown. His pride was manifested not in the breaking of moral law but in the desire to know the power of the mind.

Verlaine was the more typical poet of the nineteenth century, the man of changing complexion who discovered a temporary equilibrium in his religious faith. But Rimbaud was the example of boy-poet-prophet who abandoned everything: his family, his country, his religion, his art. The story of Verlaine and Rimbaud in London and Brussels is one of the literal epics of our age, in which the myth of the modern artist is related. It is the same story recast fifty years later by James Joyce in the Dublin odyssey of Leopold Bloom and Stephen Dedalus. The two men, one older than the other, are really one man, and the dual search for love and knowledge is one search.

5

Europe
1874–1880

THE VOYAGE is one of the most persistent of literary themes. Homer's *Odyssey* in antiquity, Dante's *Divine Comedy* at the end of the Middle Ages, Rabelais' *Pantagruel* in the Renaissance, Baudelaire's *Voyage* in the nineteenth century, and the *Anabase* of St.-John Perse today are examples of the voyage-symbol. Even if the major modern novels of Kafka, Proust, and Joyce are static and voyageless, the modern poets, under the pervading influence of Baudelaire and Rimbaud, are constantly narrating a voyage in their work. St.-John Perse's *Anabase, Exil, Amers,* and *Chronique* are voyages, not literal in a geographical sense, but explorations of the spirit, moments filled with the action of progress and conquest.

Rimbaud's *Une Saison en enfer* (1873), Apollinaire's *Chanson du mal-aimé* (1913), Eliot's *Waste Land* (1922), and St.-John Perse's *Amers* (1958) are spaced like landmarks of the modern epic. They are voyages in the Baude-

lairian sense (*Le Voyage, Voyage à Cythère*) where the goal
is self-exploration and a quasi-mystical experience. The
means of accomplishing such a voyage is a derangement of
the senses, according to Rimbaud's formula: *Il s'agit d'ar-
river à l'inconnu par le dérèglement de tous les sens.* The
hero of the modern epic is not comparable to Ulysses or
Dante whose voyage was progress or home-coming or spiritual attainment. Today's epic hero is the artist whose
voyage is a way to self-knowledge. The modern poets
learned Baudelaire's lesson that exterior nature is a source
of symbols and a repertory of analogies. In the poetry of
Claudel and St.-John Perse, the exterior world of the ro-
mantics and the inner world of the symbolists are fused.
The beauty and the meaning of the exterior world are
spiritual.

Soon after Rimbaud gave up the writing of his personal
epic poetry, his life itself became an epic and he literally
lived the voyages and the flights he had written about as the
voyages of his memory and his imagination. The years between 1874 and 1880 were spent in a series of attempted
flights.

Rimbaud turned twenty in 1874. In March of that year,
he was in London with Germain Nouveau. The two
friends had left Paris that spring, in accordance with their
earlier agreement to travel together. They occupied a
room on Stamford Street. How they supported themselves
is not known. Nouveau published articles and poems, and
Rimbaud worked on new and old prose poems destined
to become *Les Illuminations.* Abruptly, in June, Germain
Nouveau left Rimbaud and returned to Paris. There had
been no trace of sexual intimacy in their relationship, but
Nouveau may have been worried that gossip would begin.

Rimbaud, depressed by his solitude, called upon his

mother to join him in London. With her sixteen-year-old daughter Vitalie, she arrived on the 6th of July. Arthur guided them about London for a few days, but then left them to their own resources and resumed study in the British Museum. Many details of this month of July, 1874, are recorded in Vitalie's journal. Mother and daughter stayed on in London, without pleasure, hoping day by day that Arthur would find work.

According to Vitalie's entry on July 31, her brother left London that day, but it is not known where he went. In the Rimbaud Museum of Charleville, there is an advertisement in his handwriting asking for a position as a traveling companion and giving an address in Reading. This advertisement was printed in the *Times* of November 9, 1874. He was probably home in Charleville by Christmas. He may have returned to France because of military service, since he was now twenty. But he must have learned, once in Charleville, that his brother Frédéric's five-year military service released him from military service.

Verlaine left prison in January, 1875. He had hoped to live again with Mathilde, but a legal separation had been granted to her. He turned once again to Rimbaud, who had gone to Stuttgart in order to learn German. Delahaye provided Verlaine with Rimbaud's address, and he reached Stuttgart probably in early March. He showed Rimabud his new poems of religious inspiration, and Rimbaud may well have given Verlaine at this time the manuscript of *Les Illuminations*. At least in one letter to Delahaye, of March 5, Rimbaud showed scorn of Verlaine and expressed distrust for the sincerity of his friend's conversion. *Verlaine est arrivé ici l'autre jour, un chapelet aux pinces.* But soon Verlaine went to England to accept a position of French teacher at Stickney. The encounter at Stuttgart was the last time they saw one another. Rimbaud had been scathing in his remarks on Verlaine's religious attitude, and Verlaine, despite his tone of mockery in letters to Delahaye, continued for some time to hope for a resumption of his friendship with Rimbaud.

Rimbaud left Germany at the end of April. By train he got as far as Altdorf in Switzerland, and then continued on foot to Milan which he reached in a state of exhaustion. He was totally without funds. Both Germain Nouveau and Delahaye knew of the movements of Rimbaud in Milan, and in their letters spoke of his living with an Italian widow, a cultivated Francophile, who helped him and nursed him back to health. Rimbaud left Milan after a brief sojourn there. On the road between Leghorn and Siena, he suffered a sunstroke. He was hospitalized and repatriated to Marseilles by the French consul in Leghorn. Delahaye, in his letters to Verlaine at this time, speaks of Rimbaud's desire to join the Carlist troops in Spain. Efforts on the part of Delahaye were obviously being made to bring about a reconciliation between Verlaine and Rimbaud, but to no avail.

In July, Rimbaud was back in Paris where he saw some of his former friends, including Forain. Thanks to Vitalie's journal, it is known that Mme Rimbaud and her two daughters came to Paris on July 14, 1875, to consult a specialist on the synovitis from which Vitalie had been suffering. For a time at least in that summer Rimbaud worked as a *répétiteur* in the town of Maisons-Alfort, near Paris. Both Delahaye and Nouveau took positions in schools in October, Delahaye in Soissons as *répétiteur,* and Nouveau as *surveillant* in Charleville. Nouveau seems to have been discharged almost immediately.

Rimbaud returned to Charleville on the 6th of October.

Delahaye joined him there in November, and the two friends resumed their walks together. Rimbaud was studying music, both solfeggio and the piano, and various languages, including Russian and Arabic. He isolated himself from everyone for long periods of work. At the end of the year, Verlaine made a final attempt to patch up the differences between them. He wrote a letter from Stickney in which he spoke of his new religious life and advised Rimbaud to return to his early faith. A few days after Rimbaud received this letter, his sister Vitalie died from synovitis. The year of 1875, which had been filled with so many events, ended with days of mourning for the young sister who had grown to look very much like her brother.

When, in February, 1876, Delahaye moved to Réthel to teach at the Collège de Notre-Dame, Rimbaud was again alone. With the coming of spring he too left Charleville, this time in the direction of Austria. A letter of Germain Nouveau in April establishes the date Rimbaud was in Vienna. He was robbed soon after reaching the Austrian capital. In order to survive, he became a street hawker but was soon apprehended by the police and expelled as a foreigner without money and without the necessary papers. He was escorted to the Bavarian frontier, and from there made his way on foot back to Charleville.

Unwilling to spend the summer in Charleville, he set out for Holland. In May, in Harderwijk, he signed up for three years in the Dutch colonial army. Many foreign mercenary soldiers were joining the army at this time. He was embarked on the ship "Prinz van Oranje" which left Holland on June 10. In July, when the ship stopped at Djakarta (once called Batavia), a port on the island of Java (Indonesia), he deserted. A few weeks later, at the end of August, he left from the port of Semarang (on the north coast of Java) on a Scottish sailing vessel. Because of a storm, the ship went off course, sailed close to Ireland, and reached Liverpool on December 17. Rimbaud was back in Charleville by the end of the month.

He spent another winter in Charleville where he resumed study of languages and music, and then again, in the spring of 1877, left the Ardennes. Briefly, in Cologne, he served as a recruiting agent for the Dutch army. In Bremen, in May, he made a request to join the American navy. There is one sentence in English in a letter Rimbaud wrote in Bremen: "Recently deserted from the 47th Regiment of the French Army." If this fact is true, it is startling because the 47th had been his father's regiment. This is pointed out by Matarasso and Petitfils in their *Vie d'Arthur Rimbaud*.

No reliable proof has come to light that Rimbaud was associated with the Loisset Circus in Sweden, although Delahaye mentions his drinking with a white bear, in a letter of August 6, 1877. The paucity of documents on this year makes it impossible to date Rimbaud's return to Charleville (although it was probably at the end of August), and impossible to ascertain the reasons for his return. In the fall, Mme Rimbaud was living in Saint-Laurent, a town near Mézières, and presumably Rimbaud was with her and engaged in studying languages and engineering sciences. He had grown more and more silent, more and more incommunicative. The drawings of his sister Isabelle, done at this time, show considerable physical change in Rimbaud. With the coming of winter, he went to Marseilles and set sail for Alexandria. He fell ill on the boat, and was put off at the Italian port of Civitavecchia. He returned to Roche where he spent the winter.

There are many suppositions concerning Rimbaud's activities and voyages during the spring of 1878, but none can be substantiated. According to a letter of Delahaye to Verlaine, he was seen in Paris, in the Latin Quarter, at Easter time. That summer Mme Rimbaud settled down for good in Roche, and Arthur presumably helped his brother Frédéric with the farm work and the harvesting. From Geneva, on November 17, he wrote a long letter to his mother, in which he describes his crossing the Saint Gotthard range in a snowstorm. This letter, from which an extract is printed in Matarasso's biography of Rimbaud is remarkable for its detailed description.

Once again, he sailed for Alexandria, which he reached on December 10. From there he traveled to the island of Cyprus, where he undertook work as an interpreter. He directed and helped a large group of workers in an isolated quarry. They were men from many countries: Arabs, Turks, Cypriots, Greeks, Syrians. There, despite the heat, Rimbaud found the climate and the simple life he wanted. He was fascinated by the various tongues of his rough companions, and enjoyed the beach for relaxation and the sea for swimming. After a few months of this work, which was to his liking, he fell ill with fever and returned to Roche in June, 1879. His employers in Cyprus, Jean et Thial fils, wrote a good letter of recommendation and praised his loyal services. At home, his illness was diagnosed as typhoid fever. There he spent the summer in a family atmosphere.

Ernest Delahaye, who visited him in September, had not seen Rimbaud for two years, and wrote about the shock of finding his friend so changed: his rosy, boyish complexion had disappeared. His skin now was dark. Rimbaud spoke easily to him of his life of the past two years and of his plans to return to a warm climate. He was proud of the recommendation of his recent employers, and intended to return to Alexandria from where it was easy to secure work. Delahaye asked him if he ever thought now of literature. Rimbaud's answer was scornfully negative. *Je ne m'occupe plus de ça.* This was the last time Delahaye and Rimbaud were together.

The winter was difficult. Rimbaud tried again to leave the country, but fell ill in Marseilles with the same persistent fever and retreated to Roche where he suffered from the extreme cold. When he left in March, 1880, he repeated the itinerary of the year before: Alexandria and Cyprus. This time his work in Cyprus was more difficult, and he abruptly left the island in July, 1880. On the governor's palace on Cyprus, a commemorative plaque bears Rimbaud's name and the slightly erroneous date of 1879.

The two visits to Cyprus marked the end of Rimbaud's early wanderings. In October, 1879, he was twenty-five. Those who saw him at that time remarked on the fire in his eyes and the animation of his spirit that prophesied longer and more determined flights.

6

Africa
1880–1891

WHEN RIMBAUD reached the continent of Africa, in the summer of 1880, he entered upon a period of ten years, the last years of his life, which he was to spend largely in Aden, on the southern tip of Arabia, and in Harar, in eastern Abyssinia. He was to leave this region only when death became imminent.

The extreme heat of Aden and the lack of drinking water turned him against the city, but he stayed on in August with the hope of finding lucrative work. In November he signed a contract for three years with the merchant Pierre Bardey, to work in an agency at Harar. He looked upon his new position as that of an explorer and organizer. For a long time he had dreamed of working among primitive peoples. He wrote to his mother to send him technical books on hydraulics and metallurgy, on masonry and mineralogy. Harar was an exciting discovery for him, when he reached it on December 10. He found it to be an Islamic

city, with very few white people. Almost immediately he
was struck by the poverty and filth of Harar. His letters of
January and February, 1881, are far from optimistic. He
feared the climate and illness as much as the lack of co-
operation from the Egyptians there and the surliness of the
natives. When, in March, Alfred Bardey, Pierre's brother,
came to take charge of the agency, he found an irritable,
sickly Rimbaud, who had grown despondent over not having received books and instruments he had ordered from
France. Rimbaud resigned from his work in September,
but actually did not leave the Bardey agency until December 15.

At the beginning of 1882, his letters, especially the one
to Delahaye on January 18, show Rimbaud's determination to be an explorer rather than a merchant. He planned
to write treatises for the Société de Géographie, and turned
to his friend to help him procure books and instruments.
He was in Aden through the first months of 1882 and
ceaselessly complained of the heat and discomforts. As soon
as a camera reached him, he sent pictures of himself and
his surroundings, from Harar (where he had returned in
the employ of the Bardey agency in March, 1883). By this
time, he looked more like a Greek than a Frenchman. In a
letter of May, 1883, he wrote especially of his loneliness,
of the foreign languages with which he had crammed his
mind, and of his wish that he might have a son to bring
up and educate and train as an engineer.

During 1884, he went on a dangerous expedition for his
employer, into the province of Ogaden which lies between
Somaliland and Harar. The detailed report he wrote, deal-
ing in particular with geography, ethnology, and econom-
ics, was published by the Société de Géographie in February, 1884, and noticed by geographers and specialists.

Warfare between the Egyptians and Moslems forced the closing of the Bardey establishment in Harar, and in April, 1884, Rimbaud returned to Aden, where he was praised and rewarded for his services of four years. He had been a good director, and his skill as writer had enabled him to draw up accurate and succinct reports.

At first, without work in Aden, although his contract continued until June, he complained of the boredom of his existence and the climate. He worried over the apparent impossibility of saving money and becoming rich. When the Bardey establishment was reorganized, he was hired again, for six months, to the end of 1884. Business conditions were poor in Aden, and Rimbaud had no alternative. Alfred Bardey and others have mentioned the fact that Rimbaud was living at this time with an Abyssinian girl he had brought with him from Harar.

Despite his disgust with the political role of England and France in Africa—this was true for most Europeans living there—Rimbaud decided, in January, 1885, to prolong his contract for a year. He was tempted in October to engage in the risky business of gun-running in Shoa. He broke with the Bardey brothers, who warned him about the perils of such an enterprise. His letter to his family on October 22 announced his decision.

At this time there were two contestants for power in Abyssinia: John, emperor of Ethiopia; and Menelik, king of Shoa. Rimbaud, believing he would become rich in a few years, engaged in the traffic of arms with King Menelik. He was directed by a Frenchman, Pierre Labatut, in whom he had confidence. After innumerable delays, he finally started out on an expedition through the territory of the savage Danakils. From Tadjoura, in January, 1886, he wrote that the road ahead was impassable. He was on the point of continuing the expedition in April, when he learned that the importing of arms had been forbidden.

This was the mere beginning of a series of disasters and hardships for Rimbaud during which he was cheated by the widow of Labatut (who himself died of cancer in September) and by King Menelik, whom he encountered, not in the capital of Ankober, but in the town of Antotto. A seasoned explorer, Jules Borelli, wrote in his journal of February 9, 1887, that Rimbaud suffered from every possible mishap: disloyalty of his men, dishonesty of his camel drivers, lack of water, intrigues and plottings against him. Borelli lauded Rimbaud's knowledge of languages, his dogged will power, and his patience.

As soon as Rimbaud realized that Menelik was going to cheat him as much as he dared, his one thought was to get back to Harar as fast as possible and salvage what could be salvaged. He set out on the first of May, accompanied by Jules Borelli. Both Borelli and Rimbaud have described this voyage, Borelli in his ornate style, and Rimbaud in the terse, unaffected style of a geographer. After Rimbaud was paid in Harar, he left for Aden, which he reached on July 25, 1887. In a letter to the French consul at Aden, on the 30th of July, he estimated that he had lost 60 per cent of his investment and had lived through twenty-one months of constant fatigue and harassment.

He decided abruptly to leave for Egypt and reached Cairo on August 19. In a letter home, written a few days after his arrival, he describes his hair as gray, and he laments his inability to adjust to the life of a city. He had been carrying in his belt his entire fortune: eight kilos of gold pieces, which in Cairo he deposited in an account at the Crédit Lyonnais. The report on his recent expedition was published in *Le Bosphore égyptien,* in the two issues of August 25 and 27, 1887.

Early in 1888, Rimbaud made another expedition to Harar, with a cargo of rifles. The merchandise was delivered and he was back in Aden within eleven days. (March 20–April 4). Then once again, and for the last time, in April, Rimbaud went to Harar as the representative of an Aden merchant, César Tian. This was a sojourn of three years, during which Rimbaud was on good terms with his employer, on better terms than he had ever been with the Bardey brothers. Except for a Catholic priest, he was the only Frenchman in Harar at that time. He led an active life, but became increasingly depressed by his solitude, by the absence of family life and of any intellectual life. He was reduced to silence because nothing in his life seemed noteworthy. However, he did carry on correspondence with Europeans who lived in Abyssinia or who visited there. He became a good friend of the priest in the missionary center, le père Jean, an intelligent man who became, in 1900, Monseigneur Jarosseau, bishop of Harar.

But Rimbaud was as unadaptable in Harar as he had been in Charleville. There is no doubt that he was esteemed and liked in Harar. On a few occasions, by men coming from France, he was told that his poems were being published in Paris and that attention was being paid to them. He seemed disgruntled and even disgusted that such a thing should happen.

These ten years in Rimbaud's life represented the triumph of the avaricious Ardennes peasant strain in him. He revealed, to a certain degree, the personality of his mother against whom he had revolted as a child and adolescent. The hundred letters that Rimbaud wrote to his family between the 17th of August, 1881 and the 30th of

April, 1891, are those of a hardheaded, practical business-man. There is no reminiscence in them of a poet's style or a poet's sensibility. They describe the existence of an employee determined to amass a fortune and thereby attain independence. It would seem that Rimbaud had appropriated the bourgeois virtue of security. He lived in an austere manner, he worked hard and uninterruptedly, and he saw very few people in a social sense during his foreign solitude. There is no indication that he was fascinated by the exoticism of Abyssinia. He remained the trader bent upon enriching himself, and in this he failed miserably. After ten years of labor and sweat in the intense Abyssinian heat, he had saved a derisively small sum of money.

At every period in his life, Rimbaud was an absolutist. As a child he was either the outstanding pupil or the out-and-out rebel. As an adolescent he was a poet in an absolute sense because he demanded everything of poetry. The same sin of pride explains his absolutism as a trader, a way of life into which he converted all his power, all the strong determination which had once made him a prize pupil, a rebel, a poet.

The last nine months of Rimbaud's life were a nightmare of suffering. The first time he mentioned in a letter to his family serious trouble with his right leg was on February 20, 1891. He calls his malady varicose veins and rheumatism. A more explicit description of his suffering is in a letter of July 15, when he describes the pain and the swelling of his knee. From March on, he had been unable to use his leg and directed his workers from a horizontal position. He lost weight rapidly. When he was certain the tumor on his knee was growing, he liquidated his affairs in Harar, at a great loss, and set out for Aden. For this painful journey, he had a litter constructed, according to his own drawing, and hired sixteen porters to carry him. He kept a journal during this trip, which lasted from April 7 to April 24. In the European hospital at Aden an English doctor advised him to return to France immediately for an operation. He settled his affairs with César Tian. On reaching Marseilles by boat, he entered the Hôpital de la Conception on May 20. His malady was diagnosed as a cancerous tumor. He was told that an amputation was necessary, and he wired his mother for her or Isabelle to come.

Mme Rimbaud arrived at the Marseilles hospital on the 23rd and helped her son to face the ordeal which took place on the 25th. The wound healed quickly, but Rimbaud was unable, during his convalescence, to shake off a sense of discouragement and failure and future misery. Mme Rimbaud had to leave Marseilles in early June. Before the month was over, another serious worry was added to Rimbaud's pitiful state of anguish. He learned from letters from Charleville that the military authorities were trying to find him for having avoided military service. Rather than telling the truth, Isabelle and her mother had claimed that Arthur was still in Arabia. In order finally to put an end to this worry, Rimbaud explained his case to the appropriate military official in Marseilles and asked for his release.

The letters exchanged between Isabelle and Arthur at this time are moving documents. He confided in her his deep dismay at being a cripple, his distrust of doctors, the ineffectiveness of crutches, and his inability to wear a wooden leg. Then, abruptly, in July, he decided to return to Roche. He left the hospital on the 23rd. Once back at

Roche, he was cared for by Isabelle with the utmost devotion. His physical and moral state grew increasingly desperate. The stump of his leg swelled, and the left leg became infected. He grew obsessed with the idea of returning to Marseilles, and from there, if he recovered, he would leave for Aden.

Rimbaud left Roche on the 23rd of August. Isabelle went with him. Her narration of the tragic journey is the only document of this period. Her brother's physical suffering was constant. There were endless delays and discomforts of all kinds. In Paris, he boarded the express to Marseilles. The joltings and movements of the train caused him uninterrupted agony. The doctors at Marseilles gave no hope for his recovery and claimed he could not last through the year. Rimbaud himself was not told this, and his spirit vacillated between hope and discouragement.

Isabelle refused to leave his side. He needed her more each day, and she spent each day with him, trying to ease his mind and give what comfort she could to his body. She prevented, for example, the madness he conceived, of sailing for Algiers or Aden. One of the drawings she made of her brother at this time shows Rimbaud standing. He is wearing on his head the patient's white skull cap (*la calotte*). His features show the intense suffering he had gone through. It is impossible to say whether there was any deep affection between Isabelle and Arthur. She was concerned over the physical suffering of her brother who had become a stranger to the family, but she was especially concerned over the suffering of his spirit. She wanted him to know, before his death, the help of the sacraments.

The only existing documents on the final weeks of Rimbaud's life are letters exchanged between Isabelle and her mother. The central theme of these letters is Arthur's deathbed conversion. Most objective students of the poet are convinced that this event and Rimbaud's final religious attitudes were grossly exaggerated by Isabelle. It seems probable that Rimbaud received the visit of a priest and made his confession. But what the real significance of these religious acts was for him will never be ascertained.

Isabelle was at his bedside when death came at ten in the morning of November 10, 1891. The death certificate called his illness generalized cancer (*carcinose généralisée*). Rimbaud's body was taken to Charleville where he was buried. The funeral service was a High Mass. Only the mother and the sister accompanied the coffin to the cemetery. Ten years later, in the square of Charleville, a monument to Rimbaud was unveiled. The statue was damaged twice, by the German invasions of 1914 and 1940.

Catholics, affected by Rimbaud's work, men like Claudel, Jacques Rivière, and Daniel-Rops, have interpreted much of the boy's poetry in the light of what they believed the man's religious conversion. It is impossible to judge the sincerity of Rimbaud's conversion, if indeed there was one. His poetry is not religious in the literal sense, as is Péguy's, or Claudel's, or Hopkins'. Whereas the religious problem is present in much of Rimbaud's work, it is unsolved and exists as a threat to secular peace or vision. Even if it is true, as in the version of Isabelle, that her brother at the end of his life came to the end of his journeys by accepting the religious faith of his early childhood, his art remains a poetic work of quest and flight, of blasphemy and prayer, of innocence and hell.

Part II

Poetry

The Example of Rimbaud

IN COMPARING Rimbaud's effect on French literature to that of a flashing meteor in the sky, Mallarmé created, among the earliest testimonials, one that is still provocative, even if it has been employed countless times since. Writing expressly for the American periodical, The *Chap-Book*, in a letter addressed to Harrison Rhodes in April, 1896, Mallarmé summarized his memories of Rimbaud, biographical far more than critical, but judicious and condensed in the rich style of his critical essays.[1] Only one meeting occurred between them, in June, 1872, at the monthly dinner of the literary club, Les Vilains-Bonshommes, probably held at the Hôtel Camoëns on the Rue Cassette in Paris. The older man was thirty, and the adolescent from Charleville was barely eighteen.

---

[1] Mallarmé, *Arthur Rimbaud*. A letter to Harrison Rhodes. *The Chap-Book*, Vol. II, No. 1, Chicago, May 15, 1896. Published in *Divagations*, Fasquelle, Paris, 1897. Appears in the Pléiade edition of Mallarmé, 1945, pp. 512–19.

The company was too large for any personal exchange between the two poets, but Mallarmé preserved a vivid memory of the boy whom he described as tall and strongly built, with the oval face of an exiled angel, light brown hair in disorder, and pale blue eyes that seemed troubled. He betrayed the awkwardness of a peasant girl, and his large red hands might have been those of a laundress. Around the mouth were lines of a possible sulkiness or craftiness in temperament.

At the time of the meeting, Mallarmé confessed that he only knew of the existence of Rimbaud's poetry, which was still unpublished. Between then and 1896, Mallarmé unquestionably read the poems published by Verlaine in the articles on *Les Poètes maudits* of 1883. The article on Rimbaud preceded the one on Mallarmé himself. He must have read also *Les Illuminations* as they appeared in *La Vogue* in 1886, a periodical to which Mallarmé himself contributed. The older poet is not too much in error when he states that during those years Rimbaud's poetry had little effect on other poets, save perhaps on Verlaine. What counted the most for Mallarmé was Rimbaud's presence, the eruption of his personality and its sudden extinction. He claims that the name of Rimbaud was not mentioned, and perhaps deliberately omitted, from the Tuesday evening gatherings at his house on the Rue de Rome. Rimbaud's case was known to the poets of the symbolist period when Mallarmé presided as the leading poet in Paris, but especially in its anecdotal aspect.

In a few paragraphs only, Mallarmé reviews the principal phases of the Rimbaud myth, phases which since his time have been deeply explored but which have not been adequately explained. To describe the perverse and strong-willed puberty of Rimbaud, Mallarmé recalls his several trips between Charleville and Paris, the character of Rimbaud's mother, the early disappearance of his father, the irresistible attraction of Paris and Verlaine. He stresses the prestige of literature for Rimbaud and the long hours spent in libraries reading. The intense precociousness was manifested in the unusual subjects of Rimbaud's writings, in his quest for new sensations and the exotic, in the illusions offered by unexplored cities.

Mallarmé's sources of his knowledge of Rimbaud in 1872 would have been unquestionably Théodore de Banville and Verlaine. Only one anecdote is recalled in his article, and that about the goodness of Banville in renting for Rimbaud on the Rue de Buci a garret room with a white bed and a table with ink, pen, and paper. Soon after taking possession of the room, Rimbaud appeared at the window, naked, and began to throw out his clothes. Banville, feeling some responsibility for the scene, investigated the cause of this behavior and heard from Rimbaud's own lips that the boy could not stand living in such a clean, virginal room while he was still wearing his old clothes infested with lice.

The rest of the biography is sketched with brevity: the months spent in London with Verlaine, the Brussels episode and the subsequent imprisonment of Verlaine, the linguistic studies and the farewell to Europe, the voyages and the Abyssinian period, the illness and hospitalization at Marseilles, the sister's piety and help. Mallarmé wastes no time in lamenting over Rimbaud's infidelity to poetry. He simply records Ernest Delahaye's question, asked about 1875. The friend had questioned Rimbaud at that time whether he was writing or planning to return to literature, and the answer had been negative. To have prolonged such a work as Rimbaud's might have harmed its uniqueness.

Mallarmé's little essay is a meditation on the personal case of Rimbaud the poet rather than a study or judgment of the poetry. He could hardly have guessed that the poetry of France, and even some of the poetry outside of France, was to be ignited by the meteor he had described. There is some degree of awe in his voice as he speaks of the *passant considérable* of Charleville, but there is no indication that he had experienced anything comparable to the revelatory shock which Claudel felt when he first read *Les Illuminations* in 1886. For Claudel, the example of the poetry counted far more than the example of the poet.

Today, more than seventy years after his death, Rimbaud's fame is greater than ever and the influence of his poetry is felt everywhere. Editions of his work multiply each year. More than five hundred books about him have been written in all languages. Perhaps never have works of art provoked such contradictory interpretations and appreciations. One hears of his legend everywhere, and underneath the innumerable, opposing beliefs one continues to follow the legend of a genius who renounced his genius to embrace silence and conceal whatever drama tormented him. He was the adolescent extraordinarily endowed with sight and equally endowed with speech, but with the advent of manhood he deliberately renounced the prestige of letters and a poet's career. The period of wonderment about his life and his flight from literature is all but over now. In its place, the study of the writings themselves is coming into its own. The verse of Rimbaud and the images of his prose are now fixed in our minds. With Mallarmé's, it forms the most difficult work to penetrate in French poetry, and the most rewarding to explore, because for both of them poetry was the act of obedience to their most secret drama.

No single solution and no single system explain the poetry of Rimbaud. The temptation of each critic has been to elucidate Rimbaud by means of one theory, to reduce his work by wilful unification. But the three works, the poetry, *Une Saison en enfer,* and *Les Illuminations,* are very different from one another. They are the writings of the same poet, but they reflect different moments and intensities and preoccupations of his character. His abandonment of poetry, about the age of twenty, more than anything else in his career, has mystified and intrigued the critics. Except for a few possible passages in *Une Saison,* there is no proof that Rimbaud, when he was writing between 1870 and 1874, ever contemplated such a reversal. During his earliest period as a poet, he ardently solicited attention and recognition, from Izambard, Banville, Verlaine, and others. And it is certain that once he stopped writing, about 1875, he manifested no further interest in his work. The professional man of letters disappeared completely from his life and character.[2]

The work, left to itself, has not undergone so strange a fortune as some have believed. For approximately ten years after the last lines were written, the work was both rejected by the poet and ignored by the public. Verlaine's article, in *Les Poètes maudits* of 1883, helped to create the first real interest in Rimbaud in literary and artistic circles. Verlaine had first introduced the boy, in 1871, to some of the poets in Paris, and in 1883, his article, rather poor in style and information, called attention to the neglected poetry. This was the moment when symbolism was becom-

---

[2] This point, of Rimbaud as "man of letters," is developed centrally in *Arthur Rimbaud* by Daniel de Graaf. See Bibliography.

ing something more than café bohemian meetings. It was affirming the first traits of a literary movement, and it was a far from negligible force a few years later, in 1886, when Verlaine published in *La Vogue* the prose poems of *Les Illuminations.* These attracted a wider public, but Rimbaud was still grouped with other strange, isolated contemporary poets, with Corbière, Laforgue, and Mallarmé, those whose writings elicited either violent enthusiasm or total disapproval. During the next ten years, the symbolists were attracted toward Rimbaud much more through the unusualness and mystery of his case and career than through a feeling and sympathy for his work. In fact, Rimbaud's influence on the symbolists is fairly weak. They were aware that his writings were different from the splenetic laments of Laforgue, from the amorous, nostalgic chant of Verlaine, and from the metaphysical dream of Mallarmé. Because of *Le Bateau ivre,* Rimbaud was essentially for them a sea adventurer, a modern Ulysses or Merlin. They could easily associate *Le Bateau ivre* with *Le Voyage* of Baudelaire and *Brise Marine* of Mallarmé. Many knew that Rimbaud was living at Aden, and they could interpret this as a realization of the voyage poem. Their main body of doctrine was bequeathed to the symbolists by Baudelaire and was being re-explored and deepened by Mallarmé. They had no need of Rimbaud and paid little heed to him save as an extraordinary example of poetic genius, of a poetic "meteor," as Mallarmé was to define him at the close of the symbolist period.

To the portrait of Rimbaud the adventurer, which the symbolists cherished and which was fostered especially by Charles Maurras in his *Barbarie et poésie,* was soon added the statue of Rimbaud the sanctified. A distinction should be drawn between the work of hagiography carried on by Rimbaud's sister Isabelle and her husband, Paterne Berrichon, who tried to turn Rimbaud into a Catholic by interpreting his life and works in terms of his deathbed conversion, and the broader, spiritual interpretations given by Claudel and Rivière. Whereas Catholicism counted to a marked degree in his formation and in his writings, it is foolhardy to classify Rimbaud as a Catholic writer in any literal, orthodox sense. To Claudel, reading him for the first time in 1886, Rimbaud revealed the presence of the supernatural in the contemporary world.[3] Claudel acknowledged Rimbaud as the principal human agent in his return to the Church. Rivière analyzed Rimbaud's revolt as belonging to a metaphysical order, and went so far in his

---

[3] Jacques Rivière and Paul Claudel, *Correspondance*, p. 142. Cf. Claudel's letter of March 12, 1908. "Rimbaud a été l'influence capitale que j'ai subie . . . Rimbaud a eu une action que j'appellerai séminale et paternelle et qui me fait réellement croire qu'il y a une filiation dans l'ordre des esprits comme dans celle des corps. Je me rappellerai toujours cette matinée de juin 1886 où j'achetai cette petite livraison de la 'Vogue' qui contenait le début des *Illuminations*. C'en fut vraiment une pour moi . . . J'avais la révélation du surnaturel."

In his article, "Ma Conversion," published in *La Revue des Jeunes* of October 10, 1913, Claudel writes: "La lecture des *Illuminations* puis, quelques mois après, d'*Une Saison en enfer* fut pour moi un événement capital . . . Ces lignes . . . me donnaient l'impression vivante et presque physique du surnaturel."

In a letter to Paterne Berrichon, Claudel writes: "C'est à Rimbaud que je dois humainement mon retour à la foi." This letter and the above letters are quoted in Ernest Friche's *Etudes Claudéliennes,* in the chapter devoted to Rimbaud's influence on Claudel, pp. 76–150.

demonstration as to call Rimbaud the purely innocent, a being exempt from original sin.[4]

The sense in which Rimbaud is a mystical writer is extremely difficult to define. No writer is less naturalistic than he. The surrealists, during the years between the two wars, realized this and adopted Rimbaud as an exponent of the supra-sensible, as the investigator of the surreal and the infinite. They saw him as a liberator of the imagination whose major activity had taken place on the frontiers of the unreal or on the most distant confines of the real. Rightfully they considered his *Illuminations* as a work by a genius not purely man. The surrealists would hesitate to describe any being as angelic, but they sensed in the prose poems an angelic savor, an otherworldliness. His life also, in its rejection of all compromise, resembled a purification related perhaps to that of his work. They approved of his admiration for crudities and *naïvetés,* for the *peintures idiotes* he had named in *Une Saison.* After his intensive readings, Rimbaud had emptied his mind of everything and especially of didactic procedures. He had wilfully *de*civilized himself and in that act was to inspire Apollinaire, the surrealists, and the younger poets today of Paris and New York and San Francisco.

But the aesthetics of Rimbaud the *voyant* has something almost too active and violent for the principal discipline of the surrealists, their passivity, their persistent question-

---

[4] Rivière, *Rimbaud.* See the passage on p. 45 where Rivière claims that an angel has a greater degree of reality, a greater quantity of existence than a man: "A cet égard Rimbaud est un ange. Un ange furieux. Il n'a pas été touché, il porte intact la ressemblance de Dieu, il conserve toute la dépense que Dieu a faite en lui."

ing of the unconscious. Rimbaud may well have provoked the unconscious by more voluntary means than the surrealists. A study of Rimbaud's *Lettre du voyant* and Breton's *Manifeste du surréalisme* would reveal considerable divergence. The movement and rhythm of *Les Illuminations* testify to a more deliberately conscious means of arriving at derangement. Whereas the surrealist watches and waits for the unpredictable manifestation of the unconscious, Rimbaud violates his mind and ravishes the images as they form. His poetic secrets are the result of a spiritual rape and conquest. His art is the seizure of his own reality. After the tension of war and intellectualism, the young surrealists developed and explored a veritable literary crisis initiated by Rimbaud. The adolescent of Charleville provoked in them a desire for a spiritual adventure in which all values and all achievements of man were to be questioned.

In his experience as a writer of prose, when he composes *Les Illuminations,* Rimbaud calls upon and synthesizes his former experiences as poet and visionary. Part of his exercise is the effacement of the ordinary pictures of the world. The reader is immediately disorientated because the first images he sees are those of another world. A scattered handful of images are all that are necessary to prove to us that we are lost in another world where we will have to revise our usual powers of sight and mind. But this is the poet's deepest wish, to hurl us into the center of chaos, to liberate us from the ordinary patterns of thought. In composing *Les Illuminations,* Rimbaud revived his theories of the voyant, and behind them, Baudelaire's urgent cry to find something new (*trouver du nouveau*). The experience of *Le Bateau ivre* is recast in *Les Illuminations* and deepened into a need of even broader horizons and more abso-

lute conquests. The language of the poet is the clue to the
spiritual experience motivating the poems. The very con-
densation and newness of the language testify to an experience highly inarticulate, one surely related to an eternal desire that can be translated only by vision and
rhythm. Rimbaud defined as the supreme function of art
the notation of the ineffable, the casting into form of the
most vertiginous plunges of man's mind (*Délires II*). The
only possible interpretation of such extreme statements
must concern a mystical approach to poetry. Rimbaud
seems to be saying what Anselm urges in the opening
chapter of the *Proslogium:* empty one's mind to everything save God, empty one's mind of all images save
that of God. Not only to write as Rimbaud would have
the poet write, but to read Rimbaud, one has to expel
from one's mind all trite images and all logical clichés.

Poetry is opposed to definition because it is born in the
most ineffable part of human experience. It is always just
beyond language. The words of the poet are those by which
he comes closest to seizing what is poetry. The nature of
poetry has been more widely discussed critically and philosophically than any other literary subject during the past
century. The problem is still far from being solved, but
Rimbaud's contribution to it, in his critical statements and
the example of his poetry, exceeds that of any other artist,
with the possible exceptions of Mallarmé and Valéry. Each
poet reaches in himself some private part, some extraordinary domain, by ways opened to all other men of his
period—those of culture, traditions, poetic techniques,
rules and literary movements. What is common, for example, to symbolist poets writing between 1875 and 1890
is of fairly slight significance. What does count is precisely
what makes Rimbaud different from every other poet in

the world, what makes a line of Mallarmé exclusively his and distinguishable from every other line of poetry. Each poet is unique. Each great poem is incomparable. A man becomes a poet by reaching this absolute intimacy of his own. His poetic creation will therefore be a defiance of ordinary verbal communication. Its origins lie in the ineffable part of his own being and therefore are much closer to the silence of the universe than to its noises and verbalizations.

But there is a compensation for this purely personal element of poetry. It is the form of the poem which is stable and communicable. It is the part of the poem which makes us forget temporarily its indecipherable origins. Form is communicable, and yet what it communicates is always different. No two readers read the same poem in the same way. A poem is therefore a figure of inexhaustible suggestiveness. By itself a kind of night, when it is read it is capable of breaking into an indefinite number of dawns. In each reader the same poem comes to life in a different way.

The almost terrifying directness of Rimbaud's poetry takes over the reader and holds his attention. This time the poet has succeeded in transcribing immediately his vision. The shock of Rimbaud's poetry comes perhaps from this quality. When Claudel first read *Les Illuminations,* the shock was one of an unpredictable revelation. He believed he saw in the prose poems an elucidation on the very meaning of poetry, which he was to call the recreation of everything that exists, a new birth of the world and of one's self. In addition to the Christian and surrealist interpretations of Rimbaud, in the writings respectively of Rivière and Breton, there are other far more rigorous systems by which the poetry has been explained. Rolland de Renéville at-

taches Rimbaud to the mystical doctrines of India, although there is no proof that Rimbaud ever possessed a
profound knowledge of Hindu philosophy. Etiemble sees
Rimbaud especially as a social revolutionary, a *communard,* and a savant. Gengoux, in one recent study, explores
the meaning of the work in terms of the occult. C. A.
Hackett has published an excellent study on Rimbaud the
child. The work remains one of the most ambiguous and
mystifying, precisely because it is so close to the original
vision of the poet. The images of *Les Illuminations* seem
to be dragged up from the unconscious by a boy who does
not know what he is doing. The words he uses to transcribe
the images are the first that come to mind, and the transcription is made with the minimum of change. The exact-
ness of Rimbaud's language explains the bewildering effect
it leaves.

But the poet was a boy. He was not protected and supported by individuals or by a group or even by a tradition.
His singularity, his solitude were very deep. The visions
came to him, but not without intervals between them.
There, in the intervals where he was alone and unguided,
his failure waited. Because of his mystical solitariness and
his exceptional precociousness, Rimbaud's failure was to be
as absolute as his poetry was pure. He first protected his
visions from any contamination as violently as he was later
to protect his life from literature. Rimbaud's early tendency to lewdness, sullenness, and debauchery was a perverted form of asceticism, as it is in most adolescents, a
means of purification and protection. The *voyou* and the
voyant are the same being in Rimbaud, the same poet anx-
ious not to mature in order to salvage his vision which is
that of a child.

The poems are Rimbaud's first representation of his life

(*Poètes de sept ans* and *Mémoire*) and his first visions (*Le Bateau ivre*). They are the part of his work that remains closest to literature and to literary models. *Une Saison en enfer* is fairly devoid of visions. It is almost a retraction, an effort to understand his past, his revolt against Christianity. It is his confession of failure. *Les Illuminations* is a new movement of hope, of almost mystical belief in himself as poet and visionary. In the earlier works, the poet learned his language of *voyant* and something concerning the failure of living as an artist. *Les Illuminations* has behind it an experience comparable to the mystic's initiation to failure. For a mystic, failure may take on the proportions of catastrophe. The prose poems are all illuminations of a secret catastrophe we can only guess at. Their universe is incoherent. Their fragmentariness, despite the frequent sumptuousness of their language, sets them off from our familiar world of appearances. Their element is discontinuity. Each poem is separated from all the rest, and strains to discover again its context. By comparison, *Une Saison* has a remarkable logic and sequential flow. Pictures that are incompatible with one another, farewells that may be preludes, visions that are both mystical and erotic, explosions of anger and introversions, these are the themes of *Les Illuminations,* which applies the theories of the letter-manifesto of May 15, 1871.

Rimbaud's whole life and way of living are in the prose poems. The Christian mystics were never completely alone with their vision. They had always behind them the daily practices of the Church. But Rimbaud was alone with his vision. After going through, in *Une Saison en enfer,* an experience which some would equate with damnation, in *Les Illuminations* Rimbaud learns something of the greatest catastrophe for an artist, that of incommunicability. The

possible anguish of such an experience may have been
enough to explain the poet's silence which began after *Les
Illuminations* was completed and which lasted until the
poet's death. The impatience of the adolescent theologian,
narrated in *Une Saison,* becomes a more frantic impatience, in *Les Illuminations,* over the discontinuity and the
ellipsis of the visions. Adolescence can never plumb its secret, because by nature it is change. Before carrying the
memory of adolescence into his maturity, Rimbaud tried
to express it as it came to him, in discontinuous, cryptic
utterances and visions. The early poems were written close
to his mother, whom he loved and hated without distin-
guishing between the sentiments, and *Une Saison* was written close to the memory of Verlaine, whose love also had
turned to bitterness. Rimbaud was more alone in writing
Les Illuminations, more spiritually motivated perhaps
than at any other time in his life, but disorientated, abandoned to his own ingenuousness where no secrets were de-
ciphered. As a boy and in early adolescence, Rimbaud had
been incapable of accepting any of the familiar forms of
reality: mother, school, catechism, war, love. These he considered traps or compromises for the purity of spirit he felt
in himself. He opposed them, as one opposes an enemy,
until they were repulsed or vanquished or forgotten. He
fought his way to an exceptional solitude which was propitious for *Les Illuminations.* But the prose poems too were
temptations and tantalizing deceptions. They had, after all,
an alliance with literature. They were expressed in the very
words from which he had struggled to liberate himself.
Then, finally, he left them too, and the solitude out of
which they had grown, to forget them utterly in scenes of
a new life.

The three works of Rimbaud represent three degrees of

hardness, each more absolute than the preceding one. There was hardness in his will to escape his mother and Charleville, hardness in his treatment of Verlaine, where his cruelty was more direct and deliberate, and a still different hardness as an artist in his will to draw up from his incomplete vision the pictures—the colored plates, as Verlaine called them—which testify to the extent of Rimbaud's power as a visionary. *Une Saison* is closer to the constraints of civilization and institutions, and its dramatic quality is Rimbaud's effort to liberate himself from such constraints. Just beyond its pages of a notebook is the desire to return to a primitive innocence, to recapture a state of being the poet had never forgotten. This desire finds its expression and form in *Les Illuminations,* where there are far fewer traces of spiritual struggle and more direct notations on some future happiness. This state of innocency, remembered from some former existence, if not known in childhood, lost in the forays with customs and civilization, and then sought after, explains the poetry of Rimbaud and his final dissatisfaction or discouragement with poetry.

Implicit in the images and the utterances of *Les Illuminations* is the abandonment of such an enterprise. This lends the work its quality of independence, its lack of literary intention. The phrases are generated by chance, as if there were little care on the part of the poet to pursue such a game. In the very ornateness of its language and in its incoherence, the work announces its abdication. The search of such a world was predicted in *Une Saison,* but *Les Illuminations* seems to prove that it can be seen only once in a lifetime. The poet, for such visions as these, pays up with a kind of abdication, with an escape to other work and other countries. The gift of the visionary brings with it its own death. The necessary solitude for such a vision creates an even greater solitude in its wake, but one that is visionless.

The work of Rimbaud is far more knowable than his life, but in his case especially the one cannot be dissociated from the other. The example of his human existence has counted almost as much as the influence of his writing. Breton named him a surrealist by his life, and Rivière named him the supreme type of innocent—although it must, in all justice, be noted that Breton modified his earlier view and called Rimbaud an apostate, one who renounced his discoveries and called them "sophisms." Nerval's suicide and Lautréamont's total disappearance pleased the surrealists more than Rimbaud's final choice of another kind of life than that of poetry.

The difficulty of classifying Rimbaud as a type is the key to his character. He was no recognizable type. No one could live with him, and he, in his quality of constant revolutionary, could abide no one's presence for long. He was outside the law and outside the human community. He was too lucidly aware of the absurdity of beings and things to lead any kind of adventure save that which took him far away from them all. *Une Saison en enfer* will remain as the great document on his life and character, where he analyzes his past and his future, his dreams and his punishments, his peasant ethics and his angelic metaphysics. His fall has a Luciferean magnitude. His memory of an angel's existence is never abolished even at the moments when he is closest to the void. His will to face the mystery of the void is in itself superhuman. The temptation of any study of Rimbaud will always be to isolate him too completely from the world of humanity, from the real and the contingent.

The poet's world in *Une Saison* is made up of contradictions, and especially the major contradiction between the claims of Christian theology, which Rimbaud learned in catechism class and in his early religious devotions, and the claims of his pagan ancestors, the Gauls, perpetrators of witchcraft. Rimbaud felt himself simultaneously Christian and pre-Christian. But this contradiction is softened or diminished in *Les Illuminations*. Here the world is made up of discontinuities. The experience with Verlaine is practically forgotten, replaced by the deeper experience of the city. Behind the city, and returning as in some ineluctable law, is the experience of the mother and childhood. The landscapes and settings of *Les Illuminations* are those created by Rimbaud's childhood, which had been suppressed temporarily during the Paris and London adventures, only to return in the new solitude after Brussels, as the permanent exaltation of his genius.

The literary sources of a poet are far less important than the particular joys and sufferings he knew as a child. Every episode of childhood, every act and emotion, is recorded in such a sensitivity as Rimbaud's, and grows into some metamorphosis of unusual size and importance. Such are the distant origins of works of art. A child is a complex and tormented being who willingly believes, especially if his parents repeat it to him often enough, that he is a monster and that each day he is growing more monstrous. *Parents, vous avez fait mon malheur,* wrote Rimbaud in *Nuit de l'enfer.* Rimbaud's mother insisted daily on such predictions. Her part in the formation of the boy's sensitivity is unfathomable. Izambard saw in him at the Collège de Charleville a type of intellectual and a youthful poet vibrating with lyric passion. By this time, when Rimbaud was fifteen, he had developed the particular hardness of pride which characterizes youthful genius and makes it appear intractable, irreducible.

The world that had marked him the most profoundly was the closed, restricted house dominated by his mother. It is the world he describes in *Les Poètes de sept ans,* where the boy lived with his mother, fearing and hating her at the same time. He could see no one else, because she forbade his playing with any friends. The solitude was austere and puritanical. Rimbaud's sister, Isabelle, later described it, and her description justifies the poem on seven-year-old poets. Mme Rimbaud permitted her son no pleasures. He did his best at one time to obey her, but she was never satisfied. At school, especially during the last years, 1869, 1870, Rimbaud did extremely good work and won some of the principal prizes. He was admired but neither known nor loved by his schoolmates. At home, even during the period of scholarly attainments, he remained the little boy tyrannized by his mother, who wanted to mold him in accordance with her own ideas and who never realized that life was molding him at the same time, the life of solitude and suppressed hate and awakening ambitions. His revolt was fated to be total; and, likewise, the mother's unwillingness to bend to the revolt or to try to understand her son remained total until the son's death, until her own death, in fact. She did her duty, as she conceived of it, until the end. Her love of Arthur was that strange and cruel kind of love that has no understanding of the one loved. Perhaps it is wrong to call it love, because its results are so disastrous. One reads of such a mother's love, and thinks instinctively of the myth of parents who devour their own children. Rimbaud's childhood was unresolved because it was of such an upsetting nature. His return to it in *Les Illuminations* was an effort to resolve and accomplish it, to ask for the playthings he had been denied as a child, to recover and repair his earliest experience in the world.

Rimbaud's example will remain that of the poet opposing his civilization, his historical moment, and yet at the same time revealing its very instability, its quaking torment. He is both against his age and of it. By writing so deeply of himself, he wrote of all men. By refusing to take time to live, he lived a century in a few years, throughout its minute phases, rushing toward the only thing that mattered to him: the absolute, the certainty of truth. He came closest to finding this absolute in his poet's vision. That was "the place and the formula" he talked of and was impatient to find, the spiritual hunt that did not end with the prey seized. Rimbaud's is the drama of modern man, as critics have often pointed out, by reason of its particular frenzy and precipitation, but it is also the human drama of all time, the drama of the quest for what has been lost, the unsatisfied, temporal existence burning for total satisfaction, for total certitude. Because of Rimbaud's universality, or rather because of the universality of poetry, the Charleville adolescent can seemingly appropriate and justify any title: metaphysician, angel, *voyou*, seer, reformer, reprobate, materialist, mystic. The poet, as Rimbaud conceived of him, is, rightfully, all men. He is the supreme savant. The private drama of one boy, which fills the poignant pages of *Une Saison,* is always deepened into the drama of man, tormented by the existence of the ideal, which he is unable to reach. And likewise, the pure images of *Les Illuminations,* which startle and hold us by their own intrinsic beauty, were generated and formed by a single man in the solitude of his own hope to know reality.

The persistent dilemma involving all study of Rimbaud comes from the fact that he is read by men, and that his work is the complex, introverted work of an adolescent mind still overcome by the drama of childhood. No precautionary method can be adopted for studying a mind that reveals not the imprint of a learned logic, but the chaotic, unsystematized experience of a primitive. To explain Rimbaud is futile. One has to learn how to understand him, and that goal far exceeds the narrow, limiting truths of a thesis.

Une Saison en enfer

U NE SAISON EN ENFER is a major text in the history of
the modern spirit. It is a work of "confession," and
like other confessions, Saint Augustine's, Cellini's, Rous-
seau's, Chateaubriand's, it involves autobiography and
history, philosophy and psychological notations. Rimbaud's confession differs from the others because of its
brevity and the explosiveness of its language. *Une Saison*
is a confession in the form of a prose poem or a series of
prose poems. The violence of the work is not so much in
the narrative elements and in the ideas as in the rhythm of
the phrases, in the symbols and allegories that exist in
themselves and not merely as commentary on the poet's
experience. By definition, this form of writing deals with
the theme of evil, with the struggle of an individual against
a world of evil. *Une Saison* is a narrative where metaphysics is of primary importance and where the meaning of
evil is constantly being converted into the meaning of action and the meaning of words. Poetry is that art where the
physical rhythm and breath of a phrase are merged with

the meaning of the words in the phrase. In *Une Saison en enfer* the meaning of human suffering is communicated by the tempo of the sentences: by their violence and unevenness, by their delicacy and secretiveness.

The opening page bears no subsidiary title, but it is obviously a preface in which all the themes of the work to follow are audible. It is made up of images and characters who become familiar and meaningful as the work progresses. The confession is to cover the span of Rimbaud's nineteen years: from the most recent escapade (*tout dernièrement . . . le dernier couac*), that doubtless refers to the Brussels drama, to the earliest happy memories of childhood (*Jadis . . . ma vie . . . un festin*). This period, of which Rimbaud has no exact recollection but which existed as with every child before he was aware of the world, was violently terminated when the boy realized at one specific moment (*un soir*) that the traditional conception of beauty held no significance for him (*j'ai assis la Beauté sur mes genoux . . . et l'ai trouvée amère*). This phrase marks the beginning of Rimbaud's drama. It lends itself to more than one meaning. Many interpreters of Rimbaud see in it an announcement of sexual aberration. An aesthetic interpretation would seem to be more justified. Rimbaud the young poet is turning against the type of beauty illustrated by the Parnassian ideals of his day.

Rimbaud has the sense of becoming a victim, of becoming vulnerable, and this characteristic of the victim is the first mask of the poet. He calls himself the hyena, and this beast is reminiscent of Vigny's wolf, of Musset's pelican, of Gautier's hippopotamus, of Baudelaire's albatross. These are the roles for the artist, victimized and even sacrificial. The artist is the scapegoat for the ordinary citizens who, horrified by their dreams, camouflage them with respectability and easily assume the role of executioners.

This initial page, then, introduces the poet as victim and describes the moment when the characterization began. It also announces the goal to be attained in the enactment of the victim's role, and this goal indicates that the victim is, in the deepest sense, a rebel. The poet's flight from the conventional world (*Je me suis enfui*) into his own inner world (*O sorcières, ô misère, ô haine*) turns out to be more a search than a flight. In every experience of his unconscious, Rimbaud will seek and track down his innocency. He calls it first his *trésor* which has to be protected within himself: in "witchcraft" (the mysterious form of poetry), in "poverty" (the usual danger of exile), and in "hate" (which is manifested by revolt). Art is a retrogression in time, an effort, visible in countless signal instances, to recapture childhood and its oneness with the universe. Pavel Tchelitchew has painted this theme in his work of metamorphosis called *Cache-cache*. It is a leading theme in Joyce's *Finnegans Wake* and in Eliot's *Little Gidding*.

Mauvais Sang

In the first section of the work, which is the longest and richest, the poet describes himself as bound inextricably with his past. From his Gallic ancestors he inherited physiological weaknesses and spiritual habits of thought that determined and shaped his specific drama. He refers to two kinds of past: the distant past of pagan Gauls (*les Gaulois étaient les écorcheurs de bêtes*) and the immediate past of the nineteenth century with its bourgeois ideals by which each son inherits his father's fortune and then transmits it to his son (*J'ai connu chaque fils de famille*). The inferior race of Gauls were turned into crusaders, and then helped

create the three centuries of modern France, elliptically
designated by the three words: *la raison, la nation et la
science.* These were the stages of progress: reason in the
seventeenth century, the nation in the eighteenth century,
and science in the nineteenth. And now in Rimbaud's immediate past, dominated by the scientific method, he asks,
almost as if he were writing in the twentieth century,
whether science has not reached an impasse and whether
the world may not reverse itself in some cyclical revolution
(*Le monde marche. Pourquoi ne tournerait-il pas?*).

The vision of the poet as microcosm in which he sees
himself in several historical roles of the past: as leper (of
biblical times), as Gaul, as crusader (of medieval times), as
son-heir (of modern times) is abruptly supplanted by a vision of the poet as macrocosm when he sees himself in the
future. This passage of pure prophecy is almost unprece-
dented in literature. At the age of nineteen, Rimbaud
wrote with an awesome accuracy about his future. He fore-
saw his flight from Europe (*je quitte l'Europe*), the tanning
of his skin under tropical suns (*les climats perdus me tan-
neront*), his return to Europe with gold pieces in his money
belt (*Je reviendrai . . . J'aurai de l'or*), and his state of in-
firmity, nursed by women (*Les femmes soignent ces féroces
infirmes retour des pays chauds*).

Between the past and the future, Rimbaud is immobilized by the present (*On ne part pas*). To the image of
the poet as victim is added the image of convict (*forçat*)
chained to a wall. He calls the chain attaching him to the
present his vice, insoluble as fate itself. His vice has transformed him into a convict, so different from those who are
executing him that they can no longer see him. It is an apt
image, relating the struggle between reality and appearance and the torture felt by the artist as he tries to adjust

to the moral code of a society of which he is not so much a member as a prophet and interpreter.

Like Ham, son of Noah, Rimbaud feels compelled to leave his country and found another race in another land. Rimbaud's mask as convict and the color of his skin will separate him from other men and from their systems of justice which cannot apply to a man different from them. He originally planned to call the book: *Livre nègre*. This theme is the principal dilemma of *Une Saison en enfer*. Rimbaud knows that behind him in his past and ahead of him in his future, in those places where he is not, in his unrecognizable present, the secret of his being has been lost. At the end of *Mauvais Sang*, he calls it, not by the vaguer word *trésor* he used in the preface, but by its real name of innocence: *l'étendue de mon innocence*.

Nuit de l'enfer

Immediately after announcing his search for innocence, Rimbaud begins a new passage describing a realistic plunge into hell. Only the damned know fully what they have lost. Now, the literal domain of fire incloses the sinner, and it is more fearful than the convict's prison and the hyena's desert. The world had exiled the convict and the hyena because it found them repulsive and perilous to social standards. But now the poet is in the role of sinner, and this is a voluntary exile, not from the world but from the Creator. This new terror is eternal. The flames of hell are more vigilant than temporal prison walls.

In the penultimate sentence of the passage, Rimbaud states the difference between hell and the persecution of man on earth. In the world it is possible to hide, but in hell one hides and is seen at the same time (*Je suis caché et je ne le suis pas*). As in the game of hide-and-seek, the victim who is "it"—that is, the hero—hides his head against the trunk of the tree. But he is exposed to the others during the seconds he counts out. In the same way, the poet in hell is exposed to his desolation. His sin has not killed him or changed him. He is still intact, and his suffering is his sense of aloneness.

Délires I

The first of the "deliriums" has the same setting, hell, but Rimbaud is no longer alone. The meditation of *Nuit de l'enfer* becomes a drama with two characters: the infernal bridegroom, who is Rimbaud, and the foolish virgin, who is Verlaine. Except for the first and last lines, the passage is spoken by the foolish virgin, and at one point, close to the beginning, the virgin repeats the words of the bridegroom.

In its dramatic intensity, this fragment is much more than a circumstantial report of Rimbaud's relationship with Verlaine. The very boldness of this story leads the reader to believe its real meaning is in its symbolism. Rimbaud is too ornate a writer to offer a literal transcription of experience. In the literalness we read of Verlaine's love, of his renouncing his marital duty, of his following Rimbaud from city to city, of their excessive drinking, of their quarrels, of Rimbaud's sadistic pleasure in torturing Verlaine, of the madness of the relationship. The first *Délire* is the story of man which begins in a belief that his true life is somewhere else, in a place to which he must escape. *La vraie vie est absente* is an explicit formula for the romantic agony. This thought penetrates a man's heart after every unjustified and infecund experience when he asks of the experience something it cannot provide: those secrets with which to change life. *Changer la vie* is a corollary of *la vraie vie est absente,* and a further definition of the romantic void.

Délires II

The second delirium is the story of the *voyant,* of the visionary. It is the poet's drama which Rimbaud calls the "alchemy of the word." To the excessive experiences of the body succeed the excessive experiences of the mind. The theme of the two *délires* is man as procreator and artist, but frustrated in both roles, unable to re-create his body or his visions.

Rimbaud recalls elements of his early life: backdrops used by circus clowns, Latin phrases learned in church, fairy stories and pornographic books, the colors of vowels he remembered from a child's alphabet book, the water of the Oise, the workmen he used to see bathing at noon in the river. These are some of the many experiences registered in the boy's memory which emerge in his poems after undergoing a decantation and chemical change.

But Rimbaud discovered that all reality is inexpressible, and that his poems at best are imperfect replicas. He found himself therefore playing the role he believed the poet's legitimate role: the magician of hallucination who casts spells by his words. Rimbaud discovered that experience can be related only by those words that are foreign to the experience. A factory, for example, is better designated as a mosque. As the sleep of caterpillars assures their transformation, so periods of silence after an experience may produce a work of art vastly different from the original experience. This is called by Rimbaud the sacred disorder of the mind, and he designates the poet as a hierophant. Like a mystic, a poet lives through a long period of dryness when nothing is accomplished. It is the preparatory period for visions: images of death and arid neutrality (*vergers brûlés, boutiques fanées, boissons tièdes*) which precede the vision of reality. Hunger and dryness are legitimate states of being. Renunciation is the only way to possession.

At the end of the aridity, joy is the reward for the mystic, and for the poet it is a vision of which he can give only a clownish expression (*De joie, je prenais une expression bouffonne*).

L'Impossible

The four remaining passages, which are all brief, are recapitulations of major themes in the work. In *L'Impossible*, the poet speaks specifically of his flights. His reason has broken down during his effort to span the distance between East and West. He was born in the marshes of the West, and grew into what he calls Christian restlessness. And then he tried to reach the wisdom, the Nirvana of the East. The philosophical purity of Eden, Rimbaud calls a repose of the spirit, and it has almost been forgotten by men of the West.

L'Eclair

God is reached by man's spirit; without it, a man knows only restlessness coming from his assumed roles in life. These roles are flashes of attainment, deceptive moments of purity. The roles Rimbaud enumerates in this passage are familiar masks of modern man used to disguise his desire for purity and revolt: *clown, beggar, artist, bandit—priest* (*saltimbanque, mendiant, artiste, bandit—prêtre*).

Matin

In *Matin*, Rimbaud gives to the concept of hell a Christian meaning when he claims that his suffering was due to a lack of grace, and that the purity he was seeking was that of hope and of the first Christmas Mass. Hell is real only if there is salvation, only if Christ actually did open the gates of hell.

Adieu

It is autumn. *Adieu* is a seasonal farewell. Immediately ahead is the Christmas Mass and rebirth. The first sentence of *Une Saison* spoke of the wine of feast days and a child's purity. The work is the narration of the year cycle beginning with Christmas and ending with autumn, with the season of Advent. Three moments of time are reviewed, three major states in the life cycle of Rimbaud: purity (*j'ai créé toutes les fêtes*), sin (*la cité au ciel taché de feu*) and repentance (*je dois enterrer mon imagination et mes souvenirs*). These three phrases describe the feast days of purification, the burning cities of Sodom and Gomorrah, and the dying of nature at the end of autumn. These are the poet's memories of his passage through hell, of the *season* which was the summer of flaming heat. In the summer of his hell, Rimbaud remembered the birth of his purity in the ancient celebration of Christmas, and he prophesied its rebirth in a future penitence.

He speaks of having played roles of magus and angel (*Moi qui me suis dit mage ou ange*). Now he acknowledges that his destiny is not the visionary's, of a man liberated from the peasant's life and the reality of the earth. Neither is his destiny that of the angel who is beyond morality. He is simply a man before whom lies the new Jerusalem: *nous entrerons aux splendides villes*. Rimbaud is a man able to know truth uniquely and simultaneously in his body and in his soul.

Une Saison en enfer is a work governed by the metaphysical problem of being: who is man? In the opening pages, Rimbaud is asking this question. Is he a beast, a victim, or a Gaul? Is he castrated? Is he a leper? Is he a convict? Is he a man unaffected by morality? The same question is reiterated at the end: is he clown, prophet, angel? Under the influence of Rimbaud, the contemporary poet has given a new meaning to the word angel. The angel lives more with the invisible than with the visible. In *Nuit de l'enfer,* Rimbaud believes he is outside of this world (*Décidément, nous sommes hors de ce monde*). No one abode is suitable for this new hero. Rimbaud's flights are comparable to the wanderings of clowns from village to village. The poet and the clown are close to this angel as they practice skills unfamiliar to most men.

3

Poetics

In the letter to Demeny of May 15, 1871, the celebrated *Lettre du voyant,* Rimbaud states his poetic
ambition, the program of a revolutionary, of one who
wants to break with the past, with the versifiers who had
practiced a wrong kind of poetry. *Car je est un autre* ("For
I is someone else"), proclaims Rimbaud, after a few violent sentences on the history of poetry in which he salvages
only the Greek poets and Racine. There are two selves in
the poet, a deeply hidden, mysterious self who in the act
of poetry destroys the familiar self of the controlled and
predictable responses. What Rimbaud terms *voyance* is the
vision of the unknown, hidden self. It is one way or one
method of contemplating the absolute. Rimbaud speaks of
having recently watched this new kind of thought rise to
the surface of his consciousness, of having been present
at the birth of this thought. The recent violent experiences
in Paris and Charleville, during the spring of 1871, were
modes of living propitious for a new self-realization. The

excesses and violences of living had awakened in him a whole realm of sensitivity that was going to lead to a revolutionary doctrine about poetic language. It seems so powerfully new to him that he believes no poet has yet realized its scope, *auteur, créateur, cet homme n'a jamais existé!* Until then, poets had been false generators of words, hack writers, and functionaries. Everything has to be cast out: modes of thought, vocabularies, modes of behavior. For the absolute of the new poet's vision, there has to be an absolute of expression.

In these few highly suggestive words, Rimbaud adumbrates an entire theory of the genius who has to make himself a stranger to his land and society and family. The genius' rite of initiation is one of alienation. The unknown self is a stranger also to the ordinary language of the city. The *voyant* needs to become the mythic self, discoverable in the deepest recesses of earliest memory and primal fears. The derangement of the senses and the monstrous soul of the real self are that only by comparison with the familiar soul, which is an impoverishment of the original, indestructible soul. Of the two ways of knowledge, intellectual progress and self-knowledge, Rimbaud advocates the second, and lists as the major means to this knowledge of self: love, suffering, madness. These are the experiences most capable of revealing the deepest self. It is necessary to know and exhaust the poisons of life in order to retain their essence. Baudelaire, in his sonnet *Epigraphe pour un livre condamné,* had spoken of how useless it would be to read his book, unless the reader had some knowledge of evil, some familiarity with the night out of which the book had come.

The goal of such self-exploration is the unknown. Knowledge of Rimbaud's vision is the surreal, the unseen possibilities of memory before our life. Here, the poet is close to a doctrine of the soul and memory, reminiscent of Bergson's, which implies that we do not learn, we simply remember what we once knew. The supreme language that Rimbaud has in mind, is not the means of knowing, but of forgetting ordinary language, a means of losing one's self and of discovering one's monstrous nature.

The poet is Prometheus, fire thief. What he brings back with him from his exploration of self is touched with the divine. Every word is an idea. Every word contains some recollection of its divine origin. Again, as with Baudelaire, Rimbaud believes that poetic language contains all sensations: perfumes, sounds, colors. Words are magical recipes and self-contained myths. They possess a unique kind of truthfulness, not to be confused or contaminated with historical truth. The new method of attaining poetic truth is lofty and perilous. It demands the destruction of order, convention, patterns, rules. It runs the risk of leaving the poet midway between the old and the new method, of making him simply into a despiser of order, an iconoclast. The enterprise has a superhuman aspect, in seeking to reach visions that existed before the poet himself did, in reaching to his race memory. Such poetry is an *ascesis,* a power that will convert a man into a real poet, a stealer of fire. Rolland de Renéville, in his study of Rimbaud, considered these poetic experiments comparable to the exercises of the Hindu mystics by which they try to merge their will with the universal consciousness.

If the term *voyance* is taken to designate Rimbaud's method of poetry, the period in which he practiced it seems to correspond to that between the writing of the letter-manifesto in May, 1971, and his separation from Verlaine, the Brussels adventure of July, 1873. At the end of this period he writes most of *Une Saison en enfer,* of which one of the important themes is a liquidation of his poetic genius, a renunciation, at least temporarily, of his experimentation with writing. He speaks of his past efforts with scorn as if they had been failures and lies. On one level, the work does represent a divorce from himself, from the kind of man he had been and the kind of poet he had tried to become. The leading aspects of this divorce correspond to the sections in the work entitled *Mauvais Sang, Délires I,* and *Délires II.*

The last section mentioned is specifically on the problem of poetry, but its meaning is incomplete without the other two. In *Mauvais Sang,* Rimbaud represents the central dilemma of man in civilization. He has cut himself off from all attachment with the social and the religious hierarchy. He is a primitive when viewed in the light of the European caste system and the doctrine of Christian salvation. On the one hand he is the tracked beast, the victim whom society will hunt out and destroy, and on the other hand he is the baptized Christian who has felt the effects of his baptism only in the torment he has experienced at not being able to submit to it. The miracle of the baptism did not work in his case. He is even beyond original sin. These are the elements of Rimbaud's portrait as man. *Délires I* is his self-portrait as lover, but its main theme, in full agreement with the main theme of *Mauvais Sang,* is his separation from the experience of love. In it Rimbaud seems to be exorcizing himself from a bad dream, from an evil power. But he sees himself, more than Verlaine, as the evil power, and is pressed into an isolation concomitant on his isolation as false citizen and false Christian. *Délires II,* after Rimbaud's portrait as man and lover, is the poet's portrait. It is always the same characteristic of failure, the same resumption of solitude and impotency, after an extraordinary program of ambition. The great temptations of Rimbaud had been baptism, Verlaine, and poetry. They were the possible signs of metaphysical happiness, of love and hallucinations. *Une Saison* is concerned with his experience with these three ambitions, and with his recovery from them.

The title of *Délires II* is "Alchemy of the Word," and the opening sentence states that this is to be the story of one of Rimbaud's excursions into madness. The prose sections narrate his deliberate efforts to make himself into a *voyant* and the excerpts of poems are examples of the visions he brought back from the *voyance*. Initially his pride came from his embracing of all landscapes, from his scorn for the eclectic and the traditional in art: the celebrities in painting and modern poetry. The landscapes he had especially cultivated in the progress of his *voyance* were the paintings of children, signs, and circus backdrops. The literature that had fed his imagination were the forgotten, once-popular book, pornography, Church Latin, fairy stories, popular songs. These were the starting points for his dreams of voyages, of war, of enchantments. These were his studies at the end of which he would write out their most ineffable parts, the dizziness he had cultivated from such flights.

The basic exercise was a simple form of hallucination. By his new power, a factory would become a mosque and a group of drummer-boys would be converted into angels. The mere title of a play could grow into something terrifying. This was disorder, but the poet considered it sacred because of the wonder of its transformations and its endless metamorphoses. He envied and tried to emulate the periods of waiting in limbo, the sleep of caterpillars at the end

of which the magical change takes place. But his character
grew embittered. His poems were of farewells to the world.
He realized that the practice of poetry was a giving up of
the world in order to create another world. What helped
most in this strange creation were the elements in the real
world that had lost this fulness and power. He had already said that he was more helped by cheap popular literature than by the classics. For the same reason, he manifests a predilection for the desert rather than the fertile
land, for the slums of a city rather than the elegant boulevards. Hunger is more important than the eating of good
food. The luxurious and the beautiful in life have to be
abandoned. The poet has to empty his life of false acqui-
sitions and his mind of false dreams of triumph. Poetry is
the capture of the trivial and the commonplace which in
the alchemy of the poetic word emerge changed and newly
significant. After the derangement of the senses, poetry is
the creation of a new universe from sources so humble and
trite that no one save the poet himself could remember
them.

The poet is the great sympathizer with everything that
is, because he can discover in beings and in objects an
extraordinary possibility and transformation. This is the
sophistry and the logic of madness, the system which Rimbaud held and which was to exhaust him. The unreal to
which the poet is drawn has an element of the terrible in
it. Few are able to live there and remain human. Enchantments are debilitating, and poetry is best met with at the
confines of darkness where the real world disappears from
memory. To succeed as a poet is to imperil what the world
calls normal responses and normal reactions. In seeking to
recover from his poet's method, Rimbaud could well be-

lieve that happiness, in a more purely human sense, was his fate. Happiness was the defect of his poetry. After all, poetry was a seasonal thing for him, the site of a fabulous castle:

O saisons, ô châteaux!

Voyage is a cure for such a malady and such a temptation, for such a season spent in hell.

The much-discussed relationship with Verlaine, if it is considered in its analogy with Rimbaud's poetry, reveals its importance and its uniqueness which far exceed any biographical or psychological importance. The literal story, as much as is known of it, is drab in the routine of tavern existence and poverty. It is melodramatic in the intervention of Mathilde and the two mothers and the final pistol shots. It even involves court proceedings and imprisonment. The moments of happiness and elation seem to have been offset by many moments of despair and disgust. Throughout the episode, two kinds of magic preserved it: intoxication and poetry. How closely they are related can be seen not only in the ancient ritual of Dionysian tragedy, but in the attempt of Rimbaud and Verlaine to exceed ordinary living. Intoxication and poetry are two ways of blotting out the real world, of making it absent (*la vraie vie est absente*), of literally leaving the world (*nous ne sommes pas au monde*). Poetry is intoxication when, as in the case of Rimbaud, the most infernal hours of life are transfigured and redeemed.

Délires I should be read before and after *Délires II,* as Rimbaud's principal explanation of the beginning and the end of his relationship with poetry. As a document on his relationship with Verlaine, it is only of secondary importance. Its circumstantial literalness may be questioned, but its meaning has survived Rimbaud and is related to a subject far greater than the life story of any single poet.

Evil is a way of knowledge. Extreme experiences of evil awaken in most men the deepest desire to understand what they are doing and suffering in order to transcend it. Those who practice evil as deliberately and knowingly as Rimbaud and Verlaine did turn themselves into Satanic theologians much more than mere lovers. Any attempt to experience love, no matter how irregular the form it takes, is always an attempt to reach the absolute, to free one's self from the bonds of ordinary life. The mirage of love is endless because it can never be experienced solely in itself.

The velleities and the changing temperamental whims of Verlaine are opposed for all time to the pitiless, the intact temperament of Rimbaud. They are almost as far apart as the sinner is from the Creator, and almost as mysteriously joined. They were irreducibly opposed and at the same time unaccountably attracted to one another. The meaning of the struggle they waged together is related to the struggle that every creature wages with his God. But the pattern of struggle is not so significant as the richness of the aspiration, of Verlaine's to follow and Rimbaud's to lead, in the conquest of happiness. If Verlaine sought his absolute in Rimbaud, Rimbaud sought his in his role of Lucifer, of pure spirit able to induce sin in a human being. *C'est un démon, ce n'est pas un homme,* he has Verlaine say about himself (Rimbaud) in *Délires I.* The element of crime was in Rimbaud's behavior, in the way he walked (*il veut marcher avec l'air du crime*), in his domination, in his power of keeping the one he tempted outside of his own world as if it were a world of pure spirit whose atmosphere would be unbreathable for a simple creature. Verlaine believed Rimbaud had secrets for changing life (*Il a peut-être des secrets pour changer la vie*), although he knew he could never learn the secrets and was content simply to live in the wake of the superhuman power. Whatever charity Verlaine felt in Rimbaud, he knew it to be bewitched. Whatever tenderness the boy showed, the older man knew it to be mortal. Rimbaud lived too much as a somnambulist to be completely human. Before it occurred, he talked of his disappearance from the world, of his voyage to distant lands, and tormented Verlaine with such predictions. His ultimate silence was like the death of the year-god, the dying and the dismemberment. After his effort to reinvent love came his dying to language. The poet always knows that just beyond the chaos of a poem is the silence of poetry. Rimbaud was one of the very few poets who consecrated his work by a silence which has done more than any manifestoes and explanations to reveal it and to make it known.

In *Délires II,* Rimbaud speaks, with obvious disdain, as if it had been the story of one of his madnesses, of having invented the colors of vowels and a poetic language accessible to all the senses. This passage refers to his celebrated sonnet, *Voyelles,* which the symbolists about 1888 had taken quite seriously as a contribution to the Baudelairian doctrine of "correspondences" whereby a word is seen as capable of provoking sensory responses. Other critics, between then and now, have taken the attitude that the sonnet was a mere game for Rimbaud, a willed mystification. Verlaine, who believed that the intense beauty of the sonnet dispensed it from any doctrinal importance, was worried that René Ghil had gone too far in his *Traité du verbe,* of 1885, in ascribing to Rimbaud some of the major tenets of symbolism. In October, 1934, Henri Héraut published in *La Nouvelle Revue Française* an ingenious interpretation of the sonnet, based upon a school alphabet book in color, used during the Second Empire, which Rimbaud knew and remembered in ascribing the colors and figures to the various vowels: A representing *Abeille* (bee); E, *Eau* (water); I, *Indien* or *Iroquois;* U, *Univers* (universe); O, *Orgue* and *Œil* (organ and eye).

A is black and evokes the blackness of the bee. The darkness may be the shadow of gulfs (*golfes d'ombre*) where it is possible to sleep, as in the mother's womb. E was water in the school primer, and in the sonnet it quite naturally becomes the whiteness of vapor and tents, symbolic of the liquid, melting world of Rimbaud. Water was the important symbol of both *Le Bateau ivre* and *Mémoire*. In the latter poem it is associated with the mother who crushes a flower in her walk over the field. The flower, *une ombelle,* recurs in the sonnet passage on E (*frissons d'ombelles*). I is the symbol of red and Redskins (*Indiens*), the same who had nailed the haulers of *Le Bateau ivre* to painted stakes. Blood and wine are in it, all symbols of lust and intoxication. U is the universe and the French word, *univers,* gives its color: uni-*vert*. Green dominates the universe, and it dominates Rimbaud's poetry, as C. A. Hackett points out. O, in the primer, is blue and designates *Orgue* and *Œil*. Both recur in the poem, in the trumpet (*clairon*) and in the violet ray of God's eyes (*rayon violet de Ses Yeux*). Omega is the perfect word for the last line, indicating the end and the beginning, as symbol of the absolute. It is the eye that sees beyond the real world, the silence of the beyond, the end of life and the beginning of the dream. These are themes permeating all of Rimbaud's writings.[1]

> *O! Oméga, rayon violet de Ses Yeux.*

The final O, the Omega, is the circle, the appropriate symbol for the paradoxical experiences of liberation and of continuance. In his poetic language, Rimbaud freed himself from the constrictions of clichés, from the usual meanings of words, as the boat in *Mémoire* tried to free itself from the river mud, and the drunken boat from the lantern signals and from the eyes of the prison boats. O is the goal and the re-beginning. It is the animal victim, the hyena of *Une Saison,* turned mystic in the total metamorphosis that every end creates. When "the violet ray of His Eyes" reaches the poet, he is without question at that moment beyond the tomb (*je suis réellement d'outre-tombe*). O is the end of Rimbaud's long period of unadaptableness during which his vision was always discontinuous. He had been the primitive genius, bent upon subordinating words to their sounds and colors. The boundlessness of desire is comparable only to the inexhaustibleness of speech. From these two experiences, so inseparable for Rimbaud, he had protected his illusions and willingly made himself into their dupe. But he was always moving toward the final vowel, toward the O of Omega, which would be the end of illusions, the end of flight and revolt, the moment when he would slay the poet in himself.

---

[1] For a good treatment of the *Sonnet des Voyelles* see C. A. Hackett, *Rimbaud l'enfant,* pp. 116–42. For a controversial interpretation see *A-t-on lu Rimbaud?* numéro spécial de *Bizarre,* 1961.

The poetics of Rimbaud treat poetry intermittently and secondarily. He was a visionary for whom the transcription of the vision could only be of second importance. The fragmentary, discontinuous visions of the poems must be at best only imperfect replicas of the world seen by the visionary. Rimbaud is even closer to the mystics in his theory of inspiration whereby the consciousness and the conscious faculties of the poet should be suppressed for the purpose of discovering beyond them a spiritual absolute. The totality of his powers can be realized only if he succeeds in quelling the center of his inordinate consciousness. "The first study of man," he says in his *Lettre du voyant,* "is to know himself." By the destruction of his consciousness, he may reach the unconscious self which the mystics would define as that part of man open to the gratuitousness of God. The unconscious for André Breton and the surrealists is reached in the state of dreams which is the liberation of man, spending his life between the opposing states of fettered consciousness and the infinite freedom of his dream world.

The poetic theory of Rimbaud has always to be considered from the viewpoint of his final silence. This silence was more dramatic and absolute than that of Mallarmé and Valéry and the surrealists, but it is closely related to theirs. Rimbaud was at all times more capable of absolute silence because he had something of a mystic's temperament which would know that for absolute truth there is no literary expression, no recognizable formulation of thought. When the being of man reaches a total kind of concentration, whatever was his ego, his superficial self, is extinguished. This is the probable meaning of the opening sentence of Baudelaire's *Journaux intimes,* which could stand as an admirable epigraph for all of Rimbaud's theoretical writing: *De la concentration et de la vaporisation du moi, tout est là* ("Everything is in the concentration and the vaporization of the ego").

Whenever anything is said, whenever an idea is given verbal articulation, it undergoes some modification. Of all the manners of speech, poetry is that form that bears the memory of the initial, irremediable failure of all speech. Of all the poets, Rimbaud is perhaps the one who felt the most desperately poetry's fatal approximation to the absolute. The way he had elected to reach the absolute was a cul-de-sac. *Je ne sais plus parler.* The poet is the man stranded somewhere between the idea and the word. *Toute parole étant idée.* But it is a slightly different idea from the original. The unconscious, which cannot be formulated in words, participates more intimately in the absolute of thought. Because God first thought the world and then created it by his word, the creation of poetry corresponds distantly with the law of the cosmos. A profoundly creative and jealous poet, like Rimbaud, can only be impatient with words which designate and describe rather than create. Impatient with the words he puts on paper, he is always, persistently, obsessed by a veneration for the secret of words, for their unpredictable power, for the creating force they promise. To write a poem is to set in motion all the forces of the cosmos. The poetic utterance of Orpheus caused the forest trees themselves to bend down over the poet's heart. The trees recognized the poet's voice and responded. Rimbaud had read such a theory in Baudelaire's *Correspondances* (*qui l'observent avec des regards familiers*) although he scarcely needed doctrinal confirmation for the relatedness he could feel directly between the rhythm of the universe and the rhythm of poetry.

The brief section, *L'Impossible,* which follows *Délires*

II in *Une Saison en enfer,* serves as epilogue to Rimbaud's
evaluation of his experience with poets and poetry. The
very title indicates what effect such an experience represented, the impossibility of the whole attempt. It was folly,
but it had been undertaken with the greatest seriousness
and disinterestedness. He was right in cultivating his scorn-
ful attitude toward conventions, because that was part of
his escape from them. But he had forgotten one thing, one
inescapable fact, his roots in the West. He was born in the
Occidental marshes. The shred of reason left to him reminds him of that. He had tried to rid himself of Western
symbols: Christianity and its martyrs, inventions, art, warfare. He had secretly been trying to return to the East, to
the source of eternal wisdom. But that had been a dream.
A modern Westerner is the man who has harmonized
Christ with the bourgeoisie. We cultivate the fog, and intoxication, and devotions. It is another world than the
primitive wisdom of the East. What Rimbaud had dreamed
of, in his revolts and his poetry, had been the purity of
Eastern thought, the purity of the mind that leads one to
the absolute (*Par l'esprit on va à Dieu!*). The experiment
was doomed to failure. To the purity of the dream succeeded the image of man's permanent woe (*Déchirante
infortune!*). The rhythmical joy of the cosmos and its
counterpart in poetry were shattered with the realization
that they could not be sustained.

And yet they were believed in and practiced by Rimbaud long enough for pages to be written and images to
be created that have helped to sustain Western poetry since
his death. Images are products of the word. They are the
magic power of poetry. When, as in the work of Rimbaud,
they are unpredictable and sudden, they may give the
reader a full sensation of freedom, of his own complete

liberation from all the bonds of the world. A poetic image is comparable to an earthquake that will shatter rocks from their foundation. The rhythm of Rimbaud's speech and the freshness of his imagery can have the effect of liberating a reader from all the ties of his habitual life, of releasing him from the very ground on which he walks.

The most powerful of such images probably do not come from a comparison such as the ordinary simile or metaphor contains. The image which will give off the most shattering effect will doubtless come from the union of two realities that are very distant from one another in their usual appearance. The violence of the poet and the vigor of his image come precisely from the unthinkable joining of two realities, but in such close relatedness that the cosmos is suddenly reformed and re-ordered. The reader has to learn to walk differently over the surface of a different cosmos. Such discoveries, as that of a new image held firmly in a new rhythm, are made best in a night world, because there man has his deepest intuition of the void, of the limitless empire of his mind, of the eternity of time, of the innocency of the cosmos waiting for some expression of his will. Ever since Nerval and Novalis, one school of the modern poet has understood that he must be possessed by the night. Whatever union between the self and the universe can be achieved, whatever sensations can be engendered from a single sensation (as in *Correspondances*), night is the time when the superior ego (*Je est un autre*) claims its life and its expression.

The poet's mind is the site of mysteries that are constantly being enacted and celebrated, and that bear some relationship to language. When the poet writes, he recaptures from these performed mysteries the two principal acts of creation and destruction. A mystery is that which creates and destroys. It is the dramatic representation of man's personality, of his effort to construct, and his wilful annihilations. What seems real is only a mirage. The solidity of the universe is simply the result of lighting. Poetry is the communication between the world of principles and the world of facts, between mysteries and commonplaces. Poetry is that form of language which lies closest to the origins of creation. The poet and the priest have interchangeable functions. Their personality withstands a daily dissolution. But a dissolution means a re-creation. For the very reason that Rimbaud was able to adopt so many masks and to become so many lives, he is pre-eminently faithful to his mission of poet. That supreme role, composed of hieratic fervor, he imposed upon himself at the age of fifteen as if it were a question of existence, of giving an existence to the inner life he felt to be endless and primal.

Rimbaud's career gives the impression of an obedience to the dictates of an inner life, of a fidelity to a message he himself understands only imperfectly, and which will be communicated in phrases and flashes. Each work of his represents a return to this secret message and a further clarification. The interruptions were the murderous waves of existence which obscured the clearest hours, but which brought in their wake only a greater desire than ever to return to the message in its deep secrecy and silence.

Le Bateau ivre, written at the beginning of the three or four years of Rimbaud's career as poet, is not only a successful poem in itself, it is the archetype of all future work. It contains his principal themes, the order of his experiences, the evolution of his work and his poetics. According to Delahaye, it was written to dazzle the Paris poets. Delahaye saw Rimbaud just before he left for Paris, at the end of September, 1871, and has recorded this fact as well as Rimbaud's early doubts about the whole Paris campaign, about his incapacity to fit into such a world as that represented by Verlaine and Banville. He was going to the writers as if they were demigods, motivated by universal love and generosity. But the poem, in its final movement, is so strongly that of disillusion, that unconsciously Rimbaud must have felt he was wrong about the literary gods of the capital.

The poem is about the one called away from his familiar world, who leaves the land for the ocean and discovers there fresh and marvelous contacts with the waves. When the tempest comes, the sea assumes the form of a beast and the poet becomes aware of lurking monsters and menaces. He is caught in cataracts and maelstroms, in a total submersion in the wild elements. Then begins the disillusion, the period of martyrdom and fatigue. The voyager is tired of all excesses. He is on his knees now, aware of his growing nostalgia for the past, for the familiar scenes of Europe from which he had tried to escape. These awarenesses grow into a need to escape again, this time from the hell of his illusions, and to return to cities. He wills the most humble return possible, the one most lacking in grandeur and waves, the return to a child's mud puddle.

Le Bateau ivre is a less complex and less rich *Saison en enfer*. Approximately two years separate the writing of the hundred-line poem and that of the long poem in prose. But they are two condensed epics of a human existence, two works on a revolt against the pact which most men have to make with society, in the patriotic and religious sense. The motivation of the drunken boat was to find something new (*trouver du nouveau,* as Baudelaire had written), and the quest related art and a new way of living.

This was the "message" that Rimbaud took to the Paris poets in the fall of 1871, where it met with predictable coolness and the lack of comprehension that seem to be the fate of such works.

In one way, *Le Bateau ivre* is an answer to the question asked in Baudelaire's *Le Voyage:* "What have you seen?" The question was asked by a child, by a *cerveau enfantin,* and Rimbaud's answer is appropriately that of a child. The poem signifies, from start to finish, a child's world. Baudelaire had written that the great works of the creative spirit represent a recapture of childhood, and Rimbaud substantiates this theory in *Le Bateau ivre,* where at the beginning of the poem the child is eager to show his secrets, to pour them out in dazzling profusion, with the impatience and the generosity of a child. Even after the experience of bitterness and disillusion, the protagonist is still the child, but he is depicted as crouching over a street puddle, humbly immobile as he watches a paper boat. After going to all the extraordinary landscapes and enduring the ocean adventures, after passing through a cosmos exhibition of beauty and danger, the boy turns all the scenes into himself as if henceforth he will treasure their memory but not exploit them by bringing them to the surface of his consciousness and giving them a poetic articulation. He will retain them without singing them.

The child is the protagonist in *Le Bateau ivre* in his capacity for seeing the marvelous and the strange, all those things which men cannot see, and in his capacity also for storing such scenes within his memory. He may say them once, as Rimbaud does in *Le Bateau ivre,* and men will call him a poet for that, but what he says is fragile as compared with the real vision. *Le Bateau ivre* describes the bravado of a child and the return to his true weakness.

This is the poet's cycle also, and especially Rimbaud's. After the dazzling commencement of vision, the poem and the poet return to their initial state of weakness where the light is subdued and the objects only half-formed. The child lives on the fringe of society, in its shadow, and this poem likewise has a diminished coloration and finally a symbol of the utmost simplicity, a paper boat as frail as a May butterfly, left to stand for the intoxicated boat that had dared go down the largest of rivers to the sea and there pass through all the perils and beauties the sea contains.

The danger of all vision is its aftermath, the dull inescapability of the absence of vision. This parallels the danger for the child in losing his heart, in becoming depraved. This was Rimbaud's experience, especially apparent in *Le Cœur volé,* and half suggested in *Le Bateau ivre* where he speaks of the bitterness of love (*rousseurs amères de l'amour*). The naïve heart rushes to the fulness of its vision (*dès lors je me suis baigné*) only to be beaten back with cudgels. The picture of giant serpents devoured by lice and of Leviathans rotting in marshes indicates that the vision has turned into its peril. The final desire is to leave all source of light, of the moon and of the sun (*Toute lune est atroce et tout soleil amer*).

Just before the turning away from the vision, the child speaks as poet of the future vigor of his art which for a time will sleep through the nights of childhood in a kind of exile, and then the child speaks as child crouching over the puddle when the vision has receded into the night of his unconscious.

4

Introduction to Les Illuminations

THE ONLY PUBLICATION supervised by Rimbaud himself was *Une Saison en enfer,* printed in Brussels in 1873 and limited to five hundred copies, which were not distributed. The next publication in book form was *Les Illuminations,* presented by Verlaine, in 1886, in an edition of *La Vogue.* Rimbaud, in Abyssinia at the time, did not know it was to appear. A general edition of Rimbaud's work, called "complete," appeared in 1895, published by Vanier, and prefaced by Verlaine. The first edition of the *Œuvre,* by the *Mercure de France,* appeared in 1898, with a preface by Berrichon and Delahaye, and in revised form in 1912, this time with the celebrated preface by Paul Claudel.

Before the first edition of *Les Illuminations* in book form, the prose poems appeared in five issues of the periodical *La Vogue,* between April and June, 1880 (Nos. 5, 6, 7, 8, 9). When Gustave Kahn, who was chief editor, decided to publish the prose poems as a small work, in a limited edition of two hundred copies, he asked Verlaine to write the preface. It is in this document that Verlaine explains the title *Illuminations* as coming from the English, meaning *colored plates,* or *painted plates,* which Rimbaud indicated on the manuscript as a subtitle. In February, 1875, when Verlaine joined Rimbaud at Stuttgart in Germany, it is possible that he received the manuscript directly from the poet himself. But it is also possible that Rimbaud gave it to Charles de Sivry. At one point, at least, during the period between 1875 and 1886, de Sivry seems to have given the manuscript to Verlaine, according to a letter published in the Pléiade edition of Rimbaud. In the same preface to *Les Illuminations,* Verlaine affirms that the poems were written between 1873 and 1875, during travels in Belgium, England, and Germany.

On the whole, this affirmation of Verlaine on the date of *Les Illuminations,* as coming after *Une Saison en enfer,* received no credit among critics until the recent investigation of Bouillane de Lacoste, who vindicated and strengthened the earlier theory. Ernest Delahaye and his collaborator Paterne Berrichon, in their edition of Rimbaud's work (1898), ascribed to *Les Illuminations* the date 1872–73, and indicated in a brief note their disagreement with Verlaine on this point. Both Verlaine and Delahaye were fairly reliable. Most of the critics of the past twenty years have accepted the order of *Les Illuminations,* first, and *Une Saison,* second, until the thesis of Bouillane de Lacoste, who presents a skilful demonstration based on the handwriting of Rimbaud. For the years 1874–75, he discovered lists of Spanish, English, and German words, written by Rimbaud, which Verlaine had kept and presented as a gift to his friend Cazals. A valuable confirmation of this theory was discovered in the handwriting of Germain Nouveau, found on the manuscript. Nouveau lived with

Rimbaud in London in 1874. In summary, the demonstration gives credence to Verlaine's dating. De Lacoste believes that most of the prose poems were written in London in 1874, when Rimbaud was in the company of Nouveau. By March the manuscript was completed and given to Verlaine, who sent it to Nouveau. All trace of the manuscript was lost until Charles de Sivry found it in his home in 1886. A few of the pages belong to the collection of Berès (*Mouvement, Bottom, H, Scènes, Soir historique*), the others to that of Lucien-Graux.

It would be an exaggeration to claim, as many journalists and critics did on the publication of Bouillane de Lacoste's thesis, that all previous criticism of Rimbaud was based on error and loses all value. André Breton, in *Flagrant délit,* his summary of the publication of the "false" *Chasse spirituelle,* points out that the surrealists had always emphasized the importance of *Les Illuminations* and the technical evolution of Rimbaud's composition from verse to prose. Breton himself had always believed that a return to use of a fixed metrical form in poetry would have represented for Rimbaud a historical regression. He had accepted the fact of an interruption in the writing in 1873, but not the theory of a complete abstinence from writing, from that time on. Bouillane de Lacoste is concerned, both in his thesis, *Le Problème des Illuminations,* and in his critical edition of *Les Illuminations,* with problems of scholarship, the dating of the work, the fate of the manuscript, and the errors of previous editions. Only in a few instances does he intervene as an exegete or as a critic, and then he reveals a lack of profound interest in Rimbaud as a poet. A sentence at the end of his book, in which he questions the function of art as being that of "fixing dizziness," might indicate a rather basic disapproval of Rimbaud's method and art (*Mais l'art a-t-il vraiment pour fonction essentielle de fixer des vertiges?*). He is puzzled by some of the prose poems which seem to be the most important and the most intriguing in the collection.

Breton is quite right in his belief that the value of the thesis is to call attention to the year 1874 in the life of Rimbaud, about which very little is known. It was the year of Rimbaud's companionship with Germain Nouveau. Nouveau has been scandalously neglected both as a poet and as Rimbaud's companion during the year when at least a part of *Les Illuminations* was being written. It is even possible that Nouveau was closer to Rimbaud as friend and confidant than Verlaine. The absence of any real knowledge about their relationship and their exchange of poetry form the most regrettable lacuna for Rimbaud criticism.

The history of the editions of *Les Illuminations* has been written by Bouillane de Lacoste in his critical edition of 1949. It would appear from documents published in this edition that Félix Fénéon was the sole editor of the very first publication in the five issues of *La Vogue* in 1886. If one can trust the memory of Fénéon, writing to Bouillane de Lacoste in 1939 concerning his editorial work of 1886, one has to accept the fact that the order of the prose poems, the pagination of the manuscript, are the work of Fénéon and not of Rimbaud, save in the few instances when two or three poems appear on the same sheet of paper. The five issues of the magazine published thirty-seven *Illuminations*, including the two poems in free verse, *Marine* and *Mouvement*, as well as eleven poems which were quite unrelated to the work. The first available edition of *Une Saison* appeared three months after these issues of *La Vogue*. This fact, among others, helped to establish the possibly false chronology. In the first edition in book form of *Les*

Illuminations, in late 1886, with the preface by Verlaine, the order of the prose poems was completely rearranged. There is no authentic sequence to follow in the work. The next edition, that of Vanier, in 1891, contained the poems, *Les Illuminations,* and *Une Saison en enfer,* in that order. In the following edition of Vanier, in 1895, five more prose poems were added to *Les Illuminations: Fairy, Guerre, Génie, Jeunesse, Solde.* It was probably Charles de Sivry who unearthed them.

The first so-called complete edition was undertaken by Paterne Berrichon seven years after Rimbaud's death, in 1898. Berrichon had not known Rimbaud personally, but he had married the poet's sister, Isabelle, in 1896. Since Isabelle was ten years younger than Arthur, she could hardly have remembered with much accuracy the chronology of his work. Despite Isabelle's lack of sympathy for Delahaye and her indignation over an article he had published on her brother (*Entretiens politiques et littéraires,* December, 1891), Berrichon called upon him to help in the dating and classifying of the work. This was to be the first *Mercure de France* edition and was based upon Delahaye's memory of the writings. In the *Mercure* edition, the first period, 1869–70, corresponded to Rimbaud's last years at the Collège de Charleville; the second, to the years 1870–71; and the third, 1871–72. In his book *Rimbaud* (1905), Delahaye affirms that Rimbaud read to him some of the prose poems in 1872. He therefore ascribed *Les Illuminations* to 1872–73, and declared them anterior to *Une Saison.* The order had already been established, and the two editors, brother-in-law and school friend, respected it (although they referred to the date of *Les Illuminations* claimed by Verlaine in his earlier preface). For about fifty years, this date, 1872–73, was to persist. Berrichon added one further piece which he had received from Cazals, Verlaine's friend, the fragment beginning *Cette saison, la piscine des cinq galeries.* The first two words were an incorrect reading for *Bethsaïda.* In 1947, M. Matarasso unearthed two other passages in prose which were based on the Gospel of St. John and which, with the first, form a group of three pieces that seem to have no probable relation to *Les Illuminations.*

The 1912 edition of the *Mercure de France* was supervised by Berrichon and prefaced by Claudel in an essay which has become a justly celebrated critical statement. The general ordering of the work remains the same, poetry, *Illuminations, Saison,* but the poems in *Les Illuminations* are separated from the prose poems. Claudel refers to *Les Illuminations* as belonging to the "second" period of Rimbaud's work. The prose passage from St. John, which he still reads as *Une saison, cette piscine,* Berrichon places now at the head of *Une Saison,* doubtless because of the opening word. Bouillane de Lacoste believes that the fragment should be eliminated from *Les Illuminations.* With the two other passages discovered by Matarasso in 1947, *A Samarie* and *En Galilée,* it forms a series of three pieces, probably written in 1873, at the time of *Une Saison en enfer.*[1]

Of all subsequent editions, the most valuable and the most scrupulously prepared is that of the Pléiade, by Rolland de Renéville and Jules Moquet, which appeared in 1946. It alone today can be considered complete, since it contains, in addition to the already published work, the poems written at school, the *Stupra,* the *Album dit Zuti-*

---

[1] On the "problem" of *Bethsaïda* see Pléiade edition, pp. 714–15. Etiemble has some penetrating remarks on his interpretation of the prose poem in his *Rimbaud,* pp. 44–52.

que, Un Cœur sous une soutane, and the correspondence.
It also includes letters from Rimbaud's family, Vitalie's
Journal, variants and notes of great interest, and finally a
bibliography. Although the editors were aware of the research of Bouillane de Lacoste and his new theory about
the dating of *Les Illuminations,* they maintain the old
chronology. In his edition of *Les Illuminations,* of 1949,
de Lacoste succinctly points out his difference of opinion
with the two editors of the Pléiade edition. An enormous
progress has already been made in Rimbaud scholarship,
but there is still more to be done, and it may well be that
some of the problems will never be clarified beyond all
possible doubt. The discoveries of the last ten or fifteen
years prove the circumspection necessary for any dogmatic
statement about dates and manuscript readings, and even
the extent of Rimbaud's work. In 1960, Suzanne Bernard
published an excellent edition of the *Œuvre* in the Classiques Garnier series. Her notes are largely composed of
quotations from various interpreters of Rimbaud.

The theory which places *Les Illuminations* after *Une
Saison en enfer* in time makes good sense in terms of Rimbaud's poetic development. *Une Saison* is essentially a psychological drama, the history of a struggle waged between
Rimbaud the poet and Rimbaud the adolescent. It is a
modern version, and one of the most bitter in literature,
of the ancient debate between the body and the soul. *Les
Illuminations* forms a spectacle, a series of scenes which are
poems in the purest sense and which succeed the kind of
inner drama enacted in *Une Saison.* The prose poems imply a deeper understanding of human experience than the
more purely autobiographical writings. They are creations
of many elements of experience, and they possess a harmony, a beauty, and a transposition in which they tran-

scend the experience of an adolescent and create the experience of poems.

The first violence of Rimbaud was destructive. It was composed of the direct feelings of hate, despair, bitterness. The new work has violence too, but it is far more creative because it is more centrally the violence of poetry. Without completely relinquishing his roles of *voyou* and *voyant*, Rimbaud unites them in his role of poet, of the one skilled in the secret power and the ruses of words. Something of the permanent experience remains, of course, but it is extraordinarily clothed, as if its meaning could be reached only by setting it off against the world, by testing it in many varied roles. *Les Illuminations* is a poetic universe. It is true that it contains the memories of a recent past, which filled the pages of *Une Saison,* but it is especially peopled with the phantoms of a creative imagination. The scenes are fantasies. Hidden machinery offstage keeps changing them, at the will of the poet, who insists also in beholding them as if he were spectator and unknowing of the pulleys and backdrops and manipulations.

The "colored plates" come to life, and the figures move in them. No one setting remains, no one character lives for long. The poetic universe destroys and creates almost simultaneously. For each emotion of the soul there is a setting and a character, but emotions dissolve into other emotions, and the periods of waiting in between prove over and over again their inconsistency.

The monstrous and the gigantic, for example, form a theme in *Les Illuminations* which does not have its counterpart in *Une Saison.* It is a poetic transformation of the sensation of violence which was more directly described in *Une Saison.* The excessive feeling of revolt is reworked in the monstrous deformities of *Démocratie, Parade, Conte,*

Phrases. The theme of Rimbaud's aloneness and uniqueness, his lack of position in society, his lack of a real bond
with humanity is clearly stated in *Une Saison* and recurs in
Les Illuminations, where he cuts himself off from one scene
after another as if he were some angel at bay, moving with
an angel's power from setting to setting, without ever finding the precious kingdom where he might live and breathe.
The angel loses his hold upon the beings he embraces. He
cannot prolong ecstasy or fear. He is not of the world he
creates. Every scene collapses into ashes because it was created by magic. The walls in *Les Illuminations* are always
cracking open and the buildings crumbling away as if they
were as overcome by dizziness as the protagonist. Each *illumination* is a world in itself, magically constructed and
giving way in an all-engulfing, mysterious chaos to the
next world which will stand up for a brief moment as if it
were a painted picture. This is the child's world of order
that is really disorder, of a continually emerging chaos
where only the poet's mind can rescue what seems to be
reality before it sinks back into the void out of which it
first arose.

The soul of the poet is the protagonist of *Les Illuminations.* It is alternately enhanced by the appearances of the
world and harassed by the contradictions of the world. In
contrast with *Une Saison,* the writings in the prose poems
shows far fewer fits of anger and hate. It would seem that
the soul has passed through its period of violent revolt and
has come out purged to a large degree of hatred. The pose
of the *voyou* in Rimbaud grows progressively dimmer without disappearing.

The two poles between which the poet-protagonist
moves in *Les Illuminations* are order and disorder—two
separate kingdoms joined by the identity of their inhabit-

ant, a solitary inhabitant who comes to life radiantly in the kingdom of order and who dissolves in tragic brevity countless times in the kingdom of disorder. Everything that a poet can do is performed quickly and magically to preserve the order in which the poet can live and breathe. Extraordinary meetings are enacted for the bewitchment of this landscape and that, telescopings of fields and city buildings, the deliverance of words from their usual utilitarian meanings, the creation of monsters which can leap through the air and dance as do the very words which designate them.

Each *illumination* is a tale to be recited. Its rhythm demands recitation. Stripped of usual conjunctions and relative pronouns, the texts glow with the essential words of speech, with the dizzying juxtaposition of sentences and unpredictable metaphors. All is vision in these tales that defy coherent exegesis. The tales are pictures too, reminiscent of Rimbaud's talent for caricature. In one of the poems (*Villes* II), he mentions the English museum at Hampton Court and the exhibits, twenty times larger than those held there, of his imagined cities whose architecture is gigantic also. The magnificent cities (*villes splendides*) he invokes at the end of *Une Saison* (*Adieu*), are created in *Les Illuminations*.

A general impression of greater peace, of a cure of the spirit after the torments of hell, is belied by obscure but persistent notations of disenchantment and suffering. Expressions of hate also break out, but infrequently. A kind of cure has begun, but Rimbaud is still the poet close to the mingled obsessions and aspirations of childhood. A child is far more at ease in a world of disorder, and the poet is constantly destroying the order he sees and creates in order to live once again in the familiar ambiency of disorder. But disorder is the climax of the tale. Before it is reached, the poetry often transcribes a state of euphoria, flower-filled, perfumed, fervent. The vocabulary itself is of such richness that it alone would establish a kind of euphoria, where each element or each moment is separated from all the others, first, by the usual lack of syntax and grammatical relationship, and, second, by its unique beauty, as if all the loving care of the poet had been focused upon it.

Each poem seems to be called up from a bottomless chaos, and despite the magic order it finds in the poet's creation, retains always the memory of the original chaos to which it is destined to return. *Les Illuminations* is an example of "pure" poetry in the sense that it has no obvious philosophical content or theme, no didactic intention, no moral lesson. The poem represents its own emergence from chaos, and the final triumph of chaos as the poem precipitates itself into its original pristine absence of form. The most successful sections are unquestionably those which attain, just before the moment of their collapse, a clarity of order and line, a degree of limpidity, such as poetry has rarely sung: *Aube, Vagabonds, Conte.* Those that are less successful maintain the verbal virtuosity of acrobatics performed on the verge of some abyss.

The prose poems so closely approximate the ineffable that no single exegesis is possible. Because they are poems and not verbalizations of some ordered experience, their exegesis is multiple. They are unique, but not their meaning. They create out of each reader an exegete. To read them requires the application of all one's knowledge and experience, and more than that, it requires some knowledge of Rimbaud's vision. Ever since Jacques Rivière's courageous book, composed of personal flashes of insight,

Les Illuminations has been considered gravely and curiously by such critics as Enid Starkie, Fondane, and Etiemble, and, more recently, by the younger critics, Claude-Edmonde Magny, Debray, Bousquet. These are a few of the exegetes who have tried to establish original systems of interpretation. Each one has renewed the subject of the prose poems and confirmed their inexhaustibleness, their resistance to any one exegesis. A great poem is clear in the words it employs, and it is ambiguous in the meaning it suggests. Already a lavish amount of detective work has been spent on *Les Illuminations*. The lines have been examined and re-examined and turned inside out as if they were material objects that could be named and tagged. Between the extremes of Rimbaud as *voyou* (Fondane) and Rimbaud as Catholic (Rivière), the exegeses range. Each thesis is as full and as substantiated as the others. Each system is convincing, and each system is right, in its way. Rimbaud is a *voyant* and therefore bears relationship with the Asiatic mystics (Renéville). He dabbled in occultism and hence justifies the study of Gengoux. The poet's reaction to his society permits Debray to see him as a communist utopian. Magny has little difficulty in allocating Rimbaud to the descendants of de Sade, and Bousquet reveals him essentially as a reader of Swedenborg. All of these studies have some value. Even when the interpretations of Rimbaud are diametrically opposed, they should not be reconciled and thus weakened, but stand as contradictions, as renewed testimonials to the oldest debate in man, that between his soul and his body. Rimbaud is best comprehended when he is seen as being simultaneously Christian and pagan, blasphemer and Catholic, *voyou* and *voyant*, sane and neurotic, Asiatic and Marxist. The great mark of the genius is to reveal to each critic what he is looking for.

Rimbaud's phrase, *Je est un autre,* stands as the clue to this phenomenon, as sign of the irrevocable truth of ambiguity. Poetry can be fought over, argued for or against; it cannot be explained once and for all.

The familiar method of trying to explain a poem is to take it apart and to analyze it line by line, image by image. And yet poetry is precisely that object (unlike a toy) which cannot be taken apart. It has to be seen always in its wholeness, because it means what it is, and nothing else than that. Every reading of it that is total is therefore honest. Rimbaud's very syntax, in its compactness and ellipsis, justifies the feeling that here are poems honestly direct and bare. The poet seems impatient with everything that is not their essence. The words seem fated and implacable. Rimbaud appears as a kind of dogmatist in his poems, because of the tone of imperiousness that fills them. His images are his dogmas in their contradictions and nudity. They alone count; they alone are communicated. But the impatience of the poet and the direct purity of his poems are his protection against exegesis, against any method of dismemberment and analysis. Since the art itself of *Les Illuminations* is discontinuity, it is lost sight of when subjected to the mechanical, tentative, and awkward divisioning of the critic.

All the themes of Rimbaud's age are in *Les Illuminations.* It was an age of delirious and conflicting promises. The year 1870 might easily be considered as the first explosion (minor when viewed in light of the increasingly significant explosions of 1914, 1936, 1939, 1950), when the great wealth and resources of the world turned against the world's spirit and the spirit of individual man. The explosion came from the greatness of the promise and the passion in man to embrace the promise. This is also the pat-

tern and the fate of *Les Illuminations.* The adolescent of
Charleville, like the older men of his age, refused to give
up anything. To know all and to embrace all is the delirium of the poet and of the modern world.

The world grows vulnerable because of its wealth. Its
accomplishments are its perils, and the more delirious the
accomplishments, the more absolute is the peril. In seeking
to exploit its resources, it diverts its spirit from its real
goal. The art of such a poet as Rimbaud parallels the history of the world's ambition and failure. In wishing to
embrace the limitless and to know himself in the fulness of
his being, Rimbaud confronts the same danger and the
same collapse. The psychological and physiological drama
of adolescence offers a condensed and dramatic form of this
fated principle of the world and poetry. The adolescent
wills to be many things that he is not. He refuses to choose
and limit himself, and refuses to be what he is not. His
roles are innumerable and daily he invents a new one for
himself. This wilful creation and exploitation of what he
is not is the harassing drama of the adolescent. It was that
for Rimbaud, and his poetry was its faithful expression. In
Une Saison, he enumerates his roles and in *Les Illuminations* he states similar claims: *Je suis le saint . . . Je suis le
savant . . . Je suis le piéton . . .* To accept, to be simply what
he is, would be to mutilate his spirit, to reject all other possible roles. The voraciousness and the impatience of adolescence are manifested in the world's ambition for conquest and war—and in the poet's method of creation and
destruction.

Perhaps Rimbaud was primarily the peasant. All other
roles were superimposed, and finally to become again the
peasant meant the annihilation of all the beings he had become. His stolid silence after *Les Illuminations* was the re-

turn to the silence of his childhood. His poetry was aberration, but solemn, magnificent, priestlike. His first major flight, to Paris in 1870, when he carried in his pocket the manuscript of *Le Bateau ivre* to show to Verlaine and the other poets of the capital, was in its own way a flight of silence. It marked his silence over what he really was: peasant of the Ardennes. The last major flight, to Harar, was likewise one of silence, the beginning of the final silence over all that he had become and accomplished as poet. Between the two silences, Rimbaud asked of poetry what the conqueror asks of the world, to be more than he was. It is highly logical that after making such a request, one should renounce it. But that is Rimbaud's personal mystery, which does not concern us. The only thing we are sure of is the artistic success of *Les Illuminations*. Its ambiguity is both its enigma and its poetry. Its story is of a peasant boy waking up to find himself angel.

5

Themes in Les Illuminations

Childhood

BAUDELAIRE defined genius as the reinvention of childhood, the rediscovery of the child's world where the problems of man appeared first in their most lucid form. The unsolved problems of man belong so strictly to the chaos out of which he comes that the child's naturally chaotic world provides them with a clarity they lose as the experience of childhood vanishes.

Childhood is one of the worlds seen in *Les Illuminations,* seen rather than remembered or evoked, because there had been no time and no experience in Rimbaud's case for that world to have been forgotten. It is remarkably present in him. Eight of the prose poems are transcriptions of childhood, although they do not all represent the same way of considering the child. Two of them, *Après le Déluge* and *Aube,* are essentially parables, condensed stories and pictures where a dramatic action predominates. Of parables they have both the picturesque narrative and the deeply concealed significance. They are perfectly achieved unities whose meaning is as endlessly suggestive as their form is precise. Three others, *Enfance, Jeunesse,* and *Guerre,* are more poems than parables. *Enfance* is in five parts, but not dramatically conceived. It contains many themes of a child's vision. *Jeunesse,* in four parts, is a companion piece where the vision is more sophisticated, where the child sees himself as man and the man sees himself as child. *Guerre* might be considered as a postlude to the two longer poems. All three are evocations of the world of childhood. Only one of the *Illuminations* seems to treat the theme of the mother. It is *Angoisse,* centering on the ominous pronoun *Elle.* Two prose poems, *Démocratie* and *H,* reflect the violence of childhood which had served so prominently as a theme in Rimbaud's earlier writings. The first is the talk of soldiers as if overheard by a child, and the second is on onanism.

THE PARABLES

Après le Déluge   The flood has restored the world to its primitive innocence. A Franciscan simplicity has descended over everything. The flowers are growing out of the wet earth, and a hare says its prayer to the rainbow. The poem opens with the re-beginning of the earliest time, with birth, after the waters of birth have subsided. The creation reappears in its original freshness. In the earth the precious stones are still hidden, and on the surface of the earth the flowers are blossoming. But suddenly, without transition, a picture of civilization is interposed. A butcher's shop on a dirty street springs up with the same ingenuousness as the flowers did. Blood flows as soon as the waters of the flood are dried. The image of destruction follows that of creation. Three scenes of slaughter are evoked:

Bluebeard, the butcher, and the Roman circus. Blood and milk, symbols of destruction and birth, flow at the same time. But nothing lasts, not even the reign of destruction. And we see again order in nature, as the beavers build their dams, and a moment of repose in a bar where the coffee steams.

Then, as if the children were reading this story in their history book, we see them inside a big house. The rain (of the flood) is still streaming down the windowpanes, but they are lost in the pictures of what the world has gone through, as if they had not been born but were still within the warm womb. But the birth does occur, and the child leaves the house and slams the door after him. He is alone in the city square, a new Noah contemplating the aftermath of the flood. He is alone, but he is understood by the weather vanes and those high points which now dominate the rescued world. From them he can see beyond his city, and his mind moves over the universe, to the Alps, to a cathedral, to a hotel established at the North Pole, to a desert of thyme and an orchard. Gradually the spring is coming to the world, and the boy who has just been born recognizes himself and calls himself "I." A eucharis tells him it is spring. The waters rise again, and he calls upon them to form another flood because he has already grown tired of his birth, of the first order of spring, of the precious stones still hidden in the earth and the flowers that have opened. He has asked his mother, whom he calls Queen and Witch, for an explanation of the world and of himself. But she will not tell what she knows. He will always remain the child for her who cannot know more than the fairy stories tell of the earth's creation, of his own birth and of the floods that destroy the earth.

This is the parable of the birth trauma from which early

childhood spends most of its time recovering. The flood of each birth resembles the original flood when the world was destroyed and resurrected virginal. But the very virginity and innocency retain a bond with the destruction and the tearing asunder of birth. The child, at its birth, is recognized by steeple cocks, isolated sentinels placed over the world. His mother brews her potion of magic like the witches of fairy stories. She answers him only with meaningless words and recipes. He has to recover alone from the shock of the estrangement. His earliest imprisonment was warm and comfortable and natural. But the same imprisonment is within a house. It is true that the windows stream with rain, as the placenta walls once did, but the mind is troubled with questions that cannot be answered.

The world is a mother who speaks to the poet without offering any explanations of what she says. But even as a child the poet grows bored with the evasions, with the trickery of maternal speech. His birth is similar to an eviction from Noah's Ark. He comes out on the earth with a memory of cohabitation with all the animals. He can easily imagine himself an animal, a hare, for example, which he might have fondled in an earlier existence, and whose timidity he has imitated. He remembers also the violence of men because he was born in a bath of blood, and blood is the sign of murder as well as sacrifice and redemption. The new universe is hell, too. Whom must he kill in order to preserve the life that has come to him so abruptly with the subsiding of the birth waters? But to kill is to prepare the next flood, the next punishment of mankind. Already he yearns for that renewal of violence and destruction, because death may be the return to the warm, safe place he had once known and lived in without the harassing memory of birth and fears of the world. With the terror of birth, there was also the experience of its world and the discovery of a virginal world of fresh sights. But a child is not a contemplative. He is a questioner and he can only ask his mother for the secret of the existence she has given him. But the mother is herself so centrally the mystery of existence that she cannot answer questions about it. She is life and not its philosopher. The child is as alone as the poet.

Aube   The first parable is static. The child is immobilized in the prayer he addresses to the rainbow and in the final question he asks his mother. He is spectator of the world's wonders and horrors. Only his arms move round and round like those of a weather vane. But the second parable, *Aube,* is one of movement and pursuit. There exists, however, a strong relationship between the two parables. The movement of flight, described in *Aube,* is instigated as a result of the mother's failure to answer the child in *Après le Déluge.* As the first parable is related to the trauma of birth, so the second is related to the whole mythology of quest, to the life of man which begins after his birth, in his will to discover the world. This discovery, no matter how objective and geographical it appears, is really the discovery of self, carried out in order to prepare the return home, the return to the mother, or to the origin of life or to the absolute where life began. In this prose poem, the quest takes place in the very specific world of fairy stories, those which might have been told to the boy by the mother of *Après le Déluge,* in her role of queen and witch.

It is dawn in summertime. When the story begins, all nature is immobile and still under the spell of night. Nothing moves. Neither the façade of the palace, nor the water, nor the shadows. Only as the boy begins his walk, away from the palace, and as the light of dawn begins to come toward the sleeping world, does the setting become alive magically. His steps stir up the air which is warm and alive. The same precious stones that had been buried in the flood poem now look up as they are walked on. The air is so alive that wings seem to rise up with it. This is the scene of the parable. It is nature outside of the palace (of the large house in *Après le Déluge*), at first immobile and then gradually beginning to move with the coming of light and the coming of the child-poet who is going to seek in the world, by his quest of the world, an answer to his questions.

The quest is initiated and confirmed by a mysterious, unaccountable occurrence. A flower, delicately tinted, which the child comes upon in a path, tells him its name. Just as Siegfried understood the voices of the birds in his walk through the forest, a flower speaks intelligibly to the boy-poet. A real communication, or "correspondence," is established between nature and the poet. He knows that he will be directed magically in all stages of his voyage. He can laugh at the waterfall in the pine forest because it is a being for him. At its silvery summit he recognizes the goddess or the fairy queen who is the objective of the quest because she is the source of all knowledge.

But to see the goddess is not to capture her. This is the beginning of the last phase and the most frenzied, because the prey has to be chased. He catches her veils one by one. He hunts her through the cities and along the marble wharves of the canals. Finally, at the end of the chase, in a laurel wood, he comes upon her and envelops her with all the veils he has seized. Under the veils he can feel her large body. It is really she, but such reality is too great to live with, and the goddess who was dawn and her pursuer the child collapse into sleep in the heart of the woods. When he awakens, it is noon. The goddess has disappeared because dawn has changed into full daylight.

Man lives by his questions about life. Whenever he comes near to hearing their answer, he sinks into sleep or rises into rapture or into some other comparable state of which he will retain no absolute memory. The sleep of *Aube* is dreamless because it was the realization of the dream. It is the clear parable of childhood whose greatest moments are so close to the absolute that they cannot be recalled at will. Only the pattern of quest and discovery remains. The great moments of childhood are as memorable as the child's prenatal life, but they are just as subtly obscured. The parable relates also to most games of childhood, which are patterns of pursuit and hiding. They are miniature ballets where the one pursued is goddess and girl heroine. To catch her finally is to end the game and wake up in the real world. The games of a child are solemn and ritualistic. They are the first poems of the child. Under their seeming design of chance and fortuitous associations, they conceal a profound symbolism. The single game of "hide and seek," of which *Aube* is faintly reminiscent, bears analogy with the Ulysses myth of quest and homecoming. In his first games, the child actively gives himself over to his emotions and re-enacts them in familiar patterns transmitted by the ages. In his later games, which are poems, he re-enacts the same stories by means of images. Both the games and the images have their origin in the darkest regions of the child's being and memory.

Thus the two parables complement one another. In the first, we see the world from within the house of birth, at a time of great quiet. But the world to explore presents itself in its combined and confused pictures of creation and destruction. The child knows himself to be the survivor of a flood and the initiator of some future slaughter. Then, in the second, the world presents itself in an early morning freshness where the mother-image is goddess. The two poems are syntheses of dreams and actions where no one picture remains for long and where no act is ever allowed to complete itself.

THE WORLD

Enfance   Far more complicated in their form and interwoven themes are the three prose poems which analyze the world as seen through the eyes of the child. *Enfance* is the most elaborate of all the *Illuminations* and the one which best illustrates Rimbaud's method and experience, his poetics and mythology.

Part I is composed of three pictures, three superimposed "colored plates," which are three imagined and highly colored worlds of the child, totally different from the real world of Rimbaud's Charleville. First, he speaks of himself directly in his self-identification with a doll, an "idol" that is orphaned and of some strange geographical origin. This is one of the most persistent dreams of the child, to wake up and find himself not belonging to his real family and real country. He would rather be the fabulous child of a Mexican family or Greek than a boy of the Ardennes. This would be a revenge on the tyrannical family and society which misunderstands him. In a far more tragic way, Rimbaud has already stated this problem in *Mauvais Sang*, where he claimed Celtic and pagan blood and radical differences of sensibility with his immediate family. Second, he dreams of a girl, orange-lipped and seated in a virginal forest, similar to the one described in *Aube*, where the flowers burst with light and where springs add color to the sky and the sea. This is the child's idealization of nature as seen through fairy stories where a lonely princess is always waiting for him. But for Rimbaud the girl princess is always becoming the woman, goddess and mother, the very large female form of the *dames* in the third passage. He sees a whole parade of female figures: mothers, sisters, princesses, lavishly dressed, and some unhappy foreign girls. This is the fairy-story society which, despite its magic and beauty, ends by boring the boy reader. The affections are unreal. When the moment of love comes, "dear body" and "dear heart," the story has lost its meaning as the game of pursuit collapses when the pursued is caught.

Part II is a further synthesis of the fairy story world. It starts as a story about a little girl dead behind the rose bushes. The members of her family are evoked in strange, unexpected places. By the end of the paragraph we have moved outside of the story to the more familiar landscape of Charleville, to the ramparts of Mézières covered with gillyflowers, where old men are buried upright. The rest of the section is more purely descriptive and more easily applicable to the Ardennes. The general's house mentioned might be that of General Noiset who lived near Charleville and whom Delahaye reports he and Rimbaud used to visit. Delahaye also claims that he and Rimbaud used to pick gillyflowers on the ramparts. Everything is empty and desolate: the inn, the château, the church, the keeper's cottages in the park. Even the little villages have no cooks and no anvils. The sluice is opened. The death of the little girl, announced at the beginning, has drained the countryside of all signs of life. Death is not visible, but it is felt everywhere. Each element of the final sentence stresses this desolation: the calvaries, the mills that belong to the desert, the islands, and the haystacks. Into these three paragraphs Rimbaud has poured all his memory of landscapes under a spell and emptied of life, of landscapes awaiting their deliverer and their transformation. He is preparing for the four subsequent passages which are the resurrection of the bewitched land.

The beginning of the change, a few lines isolated as Part III, is in the flowers humming with insects, and in the magnificent beasts moving about. The poet refers to himself for the first time and unostentatiously by the pronoun. Only after the coming to life, in Part IV, of certain elements of the landscape, will he name himself and his roles in Part V. Magic controls the coming to life in Part IV where the song of the bird makes one blush. Everything seems directed by a stagehand. The clock does not strike. The clay pit is singled out because of its nest of moving white animals. A cathedral drops out of sight as a lake appears. This is the magic of the stage and of fairy stories. A carriage bedecked with ribbons rolls down the road, as up the road come a troupe of actors in costume. The new world is so complete that when you want to commit a crime, such as steal food and drink, there is someone to chase you. What the child wants he calls upon and then discards rapidly. What is real remains so only for a moment and then is hoisted out of sight.

With Part V the serious game begins. After the inventories of settings and backdrops where the child-poet imagines the world unfolding before his eyes, come the reincarnations. He becomes successively the character he has read of in his stories. He is the saint, first, at prayer in the midst of nature. Then he is the scholar in his library, and the pilgrim (combining both saint and scholar) who is familiar with sunsets and the roar of opened sluices. The role of the abandoned child and the vagabond is the last of the repertory and the one which Rimbaud had known literally.

The real world of Charleville is always encroaching upon his poet's consciousness and demonstrating its claim on his creation. The role of the boy vagabond and the rampart gillyflowers are autobiographical elements, as are the subsequent paths, hillocks, broom, and springs. The drama of flight and the varied characterizations suddenly collapse into a dream of nostalgia. One reaches the end of the world by going ahead. At the end is the beginning. After the fairy landscapes, the ramparts of Mézières.

Almost impatiently, the sixth and last part begins with a prayer for enough magic to rent a whitewashed tomb deep underground. Enough of expansive sites and exaggerated roles! What the poet wants now from the world is a small warm enclosure underground. By the magic of words he creates it for himself and takes up his abode. There he sits at the table, lighted by the lamp, and pores over newspapers and vapid books. Far overhead, he imagines the city with its houses, its mud, its night, its monstrousness. Very high up are the gutters, and beside him lie wonders he willingly imagines: azure pits and walls of fire. There meet all the elements of his dreams: moors and comets, seas and fables. When the contentedness of his underground retreat turns to bitterness, he imagines balls of pure sapphire and metal. With them he is master of silence. Yet even this mastery is doomed to failure. On the vaulted ceiling over his head something white glows, a spot marking a cellar window opening out to the world above. In an earlier poem, *Les Effarés,* this same object, a *soupirail* (ventilator), had been used, but then, five children had crouched outside it to look in at a baker making bread. Now the process is reversed (as C. A. Hackett has pointed out in *Rimbaud l'enfant*), and the boy-poet is safe within the warmth of the earth. He is experiencing the security of mother earth and food after having looked at it on the other side of the *soupirail*.

The prose poem *Enfance* traces the poet's passage through three major kingdoms of his childhood: the scenes of fairy stories which are called up and dispelled by magic, where the boy plays many roles; literal fragments of the Ardennes which Arthur knew and walked over; and finally the subterranean warmth of mother love, imagined as a whitened cell always threatened by a possible opening out on to the world where he would have to break the silence so totally established in the womb.

Jeunesse   This prose poem is made up of four short pieces related by their style and genre. They are condensed serious meditations, almost philosophical in nature, and appear far less successful as pure poems because they concern personal anguish. They are courageous notations on the experience of childhood, and are so full of suppressed tragic feeling that the poet must, momentarily in writing them, have moved beyond their experience in order to see them in something like their entirety and their significance.

Dimanche is a Rimbaud theme already noted in the poem, *Les Poètes de sept ans*. Here it is less directly autobiographical and more movingly universal. When the child puts aside his homework, his mind, like the house he is in and the cosmic mind of the world, becomes filled with thoughts which he describes as a rushing down from heaven (like illuminating messages of the Holy Spirit) and with memories which come to visit him as if they were Sunday visitors, and with pure rhythms which persist and beat in him as if they were settling down for a long stay. Then, as if the thoughts suddenly crystallized into images, four

slight visions pass before him: a horse running in the countryside, a woman character from a play sighing over the
desertion of her lover, bandits yearning for blood and action, children stifling their curses as they walk along rivers.
These are the images that form in the boy's mind noisily
whenever he interrupts his homework on Sunday afternoon. So he returns to his book and his sums in order to
extinguish the sights and the sounds of his dreams.

Sonnet, the second part, is a far more intricately composed piece in which the boy sees himself growing into a
man. He fears reaching only an ordinary size. His body
appears to him as a fruit hanging in an orchard. During the
days of its youth his body is a contained, useless treasure. It
symbolizes love, the peril and the strength of Psyche, who
can be loved. Youth is here the period of waiting. At a distance on a hillside there is evidence of fertility in the
princes and artists. To see them and to feel relationship
with them force the boy to ideas of crime and death. They
tell him that the world is fortune and peril, and he wants
to make it his fortune and his peril. But his problem is
what to do with the present. What he accomplishes and
knows in his present, his sums and his impatience are only
his dance and his voice, not fixed and not forced, although
strength and justice reflect the dance and the voice that are
merely appreciated at this early time. The universe of this
waiting is pictureless.

Sonnet is the unified, condensed picture of the body
waiting in the midst of a discreet humanity for some way
to reveal itself and lavish itself. Dance and poetry (voice)
would be two means for this giving of self which youth,
more than anything else in the world, wants to accomplish.
This is a deeper and more silent meditation than the Sun-

day pictures that intervene to disturb the boredom of homework.

Vingt Ans, Part III, is briefer and more mysterious still. By this time, the school lessons are like voices that have been exiled. His physical innocence, after so much time, has turned to bitterness in its accustomed complacency. Adolescence was a period of endless egoism. Its studies nourished its optimism and its ambitions. That was the season when the world was flower-laden. But now the bitterness has turned to a sense of impotence and solitude. The sounds in the world are of glasses clinking at night, and only his nerves seem alert for quest. This is a poem on the failure of experience.

The last section, unnamed, is a summary of the poem and a candid self-inquisition. The poet turns on himself in a bitter stocktaking and a denunciation of what he is. He is still living with the temptation of Anthony, which might be the temptation of the flesh. But in its already long life the temptation has shortened the boy's religious zeal, has induced nervous mannerisms of youthful pride, as well as a physical weakening and terror. What has to be done is to embark upon another temptation, the pure dream of the future where all harmonies and architectures will gravitate around him. New beings who are perfect in their way and unexpected will enter into his experiences. From the past will come the experiences of idle curiosity and luxury. He will have achieved maturity as a creative poet, and his memory and his senses will serve him as a poet. The world, then, will be different, and will have nothing of its present appearance.

After the bitter dreams of the Sunday child and the fears of growing into an ordinary man and the tedium of prolonged innocence, the poet turns inward, to conjure up the most delirious dreams of what will not happen and of what the endless dreams of youth are composed.

Guerre   The child-poet speaks to the child he is, but with the wisdom that surpasses that of the sage in its unthinking vision. He sees, not morally and philosophically as a sage, but because of the light of certain skies. His face has been modeled and colored by multiple skies as if each one were a character imprinting its trait on the upturned face of the child. To see this miracle, all the phenomena of nature rejoiced. That was his fatality, the coloring of the sky and the endless repetition of the sky. But in the period after childhood, the purity of those moments and the infinity of their vision sent him through the world where he has been respected by children, has had the affection of parents, and where he has known civic triumphs. The world into which the purity of childhood sent the poet is by comparison a disappointingly strange experience. His thoughts lead him to some image that would upset the tiresome logic of the world, and it is war he dreams of, a war of justice or of conquest that would not be reasonable. It would be as simple as a musical phrase following an ordinary experience in order to decorate and conclude it.

Guerre is half-abstraction, half-parable on childhood in the dichotomy the experience creates between the dream and the real world. The child is the beginning of the pure hero endowed with a kind of sight which familiarizes him with infinity. The real world, when he walks through it as a young man, will appear by comparison reduced and trivial. The genesis of war may have something to do with the attempt to enlarge the world by destroying it, and make it resemble more clearly the expansiveness of the early vision. War would be like an act of magic, a transformation brought about by the utterance of a phrase, of a simple melodic line.

MOTHER

Angoisse   This is the only *illumination* that seems to be specifically on the subject of Rimbaud's mother. Despite the title "Anguish," the emotional aspect of the piece is controlled. As with most of *Illuminations,* the experience is recast in images and abstractions. The lines have a deliberate clarity.

The capitalized pronoun *Elle,* with which the poem begins, might of course refer to *Angoisse,* but in the light of the piece as a whole, and especially the fourth paragraph, it is probably the mother. The same pronoun had stood for her in *Mémoire* and *Les Poètes de sept ans,* and, moreover, the equivalence between "anguish" and "mother" would not be difficult to establish in Rimbaud's case. The three firm statements of the opening sentence, phrased as half-questions, are succinctly related to Rimbaud's life at home. Will she pardon, he asks, his ambitions that had been continually stifled? Will a comfortable ending of his life replace the early poverty? (This preoccupation with money is going to increase during the years after *Les Illuminations.* The tendency to avarice, apparent in Rimbaud's early years, becomes stronger with time.) Will some final success, he continues to ask, obliterate his fateful awkwardnesses and failures? *Une Saison,* Rimbaud had spoken of his lack of manual skill and performance, of his peasant origins.

Then, in parenthesis, as if this mention of early ambitions and hope for ultimate successes suddenly flowered in him, he sings ecstatically, by aligning one substantive after another, of the dreams of his youth. They stand in groups of two, one complementing and expanding the other, and crowning the ego of the poet, *moi,* which concludes the enumeration.

After the parenthesis, a fourth question is phrased, heavy this time with a pedantic vocabulary, but significant in its relation to all *illuminations.* The poet asks whether his early candor as a child in the ambitions that drugged his mind will be justified and supported by a love of the world as he grows to know it, and by the magic of poetry as he grows in the mastery of language. He claims that as the child becomes the adolescent, the innocent, native frankness should be restored in its newer forms of poetry and love of mankind.

This has been a long question in its four parts and parenthesis, and now in form of answer, the poet speaks of the female figure as a vampire and of her role in his life as child and adolescent. Her effort during the early years had been to make him "a good boy" and behave (*gentil*), and now that she is no longer present, she orders him to continue playing with what she left him, or if not he will become more strange. This is strong indictment against her. The mother is a vampire who first bewitched and subjugated the child and who even after childhood is over continues to exert her influence. The games of good behavior and obedience can never be abandoned. If the maternal constrictions are neglected, the boy is destined to turn out a "misfit," *drôle,* a word already used in the phrase, *drôle de ménage,* to designate the London-Brussels relationship of Rimbaud and Verlaine (*Délires I*).

What "she" created in him and wants him to continue with are his mediocrity and his passive obedience. To remain obedient is a form of anguish, and to try to escape may be to experience even greater anguish. The final paragraph, a versicle, seems to announce precisely that. An escape, by water, for example, would be simply to move closer to suffering and to torture.

VIOLENCE

Démocratie   The theme of violence and revolt, so persistent throughout the early poems and *Une Saison,* is only intermittently audible in *Les Illuminations. Démocratie* is the one prose poem, composed in one coherent tone, which recalls the earlier truculence of social opposition, of ironic portraiture, of social types, of revolt against the established order.

The entire piece is spoken by soldiers who combine in their make-up brutality, obscenity, and a somewhat startling degree of pedantry in their verbal expression. They are really Rimbaud the scholar in one of his many roles. The title "Democracy" seems to apply more to the democratic spirit in the troupe than to the government.

The filth of the flag, they say, is quite in keeping with the filthy landscape, and their patois is loud enough to drown the drums as they march along. These are mercenaries, or soldiers of fortune, bent on promoting prostitution in the large cities and putting down any well-organized, sensible revolution. They will serve whatever is monstrous, war or industry. Their creed will be brute strength. Their comfort is of prime importance, and the welfare of the world through which they move is of no importance.

This is a stylized picture of the soldier, unscrupulous and coarse, who projects the child's scorn for order and organization. To massacre and thieve for one's self makes more sense than to sacrifice one's self for a cause. The word "monstrous," placed in the center of the poem, dominates it. The goal of the soldier is to create in himself a high degree of inhumanity. This is also the mask of the boy-poet who, unable to correct the evils of the world, can at least attempt to annihilate part of the world. The theme of destructiveness in *Les Illuminations* is usually associated with the motif of the monstrous. Here, in *Démocratie*, everything is monstrous: the flag, the speech of the soldiers, the filthy landscape, the philosophy of the enlisted, and the final picture of the world's collapse.

H   This may well be the most subtly conceived *illumination* and one of the most poignant in terms of childhood.

The single letter that serves as title and as the initial letter of a girl's name, Hortense, possesses the mysteriousness of a code. The last two words, *trouvez Hortense,* interrupting the tantalizing description, give the poem its form of guessing game or charade. All poems are to some extent charades, where a multiplicity of words and actions conceals a single word and a single experience, but *H* is especially that, and the poet invites discovery. He defines with an eye to mystification and a will to obscure. And yet when the right answer is found, all the parts should be suddenly "illuminated" and absurdly obvious.

Again here, as in *Démocratie* and in so many other *illuminations,* the word "monstrosity" is important and pervades much of the poem. Every element of the portrait and "case history" is sibylline. We are not told what her gestures are, save that they are atrocious. When her solitude is described as "erotic mechanics," the first clue is given. But the mysteriousness is recaptured when the girl is associated with many periods of time and is made synonymous with the ardent hygiene of races. She must be more than a girl and a single figure. She must be more than the protagonist. She seems to precede and surpass in her passions and her actions the contemporary figures, the poet himself. The final sentence is the most terrifying and obscure of all, but the qualifying adjectives point out the solution. The loves that have been described are those of a novice. The ground on which they transpire is bloody. And the hydrogen air of the atmosphere is illuminated.

At first the poem would seem to describe the life of a prostitute, but Hortense is so imaginary and is seen through such a distance in time and space, that finally it becomes apparent that she is the erotic vision of the onanist, of the boy-poet forcing a union between his fantasy and the dynamics of his body. Such an act was for certain tribes a performance of racial hygiene.[1] The artifice of solitude is the betrayal of love. What is terrifying is the self-pity in the poet and the ineluctableness of the act which seems to join him with the principle of creation and procreation. The narcissism of Rimbaud is here androgynous. He dreams of Hortense and becomes her. The mystery of the poet comes precisely from this identification of the poet and his dream-fantasy. He is what he loves. This process is as magical as the creation of a poem by means of poetic alchemy. The little girl with whom he fought lasciviously in *Les Poètes de sept ans* is now Hortense, unnamed (*H*) and unformed because she is really the poet for whom

---

[1] Etiemble, in his book on *Rimbaud,* writes, on p. 102: "Il est exact que ce narcissicisme ait été, à certaines époques, l'ardente hygiène des races. Dans les civilisations de l'Inde antique, les mères croyaient viriliser leurs fils en leur enseignant l'onanisme." Claude-Edmonde Magny holds the same interpretation for *H.* See her *Rimbaud,* in *Poètes d'Aujourd'hui,* p. 19.

the solitary sexual act is a mortification of the flesh, a personal mode of asceticism.

There is a price to pay for the visions of the poet. The exercises of the seer are exacting and relegate him to the blind in the world, to those who cannot see the real world. In the same way, the onanist provokes the visions of love, draining off from himself the potencies of his body. He is the perverse ascetic, engaged upon all the practices of fasting and labor and vigil in order to prolong in himself the illusion of being a god. His soul has to become monstrous, with full knowledge of criminals, with total adjustment to all poisons, before he can hope to transcend all periods of history in order to become a man of his own age, humbled with the new knowledge of his finiteness and his weakness.

Hortense, with its mysterious letter *H,* is Rimbaud's version of the myth of *Hyacinthus,* with its counterpart *H,* and with its comparable story of blood and sacrifice. Hyacinthus was a youth loved by Apollo and accidentally killed by him. From the blood that flowed, Apollo caused a flower to spring up. Hortense is also a flower (hydrangea), growing up from her own blood spilled on the ground. The race is renewed in every act of procreation and in every created poem. The answer to the riddle, *trouvez Hortense,* is the flower resurrected after the sacrifice, the flower that is both boy and girl, lover and god, victim and progenitor.

These eight *illuminations* narrate in their own quality and power of poems the adventure of the first part of life. It is a story of existence extending from the brilliant parable of birth trauma (*Après le Déluge*) to the dream-fantasy of Hortense. They represent the two extremes of the child's world, the two extreme forms of his solitude, his first aloneness in the womb and the later aloneness of sexuality. Be-

tween the two experiences of himself, the one barely remembered and the other frantically dreamed, are crowded
together in close juxtaposition one scene after another,
each one significant in itself and startlingly revealed in its
relations to the others. The purity of dawn (*Aube*) describes the drama of quest, but at the precise moment
when the world awakens to the child after his long sleep
in the womb. The family (*Enfance*) is seen magically transformed into the families of fairy stories, where the death
of a child stops everything and the world undergoes its
changes to create the settings necessary for the varied roles
imagined by the boy who has read the stories. The dreams
of the boy about the man he is to become succeed rapidly
to the static fairy-story world. Temptations besiege him
now, and ways of realizing the temptations. The main obstacle to his dreamed-of growth and emancipation is the
mother, ever present, ever large. Yet there is, intermittently, escape to worlds outside of him, when the mother-
obstacle can be overcome by giving full expression to his
feelings of violence. He wills, at least imaginatively, to
mingle with a troupe of soldiers who sing and do everything that is non-feminine, non-maternal.

It is the world of two quests, the one downward and
inward, secretively personal; and the other, upward and
beyond, histrionic and worldly.

The first is the theme of refuge. It is Arthur's room in
Les Poètes de sept ans, which is, especially, the whitewashed tomb underground, warm and pure, closed off from
every other place. The poet encourages the creation and
perpetuation of warm atmospheres and rooms that are
closed worlds in themselves, miniature fortresses of security.

The second is the opposite of security. It is the theme

of departure and flight where the poet is the pedestrian or the abandoned child (*Enfance*) and where the scenes are outside. In the "refuge" poems, he hears the mother's heart beating close to his, but in the "flight" poems, its noise expels him. The two impulses are extreme and antithetical. They represent a full development of the deluge trauma and the Hortense fantasy. To the terrible nostalgia for warmth and immobility succeeds the need for movement, action, conquest. The transition between the two moods is made almost magically, with the wave of a wand. The closed-in, warm places are transformed into open places, roads and paths, for the liberation of the spirit. The two moods are reflected in the early poems, in *Les Poètes de sept ans* and *Le Bateau ivre,* and they are continued in *Les Illuminations,* contraposed more rapidly and more magically than ever. Either the world must hide him or stretch out before him, in all its monstrous shapes of cataracts and storms, to be assaulted and conquered. The experience of immobility is a deepening of thought, a self-hallucination. And the experience of quest is one essentially of illumination, where scene after scene lights up and comes to life.

But the two moods can finally be seen as one, or at least as closely interrelated. Passivity is replaced by action for greater self-knowledge, for a richer return afterward to a deepening of self. At the end of the violent action of *Aube,* the child falls asleep in the depths of the forest. It is not enough merely to come to the body of his desire and embrace it. The exhaustion of such an experience plunges him into a sleep of such oblivion, of such closeness to his primal being, that he wakens in a new full light of knowledge. The hour of noon is plenitude and full light. Only the hunt at dawn and his grappling with the huge goddess will permit him such sleep and such a luminous awakening.

Life of the Poet

In its varied aspects this theme receives a more extended treatment than any other in *Les Illuminations*. In a wilful separation from childhood, Rimbaud considers what the poet's life is and what the roles are he plays as poet. His writing comes close to a kind of dramaturgy, predictable in earlier poems and especially in *Mémoire,* where each of the five sections is a minute drama different in setting and tone. The prestige of the theatre, where the poet is actor, becomes clearer in *Les Illuminations* and particularly in the ten prose poems which illustrate the life of the poet. *Conte* is a parable where the poet is "prince," engaged in a work of destruction. In the briefer depiction of roles, the poet is very often a clown or Pan or an animal, as seen in *Parade, Antique, Bottom,* and *Being Beauteous.* Three of the pieces show the poet's life on a stage, in the form of a comedy. These are *Scènes, Vies,* and *Phrases.* Two seem to deal directly with the poet and another poet. Rimbaud and Verlaine, as dual protagonists, appear in *Matinée d'ivresse* and *Vagabonds.*

In these prose poems the dreams are those of stage sets, and the principal magic is that provided by footlights and spotlights. Here Rimbaud is going to change his personality and his sex at will. He will become one of many beings, one of many landscapes. Already in *Une Saison* he had listed roles dreamed of: *saltimbanque, mendiant, artiste, bandit—prêtre! (L'Eclair),* and now he practices the ritual of metamorphosis in great freedom and fluidity. Underneath all the disguises, the poet remains constant. The poet is the supreme actor because he can be murdered and resuscitated without abandoning completely his role of murdered poet.

PARABLE

Conte Here is an elliptical story where the moral is implicit in the action, although never stated as such. *Conte* serves as introduction to the poems on the poet in much the same way as the parables, *Après le Déluge* and *Aube,* preface the poems on childhood. It is parable both in its directly related action and in the strange atmosphere, half-real, half-unreal, it creates.

The protagonist, a prince, comes from the world of childhood, but he is far more violent and tortured than the usual fairy-story prince. At the beginning of the fable, he is irritated because his life work has been mediocre. He has heretofore given himself only to perfecting commonplace, generous impulses. He has grown suspicious of those around him, of his wives especially who might have loved him more deeply. Luxury and spirituality had spoiled them and diminished the intensity of their love. He wanted greater knowledge concerning desire and its satisfaction. Since his power extended over much of humanity, he was able to begin a terrible massacre.

First he killed all his wives. The garden of the harem was turned into a bloody scene. But as the women were being slaughtered, they blessed him. He did not command any new wives, but they reappeared. Then he began to kill the men who went hunting with him and who drank with him. He slaughtered the magnificent animals of the palace. He burned some of the buildings. He even rushed upon the servants and cut them into pieces with his saber. Yet in a strange way, everything survived: the people, the gold roofs of the palaces, the noble beasts. No one opposed him. He continued to try reaching ecstasy in his slayings and to rejuvenate himself in his experience of cruelty.

One evening when he was riding alone over the countryside, a genie appeared before him, of such beauty that it
could not be described. Here was the promise of the complex love the prince had been seeking. They died together
because their happiness was not bearable. And yet the
ending of the tale tells us that the prince passed away at
an ordinary age, in his own palace. The prince was the
genie, and the genie was the prince. Our desire never has
music sufficiently complicated to accompany it.

The analogy between *Conte* and Flaubert's *Légende de
Saint Julien l'Hospitalier* strikes one immediately. Yet,
Rimbaud's parable is not of martyrdom. The scenes of
wilful destruction are not redeemed at the end by their
opposite. The supernatural aura of *Conte* leads to a psychological interpretation and never reaches the higher and
more purely mystical resolution of *Saint Julien*. The cruelty of the prince is perpetrated in order to know a total solitude. It is related, without much doubt, to the onanism
and the "dynamic solitude" of *H,* to the androgynous
dream fantasy of the boy. Hortense appears in *Conte* in the
guise of a genie, of such overpowering beauty that to lose
this being is to annihilate one's self. Love, of this order, is an
extinction of life. The same kind of scene is adumbrated
at the end of *Aube,* where the boy and the goddess die in
their embrace, and in *H,* where the body loses its form in
its collapse on the bloodstained ground. In a much less
subtle form and one that is more purely narrative and
autobiographical, a similar scene occurs in *Les Poètes de
sept ans,* where the boy, after his fight with the little girl,
returns to his room and savors alone the smells of her body.

In the pure lines of the parable, *Conte,* Rimbaud is able
to state without equivocation the identity of the prince
and the one loved by the prince. Hyacinthus, in his myth

of blood and sacrifice, becomes Narcissus in the myth of self-love and extinction. The scenes of slaughter were vain efforts to reach satisfaction. Nature grows up again after it is destroyed. There is no end to destruction, no ultimate satisfaction in it. Only when life is confounded with death, when the prince joins with the genie, can there be the pure consummation which is a death.

ROLES

Parade   If *Conte* bears some analogy to *Aube* in its form of parable, *Parade* seems related to *Démocratie* in its depiction of men or soldiers bent upon the exploitation of the world. Rimbaud emphasizes their maturity and their strength. During their marches, their eyes have taken on the lights of nature. Their faces are white and burned. The tatters they wear give the swing of their bodies a cruel appearance. The older among them can hardly be conceived of as considering the younger ones, the Cherubinos, and yet they send these youngsters who have been taught their value into the city to extract money from susceptible clients.

Here begins the strange parade which the title announces. The costumes of the younger men are repulsive in their beauty. The smile they wear, during their parade, is more like a grimace. It reveals the rage of a violent paradise. The tricks of these boys cannot be compared with the magic of fakirs or with spectacle performances of comedy. Their improvised costumes were inspired by bad dreams, and what they enact are laments and tragedies unknown to history and religions. But whatever role they play, gypsies, simpletons, demons, in their popular and maternal tricks, their attitude and their tenderness are bestial. They interpret innocence and in their prestidigitation they transform those who watch them. Everything changes: eyes burn, blood sings, bones enlarge, tears stream. The enchantment of these jugglers is either mockery or terror, and it may last a minute or endure for months. Rimbaud alone possesses the key to this mock parade.

According to Ernest Delahaye, this prose poem was inspired by a traveling circus at Charleville. It is reminiscent of many similar events that Rimbaud might have witnessed, such as a parade of soldiers or students at Stuttgart or some other city. But it appears to be much more than a street parade of colorful costumes. It is more private and Rimbaud alone has its key, he is careful to tell us. But the poem too has its key. An ordinary parade serves to dazzle and amuse. It does not transform the spectators. The purpose of this parade seems to be seduction. The poet is a new kind of comedian, a youthfully seductive type, sent out on to the street by the older, more violent part of himself. As in *H* and in *Conte,* the poet demonstrates here a remarkable self-interest. The poet is costumed as a comedian and he ends by seducing himself, the being that he was without costume. His public is himself. The poem is a tragedy, and the tragic hero is a self-perpetuating god.

Antique   The brief poem, *Antique,* is one more *illumination* on the subtle theme of role and metamorphosis. The son of Pan is addressed here in somewhat the same way that Hortense is addressed as the daughter of woman. *Antique* is the simplification and unification of the poems on self-love, *H* and *Conte* and *Parade,* because Pan is animal, man, and woman simultaneously. His son is the poet who emerges from all three sources and who preserves in himself some bond with all three.

The poem is a pure, delicate description where the three

characteristics are mingled. Like his fabulous father, his head is crowned with a ring of flowers and berries. But his teeth are an animal's. They shine in the hairy dark of his cheeks. His bare chest, like the smooth covering of an instrument, makes him appear like a new Adam, freshly created. The female part of him is in the dormant double sex he bears. Hortense was enigma and charade, a name to be guessed, but whose key, like that of *Parade,* Rimbaud alone possessed. The son of Pan, in his newly discovered gracefulness, is addressed directly by the poet, because he is Rimbaud. The final directions are those of a stage director or a dance instructor. "Walk at night," he tells himself, "moving first this thigh and then the second, and then this left leg." A new being is emerging from the old one and the first steps have to be guided. His heritage is so complete with his combined qualities of animal, man, and woman that in learning to walk he will have to transcend all distinct manners of walking and yet retain the essence of his three origins.

Antique is the parable of birth and evolution. It is on the theme of the emergence of one form from a previous form, on the development of a more human creature, who will walk upright, from a more purely animal creature. It is, then, without much extension, the emergence of the poet from the man, the emergence of the poem from the idea or the experience.

The birth of the poet was, in *Parade,* a more bawdy affair, in the costumed comedian, whose smile was a leering, and whose immediate goal was a brief or prolonged exploitation. The miracle is purer in *Antique,* with its Hellenic mythology and background, where the poet comes from Pan and his fabulous ancestors of the forest, in much the same way that Venus rises up, a complete goddess, from the depths of the sea. This is the pure birth of the spirit, of the miracle-working magician, whose character blends many traits in its inexhaustible perceptiveness, in its capacity to assume all roles, because it is all roles at the beginning.

The emergence of the new type takes place in total solitude—no parents and no assistants at the birth. The first steps are his own risk and his own self-creation. And all subsequent steps will be that also. The childhood of the poet was nourished with stories and legends. His own story was confused with theirs, and he meditated on it ceaselessly (*Il lisait son roman sans cesse médité.—Les Poètes de sept ans*). The poet is born when suddenly he dies to the existence of everyone else. At that moment he is alone, and caught between the endless visions of the future which he tells of in *Le Bateau ivre* (*O vigueur future*) and the endless reminiscences of all previous time, when even Greek antiquity is present in the boy of Charleville. At first, the men who meet him will not see him (*Ceux que j'ai rencontrés ne m'ont peut-être pas vu.—Mauvais Sang*), and when they do look at him, he will have changed into one of his multiple roles.

Bottom   This is the story of metamorphosis, of Rimbaud's *Bottom* and of *A Midsummer Night's Dream*. The poet who emerges from Pan can easily return to animal forms whenever reality is too hard to bear.

Love is no easy matter to sustain, and the lady's demands may be too exacting. A quick metamorphosis into a large bird would help the situation. Whatever the poet was, he would be something different then, flying up to the ceiling in escape and yet remaining within the lady's room and dragging his wing through the dark recesses of the evening where no light can fall on its momentary infidelity.

Then again, when the lady's bed is the central object, a metamorphosis into an animal might be helpful—into a bear, for example, not real but a sculptured support of the canopy. Rather than be the physical masterpiece, it might be well to support it merely as a strong and terrifying pedestal. Its eyes would be the crystal decorations of console tables. The room itself darkens. Whatever light is in it seems submerged and burning in the depths of water.

The third change comes in the morning—a warlike June dawn—when the protagonist is an ass neighing its grievance in the fields, until the Sabine women answer its call and come to it. Bottom turns lover in his final metamorphosis.

Being Beauteous   The most subtle and intricately written of the poems on metamorphosis, *Being Beauteous,* appears almost as a final transformation. Initially a being of great beauty stands against the snow. After this first statement, the poem is given over to a strange collapse and disintegration of beauty. The second sentence seems to relate an execution or at least a ceremony of sound and music where the worshipped body of beauty rises up, enlarges, and trembles as if it were a ghost. Red and black wounds break out in its proud flesh. Each sentence narrates an art in a gradual process of change. The third tells how the lifelike colors darken and separate from the body, that is now a vision. Then occurs a restitution. From the ground where the colors fell rise up sounds and smells from the scene confused with mortal signals and harsh music which the world, far away, hurls at the figure. It, like a maternal beauty now, withdraws and stands up. The loves of the poet are covered with a new body of love. As in *Conte,* one can draw the conclusion, even if it is not stated, that beauty is the poet and the poet is beauty.

As in *Parade*, a final sentence serves as mock cry and key to the poem. The execution is a suicide. The face of beauty is ashen, the body is stifled with sawdust, the arms are crystal. The cannon, over which the figure has collapsed, is in the center of a combat between the trees and the air.

The poem begins with a metamorphosis and ends with an unmasking. The first vision is one almost out of the world, a surreal vision. Then gradually the world rises up around it, bringing to it its mark of vulnerability, and sound and death. But the world's attack this time is waged against a beauty it cannot utterly destroy. The beauteous body, like a statue, falls apart, but the death spell, the whistle, the cannon shot, and the wound are shaken off by the poet who has learned to live through many deaths. To see beauty is to risk seeing it disintegrate. Simply to see, for a poet, means to dislocate and disorganize the universe. He has to see through the universe into its original incoherence and chaos.

SETTINGS

In three instances, the poet sees the world as a comedy in which he plays a part, not so much as actor as stage director. Here he is the creator of a separate universe, autonomous and displaceable. An elaborate machinery, of marvelous precision, controls this universe. The poet's creation is the working of levers and pulleys, the changing of scenes, the mechanic's job of curtain-raising, the electrician who can highlight a scene or darken it, the designer who can represent a forest or a night club or an Oriental harem. Everything is possible because everything is artificial.

Scènes   Comedy, in its long history, pursues its action either on the boards of an improvised stage in the midst of a city or in the country where a traveling circus can set its activities and exhibit them. Whether it be the city or the country, the same idyls are narrated and the same harmonies reached. And always the "scenes" are isolations from ordinary life, piers jutting out into the sea. A row of trees, when lanterns swing from it, is changed into a dark corridor. The comedians, like birds, swoop down on the stage which sways like the deck of a boat, and all around, the spectators are in boats too because they sway in the changed atmosphere. Wherever there is a song and recitation, in a stylized Oriental theatre or in a modern clubroom or night club, settings are contrived even in the ceilings. Stagecraft can work wonders everywhere, at the summit of an amphitheatre, in the forest of Boeotia, on farmland. The stage is geometry. Between the gallery and the footlights, and beyond the footlights on the stage, the *Opéra comique* lies stretched out in a mathematical plan.

Vies   In this important prose poem, the poet moves from the immediate geometrical wonder of stagecraft and state transformation in order to consider the plans and architecture of his mind and his memory. This is the Rimbaud of *Une Saison* and especially of *Mauvais Sang*, the poet whose thought is in exile from the past and future, and who sees both, microcosm and macrocosm, in the literal scenes of the stage.

I.   The first section is the most difficult to follow. Its theme is the expansiveness of life when the thoughts of the poet turn back to his own past and especially to his memories of a past he never literally lived. There everything was different: broad avenues of the Holy Land and wide tem-

ple steps, profundities of holy writing. What is comparable
to those distant memories is the childhood experience of
freedom in the fields, of sun on the river, of the expansiveness of such a scene as Rimbaud has described in *Mémoire*.
There nature manifests the bounty and protection of love.
The hand on the boy's shoulder is literally that of the
countryside (*la campagne*) and not of a companion (*la compagne*) according to a correction made by someone on the
manuscript.[2] The caresses he remembers are those of nature in the fields. A flight of pigeons was so startling to him
that it now thunders red in his thought. The poet's present
is an exile from that wonder and that love of the world. To
recapture it, a stage is necessary where the miracles of the
past can be re-enacted. There, to his spectators, the poet
could show unheard-of wonders, and there he could watch
on the faces of the spectators and in their hearts the treasures they discover on his stage. In them the dramas will
continue to live and to grow. What he devises for the stage
is his accumulated memory and wisdom, but it is only
chaos compared to what the spectators will make out of it.
They will scorn what he knew by converting it into something more profound. His message is lost in time and nul-
lified as soon as it is caught up by the spectators, by the
newer poets following in the dark the ancient dramaturgy
and eager to reanimate it with their freshness, their amaze-
ment. The death of the poet comes at that moment when
his art transcends his past and his memory, and is seized by

---

[2] On the manuscript of *Vies I*, belonging now to M. Lucien-
Graux, Rimbaud wrote *campagne*. The *a* of *campagne* was
changed to *o* in pencil. This is indicated by B. de Lacoste in
his critical edition of *Les Illuminations*, p. 75. In the Pléiade
edition (p. 173), the text reads *compagne*.

the spectator or the reader in a new understanding which is a new creation. The work lives by undergoing successive deaths. The poet succumbs when his work is understood by those who have nothing to do with him and who have no way of knowing what he meant by his work.

II. To see one's self at any given moment in a lifetime necessitates the invention of a part. To see one's self is equivalent to writing a poem about one's self and therefore becoming a musician and discovering a key. Even now, at a moment of maturity, in relationship to the countryside he spoke of in the first part of the poem, Rimbaud sees himself as a country gentleman remembering a childhood of begging, of former marriages and wild parties where he was never equal to the gaiety of his companions. But he does not regret his early youthful gaiety. The barren countryside encourages his fundamental scepticism. Unlike his early elation, this recent scepticism cannot be re-created and used. Besides, a new preoccupation has seized him. Isolation and age may well convert him into a wicked fool. . . . The expansiveness of the landscape in the first part of *Vies* becomes, in the second part, the life span of thought. Rimbaud can think back to his roles as a child, as beggar boy or apprentice. He can imagine what he should be in the present, a kind of country squire in a site which has grown dismal to him and which has embittered his spirit. He can see ahead to a new phase, in the future, of madness, which he expects with a growing sullenness.

III. In the final section of the poem, Rimbaud narrates his life and his lives much more specifically and with much greater accuracy. His memory of the twelfth year is similar to a passage in *Les Poètes de sept ans,* where the boy in his room, closed away from the world, imagined it in the illustrations of his books and magazines. At twelve, according to *Vies III,* he was locked in an attic where he knew the world and illustrated the human comedy. This "life," as well as the others, is a further exercise on expansiveness and great breadth. History, which most boys learn at school, Rimbaud learned in a wine cellar. History is inebriation and the exercise of imagination rather than the acquisition of factual knowledge. The women he met at some night festivity in a northern city turned out to be the wives of former painters. The wives or models of old painters could easily be the poet's initiation to the world of womanhood. He learned the ways of science, not in a modern laboratory, but in an old passageway in Paris. When he wrote, as a poet, his imagination was so powerful that all the Orient surrounded his dwelling. Its extent was as immense as his work. And the retreat he made after his work was spent in the same place. Such moments as these had already been felt in *Une Saison en enfer,* and the ending of the prose poem is strongly reminiscent of the earlier work. Each of the final phrases, brief and forceful, renews the poet's present state of feeling and announces his future direction. It is Rimbaud's persistent theme of abandonment. His blood is heated. His duty has been revealed to him in two parts. First, he must stop thinking of all that he has been cogitating over. Before the final, irrevocable interruption of literary work and poetic thought, Rimbaud must have felt many similar impulses. He must have been led gradually to the final abdication of thought. Without the thought of his past and his future, he will be beyond the tomb, in another world, where no duties and commissions can be given him. This is the second injunction, absolute in tone and statement. Once more, Rimbaud announces the life he is going to lead, beyond all the lives of the poet.

Phrases In its form throughout and in the theatrical magic of its final sentence, this prose poem appears quite unlike the others. The "sentences" of the two opening passages seem to be spoken by someone else, as in *Délires I* where the "foolish virgin" speaks almost exclusively. Here too it is a girl speaking to the poet. She uses the formal pattern of address, *vous,* and yet her language is that of lover. She speaks of the reduction of the world into a single setting, a wood, a beach, a house, which would exist only for the two of them, and where she would be sure to find him. She looks ahead into the future when the poet is an old man, of noble appearance and toward whom the world has been indulgent. This is the scene of security and fidelity, opposite to Rimbaud's real life, but a scene he had dreamed of and testified to in letters as well as in this *illumination.* In this advanced stage, when she has made real all his memories and tied him down to them, then she will stifle him and his life will be complete. She continues to speak, in the same vein of prophecy. In their strength at being one and growing old together, there will be no turning back; in their happiness, no ridicule; in their wickedness, no punishment. Love will rule, in its adornments and dance and laughter. It will not be expelled.

To these "sentences" of the girl succeeds a strange transitional versicle (the third), when the poet speaks and answers the girl by using the familiar form, *tu.* He sees her as a being quite different from the one she had considered him. He calls her comrade, beggar girl, and monstrous child and then lists all the matters toward which she is indifferent, and which, by implication, count for him: other wretched girls, the maneuvers of words and stagecraft, the embarrassment of creation and performance. She is outside all these relations of the poet, and he suggests that she join

herself to them with her "impossible voice." Her voice
would be the flatterer of all that composes his despair.
With this request, he asks her to serve as accompaniment
rather than as the vital force she herself describes.

After these four lines of transition, the scene of the poem
begins: *Une matinée couverte, en juillet.* The curtain has
just gone up, and the insistent voice of the first part is lost
in the wonder of the stage and the noise of the action. We
learn the time of day and the season, the atmosphere, the
smells from the canals and the fields. But such things are
not on the stage, nor in the inner landscape of the poet. In
the two words, "playthings and incense," he calls upon the
mirage of the theatre for the total recreation of the work.
The struggle has begun between nature and art, between
the natural and the theatrical.

The last four versicles are devoted precisely to that
struggle between appearance and reality, between the effort to create the stage and the will to see on it a universe.
The real ropes, extended over the stage for the curtain and
the drops, he sees, in his mind, stretched from steeple to
steeple, stretched as garlands from window to window, as
golden chains joining the stars in the sky. The magic of
transformation has begun, and the poet is experiencing his
particular form of ecstasy. An ordinary scene of nature,
that of a pond with mist rising, fills him with expectancy.
The pure magic of transformation begins. Familiar elements of other illuminations recur in the questions the
poet asks. He wonders if a witch will appear in the white
sunset and what purple flowers will come down with the
fall of night. With evening the popular festivities begin and
over them bells ring, decked out in colored ribbons and
suspended from the clouds.

But the poet can stand only so much of the world and

the literal transformations the world is responsible for. The poet's night is finally covered with a black dust that separates him from the blatant jollifications. Alone he can recapture the dream of total beauty and eroticism, of Hortense, of the genie. In his own room, after turning down the lights, from the darkest part of his bed, he can see them all, the girls and the queens, all the figures he thought he had seen in the world and on the stage.

The process has the rapidity of a curtain going up and of an unexpected wonder revealed on the brightly lighted world of the stage. The act of turning off the light in his room is the same as the lowering of the house lights in a theatre—the closing of his eyes as he stretches out on his bed, and the sudden vision of the world of desire and dream. His final words, *je vous vois, mes filles! mes reines!* is like a magical incantation which will call the vision to life. The last incantation is the most effective in bringing about the transformation. But each of the versicles has a comparable sentence destined to provoke and create a vision.

DRAMA

The great intoxication of Rimbaud's life was poetry. It was an intense and delirious ambition to create with words and thereby to change himself and the world. During the five years of the experiment, Rimbaud associated himself more with Paul Verlaine than with any other human being. In one of the sections of *Une Saison en enfer, Délires I,* he gives a dramatic interpretation of this relationship. Two *illuminations* are further commentary upon the Verlaine episode. *Matinée d'ivresse* presents the violent, harsh aspect of the story, and *Vagabonds* shows a deeper sense of pity and reflection.

Matinée d'ivresse   Rimbaud sings of the good and the beautiful which he believed he possessed, even as the moments of degradation and torture which such an experience afforded. It represented both wild exaltation and the rack of pain. Rimbaud calls the experience "a morning of intoxication," and sees it as a cycle, beginning with childlike laughter and ending with the same laughter. He recalls the image of poison, already used in *Une Saison* (*Nuit de l'en fer*), and says that it will remain in his system even after he has returned to the former tedium, the former sobriety and lack of harmony. The promise that had been made to him as body and soul, he considers a madness. It was a promise to efface the tree of good and evil, to expel the tyrannies of custom and morality, and to cause to flourish the purest of loves. The beginning and the ending were disgustingly banal. In between, the two tried unsuccessfully to lose themselves in a kind of eternity.

The experiment took place yesterday, in the briefest expanse of time. And yet an entire cycle of sensations was evolved: youthful laughter, a discreetness of slaves, a virginal austerity, a horror for all that was endlessly present. Such memory of emotions is now sacred and enshrined. The beginnings of the experiment had the rustic awkwardness of Rimbaud's provincial arrival in Paris. The ending was chastisement and separation, the drama of Brussels, which Rimbaud sees presided over by angels of fire and ice.

The last six lines of the poem are comment on and interpretation of the experience. They are reminiscent of *Une Saison* in their tone of personal dogmatism, in the absoluteness with which they are forged. The period passed thus was as brief as a night vigil and, like a vigil, was sacred and ecstatic. What remains for Rimbaud from the vigil is a mask, a new expression on his face. This is the mark and

proof of the method he has learned and which he now proclaims. *Nous t'affirmons, méthode!* This method is Rimbaud's understanding and seizure of poetry which only
yesterday permitted him to exalt each one of his past ages.
(In *Mauvais Sang,* for example, he had described himself
as Gaul, peasant, crusader, marauding traveler.) Again, he
calls the result of his experience a poison which is in him
forever and in which he now has confidence. This is the
poison he swallowed in *Nuit de l'enfer,* whose venom
changed him utterly and deformed him (*La violence du
venin tord mes membres*). The invasion of the poison and
the resulting transformation have given to his being such
unity that each day he can give his entire life. The poison
of the wine has made him totally vulnerable. The world
has changed for him now into a world of assassins (or
hashish users). *Voici le temps des Assassins.* The poet is the
one exposed to all attacks, the one whose state of intoxication drives him constantly to the brink of catastrophe.

The "method" which permits the creation of poetry necessitates at the same time such an awareness of human
experience, such a clear vision into the world of men and
nature, that the poet's strength is offset by a new human
vulnerability. The "assassins" wait for the morning exaltation to diminish, when they will succeed in domination,
when the poet will be reduced to his role of inferior.

Vagabonds Of all the fragments of Rimbaud's writings
where it is quite obviously a question of Verlaine, this is
the most poignant. The style is less emphatic, less violent
than that of *Une Saison,* less elliptical and poetically
charged than the other *illuminations.* Rimbaud, in this
poem, is thinking more of Verlaine's fate than of his own.
The instinct of charity is here unusually strong for Rim-

baud, and gives to his expression a depth of personal feeling and sympathy that is fairly unique. Verlaine is the brother to be pitied. Rimbaud exploited all the older man's weaknesses. What had been destined to be exaltation and liberation turned out to be exile and slavery. And Rimbaud acknowledges that he had been willing to return to that exile even after the separation. He realizes that Verlaine had ascribed to him a very strange kind of bad luck (*guignon*) and innocence, and had given to these two traits puzzling explanations.

In this relationship, Verlaine was the satanic doctor, the older and the more learned. To him the boy answered with mockery and derision, and escaped through the window. Once free in the countryside, Rimbaud would imagine the ghosts of future nocturnal escapades, capable of forcing him back to the old pattern with renewed hopes of enhancing it. His flight had been a hygienic escape and on return he would collapse on the floor exhausted and fall asleep. Then Verlaine would rise up in drunken anger, and the dismal scene would begin again. Intoxicated, Verlaine would shout the words of an idiot and try to awaken Rimbaud.

Throughout the trying relationship, Rimbaud claims he had sincerely undertaken the mission of converting Verlaine into a greater poet than he had been, of "returning him to his primitive state of child of the sun." The enterprise was a collaboration between poets, during which the younger one who was formulating a rigorous and profound poetics sought to impose it on the older singer. It was the imposition of revolt on tradition. Ironically, the poet from Charleville, who had come to Paris to seek help and encouragement from a poet he believed in, reversed the process and set about indoctrinating the master. The wanderings of the two poets from capital to capital were the exterior sign of their quest for a personal and artistic fulfilment. Rimbaud mentions the two literal sites of their wanderings, the taverns where they drank and the roads where they ate bread, and summarizes the seasons for the continual search, by his haste to "find the place and the formula." This condensed final statement is many things at once. It is Rimbaud's key to his ardent experiment with love and poetry. It is the description of his attitude throughout the experiment. It is, finally, the only excuse he offers for the sentimental upheaval and the near-catastrophes the experiment involved.

The action and the need were equally precipitated. Decisions followed one another without interval. Hotel rooms and taverns were occupied and vacated in rapid succession. No "place" was ever found propitious for the harmonizing of two such conflicting temperaments. No "formula," no poetic creed was ever evolved sufficiently strong to answer the demanding requirements of Rimbaud and to satisfy his taste so equally formed of delicacy and violence. Vagabondage was to be the quest, the initiation to the discovery of a "place" in which to live and of a "formula" by which art would be created. But the life of the vagabond never changed into anything else for Rimbaud and for Verlaine.

Throughout this examination of ten arbitrarily arranged prose poems, from *Conte* to *Vagabonds*, one has the impression of studying always the same experiment, but in different lights and in shifting shades of meaning. The meeting of the prince and the genie in the forest scene of *Conte* is a projection of the Paris meeting of Rimbaud and Verlaine. Whereas *Vagabonds* is almost a page of autobiography, *Conte* appears as a poem or a parable which is an interpretation of a real event. In both are developed the similar themes of destruction of what is loved and the hero's effort to identify himself with whom he loves. In full health (*dans la santé essentielle*) the prince and the genie died together, and later the world realized that they were the same being. Rimbaud acknowledges in *Vagabonds* that his greatest desire is to turn Verlaine back into his primitive role of poet and sun god. In this wish he identifies himself, in his deepest ambition, with his companion. They perform the same rites together, in drinking the same wine in the taverns and in eating the same bread on the road. When they separate, Rimbaud is to die as a poet, and afterward the world will confuse them by falsely uniting them. The prince dies once when he becomes the genie, and then continues to live until an old age. Rimbaud dies once when he becomes the vagabond-poet, and then continues to live a far more ordinary life. The prince and Rimbaud combine in their temperament traits of tenderness and violence, one alternating with the other, one begetting the other according to some implacable law of creativeness. A seizure of beauty, for both the prince and Rimbaud, is followed by an overwhelming sadness.

In both poems also, as in many others where it is often expressed more obscurely, is audible the theme of promise, Rimbaud's great belief in himself, in his perfectibility. The sun god of *Vagabonds* is not only Verlaine. It is Rimbaud also, the self he would choose and teach, the privileged one, the self to whom revelations will be made. Rimbaud's sense of creative power was very strong in his relationship with Verlaine. It was an element in his conception of love, in his need to make over the beloved or to destroy him when he could not be made over, when the promise could not be realized. This aspect of Rimbaud's temperament is clearly manifest in *Génie*.

Love he confused with invention, and life he confused with a stage which can be "arranged." The religious formulas of Rimbaud's childhood reappear altered and in strange contexts, especially in *Une Saison en enfer*. The fairy stories of his childhood have a similar importance and appear in a similar estrangement in *Les Illuminations*. In *Bottom*, for example, the large grey-blue bird recalls the story of *The Blue Bird*, and the bear, the story of *Beauty and the Beast*.

All the places he passes through or imagines become hallucinated. In *Vies* he recalls many places: the site where a Brahman taught him the meaning of Proverbs, a bitter countryside under a dark sky, an attic room where he was locked up at the age of twelve. The constant changes of places, as if the poet were some maniacal stagehand, testify to Rimbaud's solitude, to his will to live always beyond the limitations of the present site. Verlaine represented in Rimbaud's life his greatest chance of escaping from solitude. When that chance was over, or at least diminishing perceptibly, the prose poems of *Les Illuminations* narrate his return to solitude. But they are suffused throughout with a fairy-like fantasy. In some of the poems the childhood fantasies are most in evidence: *Enfance*, *Jeunesse*, and parts of *Après le Déluge* and *Aube*. And in others, especially those just examined, the fantasies are more purely of the creative poet. Yet the two are never totally separated in Rimbaud. As a poet he remains close to the fantasies he created as a child.

The fantasy, suggested by the theatre, deepened between his periods of childhood and poetry. He refers briefly to it in *Une Saison*, in the section *Délires II*, when he lists the

circus backdrops and old operas among other pictorial representations he loved: idiotic paintings, signs, and popular
colored prints. (This last, *enluminures populaires,* is
doubtless what Rimbaud means by *Illuminations.*) In *Les
Illuminations* all the elements of the theatre become more
pronounced: settings, costumes, characters help to create a
world different from the real world. Rimbaud erects his
scenes outside of the familiar world and multiplies them at
will. They are usually fairy-story scenes, with castles and
carriages and princesses, but they unfold in an order contrary to the tradition of fairy stories. Whereas the scene of
enchantment and beauty in the usual fairy story follows the
scene of tawdriness and ugly realism, in the prose poems
the initial flash of beauty and of an enchanted scene is darkened at the end by some collapse, by some accident in
which the real world is seen beyond the fantasy. The
painted set is usually ripped and through it one can see the
dark brick walls of the stage and the real theatre. In *Phrases*
Rimbaud makes a complete circle and at the end returns to
the magic vision of creatures on a stage, *mes filles! mes
reines!,* whom he sees from the darkness of his room as if
he were seeing them from the darkness of a theatre.

In *Matinée d'ivresse* there is a close proximity between
Rimbaud's affirmation of a poetic method (*Nous t'affirmons, méthode!*) and his ominous announcement of the
coming assassins (*Voici le temps des Assassins*). The creation of a work brings with it the necessary death of the
poet, as in so many of the fairy stories the princess dies
when the enchanted spell is over, or the prince turns into a
beast. Likewise, in *Vagabonds,* the phrase "sun god" (*fils
du soleil*), which we take to be another version of Rimbaud's *voyant,* or which possibly means "loafer" as opposed
to *fils du travail,* is closely followed by another self-portrait,

that of the man eager "to find the place and formula" (*moi pressé de trouver le lieu et la formule*). The poem is both goal and death. The poet, in revealing his poem, reveals the very secret by which he lives. The rapidity with which a scene lives and dies in a theatrical performance is analogous to the birth of a poem and the consequent extinction of the poet's vision. The genie, appearing suddenly in the forest (*Conte*) and the tall creature of great beauty standing before snow (*Being Beauteous*) are examples of the fulgurant visions of the poet, of himself or of his fantasy realized, and of the almost immediate disappearance of the vision.

What Rimbaud creates seems always to belong to the future. He is so knowing of his method of hallucinations and of their brevity that he fears to speak of that which, when it is spoken, will cease to exist. Again, in *Vagabonds,* one sentence especially speaks of poetic creation and of its perilous existence. During his escapes from Verlaine, he used to create "phantoms of a future nocturnal richness." All the elements of the definition are significant: the creatures are phantoms, the richness of the apparition belongs to the future, and its world is nocturnal, like that of the theatre.

In between the real flights of his adolescence and the sporadic separations from Verlaine, Rimbaud learned, by a simple process of hallucination, another kind of evasion, that of the poet, taking place in total immobilization. There, the poet does not go to experiences. They come to him. They offer themselves to him. It is the inner vision of the *voyant* unfolding. An unpredictable world where everything comes to life, where stones can look at us and where a rabbit can say a prayer to the rainbow. Each *illumination* illustrates this power of the poet, his way of awakening everything that is habitually passive, of bestowing life on everything that sleeps in the real world. At the beginning of each prose poem, the curtain rises on a scene that is still and dormant. Then suddenly, with the magic lighting, the tableau comes alive, the vision takes on movement, and the action moves fast until the usual collapse comes at the end and the curtain is pulled down hurriedly. If the poem starts in hallucination and immobility, it unfolds in extraordinary movement and animation.

Vision of Nature

Nature is a constant poetic theme throughout *Les Illuminations,* and in four especially (*Fleurs, Marine, Fêtes d'hiver, Fairy*) the emphasis is more delicately insistent and other intertwining themes more subordinate. They are miniature pictures of color and movement where a scene of nature is paraphrased and poetically reconstructed or created.

NOCTURNE VULGAIRE

Another *illumination, Nocturne vulgaire,* is longer and more important, because it bears a strong relationship to the prose poems on the theatre and on fairy stories. In *Nocturne vulgaire,* the magic enchantment of stagecraft and the characters of the fairy-story world are swept aside for the pure magic of nature.

It begins with the magic of the wind which destroys the semblances of houses. The wind opens the cracks in the walls. (This *motif* of the crack or the *brèche* has been announced in other *illuminations.*) It disperses the contents of the hearthside and blots out the windowpanes. The one word, *opéradiques,* in the first sentence, derived perhaps from *opéra,* relates to the stage. Three entrances to the poet's private home world are stated in the first sentence:

the cracks in the walls (*brèches*), the hearthside (*foyer*), and the windows (*croisées*).

Then, as if the openings widened and exterior nature surpassed and suppressed the house, we are outside in a scene of a fairy story. The poet is traveling in a carriage whose style indicates its period of lushness and comfort. In two apostrophes, as if they were two waves of the wand, the carriage of escape is twice baptized and twice metamorphosed. First, as the hearse of the poet's sleep. The collapse of the walls of his familiar house was like the falling into sleep, which is always a kind of death and isolation. Then he calls it the shepherd's hut of his foolishness. As he moves over the pasture land, a shepherd's hut could easily designate the magic carriage, and the foolishness (*niaiserie*) would be the state of awakeness, opposed to sleep. But it is a carriage veering over the grass that now covers the road. Through a flaw in one of the windows the poet sees the extraordinary shapes of familiar forms: lunar figures, leaves, breasts.

With the coming of colors, of Rimbaud's favorite green and blue, the nocturne grows frenzied. The carriage rolls out of sight, and the unique traveler seems to be left behind. If he whistled now, he doubts whether the carriage would return. In its place he might call down storms, like those that fell on Sodom and Solyma, or beasts of the forest or armies. The dream becomes total when he wonders whether the carriage and the relay horses (*bêtes de songe,* he calls them, rather than *bêtes de change*) will come to life in the depths of the forest and he inside the carriage might sink up to his eyes in the bath of silk coverings. It would rush him through loud waters and spilled wine, and roll him over the yelping dogs. (This is almost the vocabulary of *Le Bateau ivre* and of its wild, unruly voyage.)

The ending is as abrupt as the opening and it uses the same phrase. A wind disperses the limits of the hearthside. The same wind, at the beginning of the poem, had begun to do this. What transpired between the coming of the wind and the dispersal, was the poem: a flash of thought, a rapid illumination, as unreal as a fairy story. The scene is built up as rapidly as it is demolished. It is composed of the fantastically beautiful (the carriage and the sights through the window) and the commonplace (the water, the wine, and the barking dogs). It flashes outside of time, because it belongs to a mental image that forms and disappears as one continues to carry out some timed and inconsequential activity.

FLEURS

If, as the title indicates, this *illumination* is principally about flowers, it involves also the theme of a theatrical setting, and, mysteriously hidden, the human theme. Each of the three versicles has its own condensed unity. In the first, the foxglove opens out before the eyes of the poet. He sees it from a golden step, draped in baroque furnishings as if it belonged to a stage set. Under the flower, and throwing it into clear relief, is spread a carpet of silver threads and points like eyes. The singleness of the flower and its coming to life in such an elaborate décor provide it with a near-human quality.

In the second versicle, it bears another name, that of "water rose" (*rose d'eau,* which phonetically is almost the same as the water reed, *roseau*). It is named at the end of the phrase, and is announced elaborately by its setting, as was the *digitale* of the first versicle. Again, the setting is theatrical and yet all the elements come from nature.

There are mahogany pillars, an emerald dome, thin stalks of rubies surrounding the central stalk of the reed.

The setting spreads out, in the third versicle, to include the sea and the sky. They are like a god with blue eyes and a white body, and so intense is their attraction that they draw to the marble terraces (the golden step of the first versicle) a crowd of young and strong roses. There the connotation is more and more definitely human. The roses, in their color and youth and strength, could be children, attracted to the bewitchment of such a setting as marble terraces opening on the sea and the sky.

The metamorphosis, in such a poem as this, moves backward. The flower becomes the human form. It is the reverse of the fairy story where the prince becomes the beast, or the myth where the girl Daphne becomes the tree. The human element is hidden but latent. Throughout the poem the colors oppose one another: (1) the gold of the sun and the green of velvet; (2) the emerald dome of leaves and the ruby flesh of the reeds; (3) the whiteness of the sky and the rosy flesh of the children. And in the same way, the human figure both rises out of the flower and opposes it in its life of movement.

MARINE

Composed of ten lines, of irregular syllabic count and unrhymed, this poem has been claimed as the first example, or at least as one of the very earliest examples, of free verse in French poetry. It is named "a marine study" and is presented as a single unified picture. The first sentence, of four verses, is ponderous in the objects it describes and the actions of these objects. Impossible to say, despite the title, whether these are boats or land-ploughs. On the one hand, they are called chariots of silver and copper, and they

raise up the roots of briars. But they also have metal prows
that beat against the foam. The same equilibrium and perfect ambiguity continue in the second sentence, of six lines,
where the flat land (*la lande*) is represented by currents
(*courants*), whose eddies (*reflux*) describe ruts (*ornières*).
The circular movements of the land (or the water) move
both toward the tall trees of the forest and toward the pillars of the wharf. Striking against the edge of the wharf, the
light falls in billows.

From a familiar picture, such as one he might have seen
in the Ardennes, the flat land, the forest, the briar stumps,
the ruts, Rimbaud creates a superimposed aquatic picture
where the ploughs are ships and the furrows are billows.
The light of the original countryside is so strong that it
transforms the real objects into their counterparts of another world. It is a brief moment, when one world grows
out of another, but does not totally disengage itself. The
two worlds are present simultaneously, the one realistically
fixed in the poet's memory, and the other imaginatively
generated by the poet's magic.

FÊTE D'HIVER

With *Départ*, this is the briefest of *Les Illuminations*. In
only five lines, the poet evokes a scene of nature that is
quite obviously artificial and theatrical. The first sentence
begins with mention of a cascade but ends with *opéra-
comique*. And the second sentence begins with the word
for chandeliers or rockets (*girandoles*) and ends with the
green-red lights of a stage sunset. The inhabitants of the
orchards and forests are nymphs, those created by the poet
Horace, but their costumes come from the First Empire.
When they dance, they form groups like those painted by
Boucher. All periods and all arts are confused to provide a

winter celebration. The effect is one of a carnival in which art creates nature. The first scene is reminiscent of Switzerland, with its mountain chalets and waterfalls. And the last scene is the deliberate exoticism of Boucher, of the eighteenth-century sentimentality in its etherealized and delicately painted scenes of foreign countries. The theatre in winter time can transcend any drab reality outside, as the *illuminations* of Rimbaud can transform the literal countryside of the Ardennes or of a European capital into a storybook scene.

FAIRY

Fairy is far more complex, in the multiplicity of natural scenes evoked and in the characterization of the young girl Hélène, whose mind reflects the fairy world. For her childish imagination plots are formed. A conspiracy grows up for her between the trees and the sky. To say "trees and sky" would be the barest reduction of what the poet says, because the conspiracy for him (and for his imaginary character Hélène) is one between the ornamental sap in the virginal shadows and the impassive light in astral silence. Thus, in the magic of language, a conspiracy such as would rise up in the imagination of a child is recreated. The true factors of the conspiracy are perfectly opposed and fused. The sap of the tree is comparable to the light of the sky, and the shadow from the tree has its counterpart in the silence which falls from the sky. The picture broadens then without losing any of its pristine elements. The light becomes the heat of summer, which is confided, as if it were a gift, to mute birds. The impassiveness of the light becomes the summer indolence which, as if it too were a gift, is entrusted to a mourning barge so priceless that it does not sail on the water but remains in gulfs formed by stories of love tragedy. One thinks of Tristan's barge, but the love element of a fairy story dies before it is allowed to form. The perfumes the young princess might have used if she had grown up to know mature love are expended on the air. The spell of the fairy world prevents the anguish of love from forming. Death intervenes and eclipses the second act of love-passion. The fairy story narrates only the morning world of ardor when the tree and the sky are significant beings, and the mourning world of death when all animation ceases and all sensory excitation is over.

There is no finite verb in the second stanza, but it lists the sounds that reach the ears of Hélène as she listened to the story. She hears the song of the women cutting wood in the forest, the sound of the waterfall, the cattle bells from the valley, and the animal calls in the desert. The third stanza has a finite verb, attached to the elements of the story which come to life and tremble for her: the shadows of the dark forest, the beasts of the poor, legends of the saints. They are the three essential elements of the fairy world: the magical setting of nature, the sentiment of charity and pity, the miraculous stories.

As in the second stanza, there is no verb in the last one which celebrates Hélène as being superior to all that she witnesses in the world of enchantment. The light of her own eyes and the grace of her movements surpass the beauties of the theatrical setting with its exaggerated speech and its deposition of Fate. The youthful reader contains in herself a fairy story more real than the one she hears. She reorganizes what comes to her and reanimates the worn-out themes and the tawdry tales. The greater magic is in the listener—in the poet, who permits no abstraction to remain as such, who personifies and concretizes all the elements of nature, who casts a spell over them far stronger than that of mere stagecraft. Many times throughout *Les Illuminations* the fairy representational world collapses, and the poet (as Hélène in *Fairy*) has to reconstruct with a purer spell of magic.

Especially in these five *Illuminations,* Rimbaud speaks to us as a child might who has mastered the pure expression of his thought. In them he appears as the youthful hero of nature, as the hero of a moment in childhood when the world is unaccountably subservient to the imagination of a single being. He is the magician building and destroying the world almost simultaneously, as a child erects a city of blocks and swiftly pulls out the foundation once the top turret is in place, as a poet writes and rewrites in order to liberate the idea and finally construct it in its absolute form. Rimbaud is docile to the ambiguous child's mind of builder and destroyer. The poet is both engineer and revolutionary. The form of *Les Illuminations* is opposed to a preconceived rhythmical pattern in order to espouse more simply and directly the subject matter of constant metamorphosis. The imperious directive of "changing life" (*changer la vie*) makes of *Les Illuminations* an extreme work where even the permanent elements of nature are tyrannized by the creative imagination of a boy stage manager.

Vision of the City

No other theme is more clearly developed and richly ornamented in *Les Illuminations* than that of the city. It rises up in the poems, as the cities rise up in Rimbaud's vision, imperatively and demanding attention. Poetry is always being born on the frontiers of other problems, deeply personal and universally metaphysical problems. The vision of Rimbaud's city is not separate from his great desire

to seize the absolute in his poetry. The problem of knowledge, in its most harassing philosophical sense, is constantly
related to his thoughts and his images. Certain pictures of
the city that occur in nine *illuminations* seem to form before the poet without his willing them. He becomes in
them the poet troubled with his own apparitions. The
ancients would easily explain this experience as being a
gratuitous gift of the gods, as marking the poet with special
indulgence.

Within the limits of this single subject, Rimbaud's imagination unfolds with its greatest intensity, in the establishing of an essential description. The theme is briefly
but sumptuously sounded in *Adieu,* the last section of *Une
Saison en enfer,* where, in autumn (*L'automne déjà!*) the
poet's boat turns back toward the harbor behind which
rises a tremendous city covered with fire and mud. The
vision here is one of poverty and pestilence. It is opposed
to the gold vessel setting out from a white beach. But the
return has to be made, and at the end of the piece the poet
feels new strength and tenderness in him. At the next
dawn, he knows that he can enter, because of his ardent
patience, magnificent cities. Briefly, and in somewhat the
same way, the same city rises up in *Enfance V,* from a scene
of enclosure and security, where the poet works underground in a whitewashed tomb. Far above him, the monstrous city, colored with the same red and black, rises up
in the mist.

Rimbaud's city is always a vision, that of a poet's unreal
city, imagined as something incompatible with ordinary
life. Its giganticism, first, separates it from the usual world.
It stands high about the port, as in *Enfance V,* or at a great
distance from him, as in *Adieu.* The life of the European
capitals may well have inspired such pictures as Rimbaud

gives in the nine *illuminations* we are about to examine. Some of the prose poems may have been written when Rimbaud was in company with Germain Nouveau, a poet and painter in his own right. Throughout these particular pieces one feels a strong fascination for the tumultuous aspect of cities, for the unceasing movement in the streets, for bizarre, magnificent constructions, such as those that would captivate a boy brought up in the Ardennes. Their basis may be in Rimbaud's knowledge of Paris, London, Brussels, but their poetic form makes them into cities of the future, dreamed of cities without real inhabitants.

By the use of the dream, Rimbaud adds his testimonial to the belief of Nerval, of Baudelaire, and of Mallarmé that the purest disinterestedness of poets manifests itself in the dream containing the secret of all creation. The dream is the "state" that procures the real power for the word. The very emergence of Rimbaud's cities from the darkness, from a lower darkness, in fact, makes them analogous to the birth of poems out of the deep unconsciousness of the poet. In order to reach the dream pictures of his cities, Rimbaud must have suppressed what the surrealists would call his conscious faculties. This is an important part of the poet's effort to realize the totality of his spiritual power, to reach some aspect of the absolute. By the destruction of his conscious state, the poet may the more easily reach the gratuitousness of his unconscious. The monstrous cities he finds there have certainly some connection with the monstrous soul he felt necessary to provoke, according to his *Lettre du voyant: il s'agit de faire l'âme monstrueuse.*

The organization of the nine *illuminations,* in order to make of them a progressive and unified study, is quite simple to establish. *Ouvriers* is the poem on the suburbs, and hence on the approach to the city, which is still at some distance off. *Les Ponts* is literally that: the bridges that seem to lead directly into the city and that give a vision of complexity and the cacophony of confused sounds. *Ville* is a sober poem, composed of deliberate and almost factual statements where the poet calls himself a citizen of the metropolis. In *Ornières* the enchantment begins, and it is closely comparable to the fairy world enchantment of other *illuminations* where an ambulatory circus metamorphoses the city. Then two more intricately detailed poems, both called *Villes,* provide grandiose synthetic pictures of the dream cities in an amazing richness of color and bold architecture. There remain in this series three poems, far more difficult to characterize and determine: *Métropolitain, Barbare,* and *Promontoire.* They are the most difficult to read in their veiled allusions and their exceptional syntax. They join to the theme of the city other more private themes of the poet which have already served in *Une Saison* and in other *illuminations.*

OUVRIERS

The strong story element in this prose poem is not so reminiscent of the *conte,* in other *illuminations,* as it is of the novel. The worker, or the husband, speaks. He describes his wife Henrika (Rimbaud has a strange preoccupation with H, as in Hortense and Hélène), in her old-fashioned dress, bonnet, and silk scarf.

The site is a dreary northern landscape in February, where a warm wind from the south reminds the man of a better country and emphasizes their poverty. His wife's dress looks like mourning. They walk through the suburb where the sky is grey and the south wind excites odors from the dried-up gardens and fields. The walk tires the man more than his wife. She points out to him tiny fish in a pool left over from January's flood.

The last and most important paragraph is given over to the city which they sense at a distance and which seems to be following them with its smoke and noise. By contrast, the other world, of sunlight and shadows, comes before him, the ideal country which the south wind evokes. The worker remembers his painful childhood, his summer anguish, his lack of strength and knowledge. He swears they will not spend the summer in this miserly place where they will never be more than orphaned fiancés, where their poverty will prevent their knowing marriage. His arm, now hardened from work, should not drag after it a beloved picture of a wife. It should, by implication, support a wife in the beauty of a temperate land.

This is a fairly realistic picture which Rimbaud knew intimately, of the north, of the Ardennes and of Belgium. A dismal suburban scene, at some distance from the city but close enough for the man to sense the horror of its industries. It is perhaps the simplest of the *illuminations*. Henrika, the wife, is described, and her husband, who tells the story, speaks of his desire to leave the north and the crowded suburb where the workers live and his life which has been vainly spent in such a setting.

This is a poem on the tolerance and resignation which most men have to exhibit during their lifetime. The "I" of the passage has probably felt many times the drama he adumbrates, and it is impossible to say whether he really will revolt and carry through the change. In the midst of the most drab aspects of life, a tormenting and yet divine shadow forms. It is the possible beginning of the poet who

will communicate, if he does emerge, the purity of his torment, which is far less a torment when known by ordinary
men.

LES PONTS

This *illumination* is more closely a poem than a passage
from a novel. The description is both realistic and highly
exaggerated. The pure accumulation of details presents a
complicated picture which "joins" the real and the unreal
worlds.

The sky is grey, as it was in *Ouvriers,* but it has a crystal
look, an effect of distance which Rimbaud notes many
times (cf. *Being Beauteous, Métropolitain, Villes* I). The
bridges over the canal are so numerous that they form a
curiously intricate design. Some are straight and others
arched. They are so long and light that by comparison the
banks, weighted down with domes, appear lowered and
diminished. Huts are on some of the bridges, and masts
and parapets on others. On one of them the poet sees a red
coat and imagines other costumes and musical instruments
to accompany it. He can almost hear the popular melodies
or concerts of some fair. Underneath the bridges, the water
is blue and grey, and broad as an arm from the sea.

Then suddenly, with the last sentence which is a separate
paragraph, a familiar trick of Rimbaud disperses the scene.
He says that a white ray falling from heaven blots out the
comedy. This effect was described in many of the *illuminations* which contained elements of a theatrical set and
the décor of a fairy world. It is the inevitable collapse after
the construction, which indicates that here too the vision
of the city is an imaginary picture. The stage, the fairy
world, and the city are all themes by which Rimbaud plays
with the familiar world and deforms at will stabilized pat-

terns and architectures. Usually at the end, an effect of light, of clouds or fog or snow, destroys the picture which he had so painstakingly traced. All of his landscapes move at his will. They are forms described only at the moment of their genesis. Their remarkable plasticity is always subordinated to a power of dynamics which is almost fiendish in its destructiveness.

Only after a long familiarity with *Les Illuminations* does one come to realize that the literal pictures described are not so important as the words that paint the pictures. They are the words of a pen, drawing up from each movement they describe a dark mystery, comparable only to the mystery of dreams. These pictures are composed only to be decomposed, in harmony with the characteristic of dreams. Language, in its form as poetry, is impenetrable. In its own way, poetic knowledge is as obscure as divine knowledge. Only flashes of the original truth appear in poetry, which temper and trick our anguish. Poetry is approximation, always approaching the absolute, and always collapsing and failing at the very moment when it seems closest to justifying itself.

The repeated lesson of Rimbaud, visible especially in *Les Illuminations,* is that the word is an action, rapid and devastating. It is the action of the mind, the gesture of the idea, that which seeks to affirm the idea. Poetry is therefore simultaneously the creation of thought and the suicide of thought. It is the seemingly masterful and actually pitiful means—but the only one—of establishing between the flesh and the spirit of man a continuity. Rimbaud's phrase from the *Lettre du voyant, Toute parole étant idée,* is the clue. Words, then, are the voice of thought. And the words of a poem remain far closer to the original thought than the words of prose, always eager to explain and therefore to modify and emasculate. Words, at their birth, must have had a closer participation with thought than they have finally on the page or in their spoken form. The poet remembers this closer alliance and suffers from the final approximation.

VILLE

Mysteriously sober is this statement of Rimbaud the citizen. He seems to be speaking of London or of some city of England. The obvious reasons for this interpretation would be: he calls himself an ephemeral citizen, who knows he will not stay long and who is quite contented; he contrasts the statistics on the longevity of life of this people with those of the "continent"; he uses the English word "cottage" in speaking of his habitation. Other elements also seem to substantiate the English site: a lack of taste in the exterior of the houses and the plan of the city; an absence of any monument of "superstition," such as that which a Latin might invent; the simplicity of the moral code and the language, reduced as they would appear to a foreigner trying to understand them; the coal smoke over the city, thick and constant.

The remaining elements of the passage would designate it as any typical city, with the standardization of the millions of its inhabitants: the way in which they were all educated, their trades, and their old age. They remind the poet of such old age that when he looks at them from his window, they seem like ghosts, and the smoke turns the setting momentarily into a dark wood on a summer's night. (The allusion is rapid but unmistakably to *A Midsummer Night's Dream*.) Ghosts they are or new figures of the Eumenides or witches. The poet's heart is the scene. Everything reminds him of Death, whom he designates as an active servant girl; of the Lover, her spouse and a despairing man; of Crime, personified as a chicken piping in the mud of the street. From the beginning to the end, the tone that is built up is one of bathos. The ephemeral citizen is disillusioned. The inhabitants of the city live in a routine of somnambulists. Death, Love, and Crime are the three characters grotesquely and comically described. The funereal sentence at the close has been carefully prepared.

Again, here, as in *Les Ponts*, the poet's method is admirably apparent. The city is always the approximation to the City of God, as the poet's word is always the approximation to the Logos. The universe, conceived by God, by God's Word, specifically, becomes degraded, but never loses completely its memory of original perfection. What the human city has become, as the poet looks at it from this window, is a trio of figures, of Death without tears, of Love that is desperate, of Crime that flutters weakly in the mud. It is the picture of Hart Crane's "famished kitten on the step" in *Chaplinesque*. In his world too, another city-poet's world, he claims that we

> through all sound of gaiety and quest
> Have heard a kitten in the wilderness.

With such intuitions of humbleness and fear, as Rimbaud expresses in *Ville* and Crane expresses in *Chaplinesque*, it is little wonder that poetry for both of them was to become the silence of words, that kind of poetry that is the opposite of sonorous power, of descriptive poetry and song. The real words Rimbaud and Crane will use in their most successful poems are those which shed a darkness around themselves. There, in the darkness created by the words, the real poem will unfold, and will bear to the poem in words the relationship which the dream bears to the state of pure consciousness.

ORNIÈRES

Rapid, because achieved in just a few brush strokes, and secretive, because it recaptures the mystery world of fairy stories, *Ornières* would serve as Rimbaud's initial experience in the city, as the one following *Ville* where he claimed the title of "ephemeral citizen."

After observing the populous section of the city, he enters the park, and immediately, as if such a site would justify such a metamorphosis, the statistically minded realist citizen of *Ville* becomes the poet. The change comes with the site and with the dawn also which awakens the foliage and the mist and the noise of the park. These are the elements of the scene in the night. On the left are slopes still covered with darkness and the countless wet ruts in the road. The word for "ruts," *ornières,* serves as the title of the *illumination,* because they are the marks on the land which call forth the vision. When he sees the tracks on the slopes, he imagines the circus parade and describes it magically in six or seven lines. All the elements are mentioned: the golden wagons containing the animals, the painted multicolored flags and backdrops, the spotted horses, the men and children riding the strange animals, the carriages as brilliantly bedecked as the children riding them and resembling the magic carriages of fairy stories. The radiant vision ends, as so many of the *illuminations* do, with the dark note of collapse and death. Here, in the procession, the poet also sees caskets with their black plumes and canopies over the carriages pulled by blue-black mares. The harsh title of the vision is justified by the final, somber picture of death.

Ernest Delahaye insists that this poem is a direct reminiscence of a traveling American circus that filled the large square, la Place Ducale, of Charleville in 1868 or 1869. He remembers the cavalcade of horses and the astonishing animals and all the accessories of an opulent troupe. This might well be the source of such a poem, or other similar parades, like those of Mardi Gras, which Rimbaud might have seen in other cities. The power of the passage comes from the seriousness with which Rimbaud considers the parade and the magical way he converts a tawdry exhibition into a wondrous fairy world experience where an ordinary cart is transformed into a carriage. Even in a city, in a secluded section of the park, the poet can recapture the enchantment of childhood. This is the process he applies to the total vision of the city in the two subsequent *illuminations*.

VILLES I (*Ce sont des villes!*)

The opening sentence is punctuated with an exclamation mark, although it has a declarative and almost defiant effect. "They are cities!" It is a necessary statement because each element of the detailed description which follows is composed both of a recognizable part of a city and of a part that is a poetic interpretation. The cities of this poem belong unquestionably to poetic vision.

The final line, separated from the main part as a paragraph by itself, is a question in which the poet confesses the source of such a vision. The "region" he has described comes from his sleep and the slightest of his (unconscious) movements, and he wonders what "good arms" and what "hour" will give that region back to him. They are the arms of embrace or the arms of labor, and the hour might be similarly described, as the one which will provide the enchantment and the creation.

Between the exclamation and the final question extends the poem itself, each sentence of which has a basis in the reality of cities and in their imaginary existence. The monstrous size of the cities is first expressed in their appearance of mountains, which the poet specifically names Alleghenies. Then a shift comes from the New World to Switzerland, indicated by crystal and wooden chalets moving on invisible pulleys as if they were on funicular railways. The craters and palm trees of the new sentence shift the scene to still another climate, and so the spectacle unfolds with an amazing ubiquity and with a constant shift of altitude from mountain to sea-level.

First the poet evokes a medieval city world, with its corporations, its banners (*oriflammes*), its mountain passes where Roland blew his horn. Then, lower down, we see cities on the ocean, with inns and masts in the sunset. Then again, far above, the fields on the hills show centaurs riding through avalanches, and immediately we plunge downward, to the sea again, with its memory of Venus' birth and the sound of precious shells and pearls. The flowers on the hillsides are so large and shining that they seem to bellow. Up from the valley ride flocks of fairy queen Mabs, and at the top, deer suck the breasts of Diana. A whole world of mythology is evoked in this poem, and always with its tenuous relationship to cities. The Bacchantes scream in the suburbs under the moon. Venus glides into the caverns of hermits and blacksmiths. Periods of history are mingled: the modern corporations of labor sing their claims on Baghdad Boulevard.

The general effect of the poem is not unlike the incoher-

ence of dreams, and yet within the details of the single
sentences every effect is calculated to astonish the reader
and move him from one part of the world to another.
Every geographical and mythological apparition is unexpected, from America to Baghdad, from Venus to Diana.
The total impression is one of power, lyric power and
magical possession. The poet sings as one possessed with
the immensity of the world, as drunk with the richness of
cities, their differences and their legends.

The words give the impression of racing to clothe the
idea, only to find that they are the idea (*Toute parole étant
idée*). Such a passage moves to a function of language opposed to that of dialectics in which ideas are simplified and
reduced and stripped of their adornment. The words of
poetry retain all the relationships with which they are created, and compose a synthesis and preserve therefore the
total idea which the dialectical process diminishes and hu-
miliates. For Rimbaud, the time has not yet come for a
universal language (*le temps d'un langage universel vi-
endra!*). His cities are the renewed expression of the age-
long history of Babel. His are the newest constructions of
the famous tower, which was to open the portal to God
and the one language. The same failure is repeated for
Rimbaud, and it will also be repeated for Mallarmé, the
other modern poet so tenaciously bent upon proffering the
immortal word. The final sentence of *Villes* I is one more
foreshadowing of the poet's failure with language, one
further instance of the poet's final torment with the multiplicity of languages. More sumptuously than most of the
illuminations, the two companion pieces on "cities" re-
produce the creating power of the word. They give the
effect of quite literally engendering the cities that rise up
before our eyes with memories of all times and all places,

real and unreal. Language seems to be responding to the desire of the poet and creating for him the most magnificent of visions. The words of the poem are far from being the careless or casual whims of a game. They are willed by a secret mind of the poet and reflect luminously the idea. Such words do not designate. They create.

VILLES II (*L'acropole officielle*)

The theme of giganticism is still more apparent in this second study, with its key word of "acropolis," its "colossal" conceptions, its "giant" candelabra, its dome 15,000 feet in diameter, its "circus" proportions in one of the city parks.

Here also the city is seen as a vast structure on various levels. Floors, stairways, domes, acropolis, all accentuate this impression of interrupted and different levels. The "high" part of the city (*le haut quartier*) has elements not usually associated with it, such as an arm of the sea. From the foot-bridges the poet is able to look down and behold the great depth of the city.

Details creep in from varied periods and places that provide an atmosphere of confusion and dislocation. Whatever the real city is that Rimbaud has in mind, it is shaken and transformed by its proximity to some fabulous city of another world. The confusions are not contradictions. They are efforts to create unique cities where classical architecture will appear with painting exhibits like those of Hampton Court, where a Norwegian Nebuchadnezzar designs the stairways of government buildings where iced drinks cost a fortune. As soon as an element is mentioned, it is cut off immediately or transposed into some opposite element. The vision is constantly changing so that in its entirety it will be incompatible with the known universe of men. The poet is both the creator of his city and the spectator of its dissolution, of its constantly renewed drama.

The ending of *Villes* II is longer than that of any other *illumination*. The note of dispersal and collapse which ends most of the prose poems is here more carefully prepared and minutely analyzed. The poet tries to imagine the police force of his city, but he realizes that the law must be so strange that he cannot define the adventurers or criminals. He moves out from the city center to the suburb (*faubourg*) where the air is made of light. He has lost sight of the city and soon loses sight of the suburban section that grows into the country. Forests and plantations have replaced the city. There, with a characteristic final delirium, the poet sees "gentlemen savages" hunting their newspaper articles under artificial light. The passage is an elaborate oxymoron where each word contradicts the other, in which an unpredictable world is created.

The myth of Babel and its great effort of construction to reach the one language are again evident in this poem, and even more strength and greatness appear in its poetic expression. When the poet meditates and writes, he channels the forces of the cosmos and endows them with a miraculous impulse. The parts of the fabulous city present themselves as a revelation to him, but as real and alive parts. Whatever fear or agony the poet may have felt at the creation of his poem, when it is completed, he must feel, at least momentarily, a singular sense of achievement. The poet is the miracle-worker. To the myth of Babel, the poet adds, in his accomplishment, the legend of Orpheus enchanting the real world, the trees and the animals who heeded him. The movement of such a poet is exciting to read and hear. It communicates a veritable rhythmical joy. But the intoxication of reading such a poem as *Villes* II must be less strong than that experienced by the poet when he created it.

MÉTROPOLITAIN

This poem is one of three *illuminations* which, while still preserving some memory of the city, break away from its domination and move in another direction.

Each of the five stanzas ends with a word of exclamation, the subject of which has been briefly prepared and enacted as a charade might be. The first is the city itself, which in its new form of metropolis extends to include the world. From the straits to the sea, and over the sand washed by the sky, cross back and forth crystal boulevards marking the limitless boundaries that contain within them the familiar details of a city: poor families and fruit-dealers.

The battle picture, which comes second, is the rout of all the elements that seem to be leaving the city. The human figures are not described. Only their helmets are named, and the wheels of their wagons, the barges, and the backs of the animals. The lines they form are another kind of boulevard, stretching over the desert and parallel to the black smoke in the sky, formed by the burning city, which appears to the poet as the mourning sign of the ocean.

The countryside, as third division, offers a series of pure fantasies. If you look, you will behold the real world made unreal by vision. This is Rimbaud's familiar process of transformation whereby an ordinary word, with a slight suggestion of change, becomes an extraordinary detail. A face, for example, under the light of a lantern, appears as an illuminated mask; a girl by the river is suddenly a simple-minded nymph in a noisy dress; shining rocks in a garden of peas are called "luminous skulls."

In compressed richness the fourth versicle revives many

of Rimbaud's favorite terms and images. Under the "sky," the word of summary, the world changes with the changing of light. The flowers behind the garden walls are "atrocious" (cf. *toute lune est atroce* of *Le Bateau ivre*). The inns never open to the traveler (cf. the *auberges* of *Ma Bohème* and *Comédie de la soif*). There are princesses too in the fairy tradition, and astrology to learn.

The large female figure of other writings, of *Mémoire*, for example, and of *Aube*, dominates the final section, and again the poet struggles with her, as if she were mother and spouse. *Force* is the culminating word and the culminating mystery animating the scene of the struggle: the snow, the green lips (of the goddess?), the ice, the black flags (of the army?), the blue rays (of the sky?), the dark perfumes from the sun. All the elements of nature are here listed, of the real and the changed nature.

The poem, this time, is almost the beginning of a story or of a parable, as in *Conte* and *Aube* and *Après le Déluge*. Yet the title contains all and limits the elements to a relationship with the universe-city. Because the wonderment of discovery is so childlike, it is constantly breaking down the boundaries of usual definition and terminology.

The title, *Métropolitain*, is not puzzling if one accepts Rimbaud's belief in the poet's function as being the destruction or the voiding of forms in order to compose a new reality. This would be for Rimbaud the poet the one reality that he seizes upon in such a poem as *Métropolitain*. In it we can see both the ruins of the first reality and the form of the new reality rising out of the ruins and their shadows. Each poem has to be a risk, an extraordinary attempt to construct a reality able to resist and to last.

By naming an object the poet gives it an existence. But then he eradicates it by a negative word. Mallarmé's *aboli bibelot,* would exemplify this, whereby he removes the object from the real world into the real world of poetry. Rimbaud too has his image of emptiness and absence. With the announcement of *la Ville,* at the end of the first part of *Métropolitain,* we move immediately to its opposite, the desert, and the objects like "helmet" (*casques*) that designate the fleeing soldiers of the city. The effect, in a sense, is one of disintegration, whereby the sensible universe is replaced by another reality.

In the poem, one after the other, the objects are named and destroyed, and always out of the ruins new objects are erected. This is the singular power of the poet. The image of a city is created by the destruction of one city and the construction of another. For the word as an image to remain, a world has to disappear.

PROMONTOIRE

One of the most densely written pages of Rimbaud and one that best illustrates his poetically charged prose, *Promontoire,* appears as one solid paragraph—almost, in fact, as one solid sentence. There are actually two sentences, the first, an exclamation of four lines, and the second, a twenty-line period, abundantly provided with semicolons, which unfolds as solidly as the rock-bound promontory which is its proud subject.

Water is the first notation. The promontory is seen from a ship, as dawn comes. In the early morning light a villa, with its smaller buildings, assumes such proportions as to resemble an island of some exotic place, Japan or the Peloponnesus.

With the beginning of the second sentence the theme of giganticism is again emphasized. Fortifications and dunes stand out along the coast. Geographical specifications add

to the preciseness of the vision: Carthaginian canals and
Venetian embankments and Etna-like volcanoes. The flowers grow along deep gullies, and water flows from glaciers.

After the mention of parks, with their Japanese trees, the
existence of the city grows more real and the promontory is
lost sight of until it returns in the final word as the
"Palace-Promontory." Even America, land of giganticism,
is represented by Brooklyn, and the railways of all countries are seen as vying with one another, and the hotels,
placed like promontories overlooking the valleys, are deco-
rated with the arts of men and overlook the world and the
travelers from all the countries of the world. The transposition in the poem has been lucidly carried out. A promontory suggests an hotel, which appears as a microcosm of the
world.

BARBARE

This is the apocryphal message, after the extinction of
the city. Its subject makes it into one of the most seemingly disjointed of the poems, one of the most hauntingly
nostalgic and at the same time one of the most violent. It
is one of the rare instances where Rimbaud repeats words
and phrases to achieve an incantatory effect.

The opening phrase makes it very clear that we have
passed beyond ordinary time and that the world of men is
over. A return to barbarism, or to a time before time, has
taken place, such as predicted in *Mauvais Sang*. Rimbaud
has always maintained a familiarity with prehistoric or
primitive times. *Barbare* is largely composed of marked
contrasts, especially in color. The red meat of the *pavillon*
(room or banner?) is contrasted with the paleness of the
arctic sea and its flowers. But the sea and the flowers do not
exist. The world, as it disappears, leaves a last flash which

joins with the new whiteness of the void. As if he alone
were left in the vanishing world, the poet recovers from
the fanfares of heroism, the useless expression of an out-
moded moralism. Those who were once assassins go down
with the world they helped to annihilate. The line of color
contrast, of blood and pale flower, is repeated, and again
the arctic sea and the flowers are canceled out as if they
were the poet's creation to designate the new void.

The word *Douceurs!* begins a new part of the poem, and
it will be repeated many times in a few lines, as if by its
very utterance it will work the necessary magic of separating the new birth from the catastrophe. The contrasts are
now more insistent than ever, and always of the same colors: braziers are coupled with frost or with foam, fire with
diamonds. The depths of the ocean is opposed to the icicles
of the stars. And the heart of the earth is burned to carbon
for the great transformation. Forms and signs of the old
world persist in the new music of the spheres and the new
sweetness of the air. From the extremes of a volcano pit and
an arctic cave the lonely voice of a woman can still be
heard. But soon, as the interrupted ending indicates, even
that will be over and a new world will begin.

The images are metallic and incorruptible. Fire burns everything in the poem, as it burns the very heart of the poet.
The new contours of the world will be pure and perfect.
There is almost a new grammar devised for the poem. The
isolated words are recognizable, but they are not joined in
familiar ways. Each word serves to create the beginning of
a new spectacle, but no single one is allowed to grow. The
total effect is one of multiple new growths and new flashes
which rise up from a burnt and burning world. This is the
end of the city.

Whatever the real city was for Rimbaud, he traces, in these nine *illuminations,* the contours of an extraordinary superimposed city and points out in the flames of a secret abyss the fate which awaits the city under itself and the magical city which will grow out of it. The inhabitants of the city are barely referred to, but the poet paints an intricate trelliswork of bridges and avenues and gigantic overpowering edifices that stand for the dreams and the ambitions of the inhabitants. Their silence and their absence are accountable for in the principal art of pictures that the *illuminations* develop.[3] The world of these cities is impermanent, but it is somehow related to man's drama of knowledge. There is no real philosophy for poetry, which is in many ways a purely gratuitous act. But its pure gratuity comes about only after a certain kind of life has been known and acknowledged. True knowledge is experimental, and the poet knows this intimately. In his city poems, Rimbaud constructs a cosmos, preserves it for a moment, and then destroys it. But during the remarkable moment of the poem, every barrier between a man's conscience and

---

[3] The landscapes invented by Jules Laforgue, especially in *Derniers Vers,* are comparable to the landscapes invented a decade earlier by Rimbaud in the way the two sets of urban pictures contain, and even release, the very complex emotions of the poets. T. S. Eliot, in such poems as *The Love Song of J. Alfred Prufrock* and *Portrait of a Lady,* will also charge urban landscapes with the psychological complexes of his characters. The combined interior and exterior landscapes of Laforgue are more controlled in the art of Eliot, more finely proportioned, but the nostalgic poetry of the *faubourg,* as a method of expressing personal emotions, was first exploited by Rimbaud and Laforgue.

the world is abolished. All opposites cease opposing one another when there is no distinction between the self and the exterior world.

Mystical Vision

In the ten *illuminations* chosen to illustrate the gravest vision of all, that which seems closest to being the vision of a mystic, Rimbaud appears the most separated from ordinary human beings; and here he is closest to the role of escaped angel which Mallarmé assigned to him and which, later, Jacques Rivière was to analyze so brilliantly. Almost a wrathful angel, we would say, impatient with the race of men and the world from which he feels himself so different in his purity, in his resemblance with God. He is the sword-bearer, appearing in a flash and disappearing with the same rapidity when his terrible message has been delivered.

The ten pictures might be considered the justification of the celebrated passage in *Une Saison* where Rimbaud claims his real life is absent and he is not in the world (*La vraie vie est absente. Nous ne sommes pas au monde.—Délires I*). Such a temperament as the one creating these particular *illuminations* would indeed find it almost impossible to belong to the world. In each of them Rimbaud states that he is constitutionally incapable of coming close to mankind. The flame in which he lives separates him from all others. And his flame does not diminish. It keeps him incased in a prodigious solitude.

Rimbaud has few characteristics of the philosopher in his writings, and that is why it is difficult to explain, in terms of ideas and concepts, his belief about his own innocency. It was a state which he felt and expressed violently in flaming images. When he did try to explain, as in *Une Saison,* he ended by confusing his thoughts and finally abolishing them all in the poignant sentence of *Matin: Je ne sais plus parler!*

In *Les Illuminations* Rimbaud does not talk about poetry; he practices it. His immediate goal has nothing personal, nothing philosophical about it, because it is the goal of the irreproachable poem, whose images will be immaculate. He wants them as incorruptible as the precious metals he often mentions, and as pure as the colors he describes. Claudel called Rimbaud a *mystique à l'état sauvage,* a mystic unsupported by dogma. This angel is solitary; those whom he meets do not see him. He says this at the beginning of *Une Saison en enfer.* The expression on his face is so vacant (*le regard si perdu*) that he may well be invisible to other human beings.

In one sense, Rimbaud's two works in prose mark him off from other human beings in two distinctly opposite ways. In *Une Saison en enfer,* he unashamedly classifies himself as subhuman, as bestial and inferior. *Je suis de race inférieure de toute éternité,* he solemnly says in *Mauvais Sang.* And this theme pervades the entire work. In the prelude, *Jadis,* he calls upon his executioners; in *Nuit de l'enfer* he is the village simpleton (*Horreur de ma bêtise*); in *L'Impossible* he claims the bit of reason he was born with has left him; *Adieu* describes his return to the soil and his peasant state. But in *Les Illuminations,* and especially in the ten chosen to illustrate the mystical intuition of the poet, he appears with another set of characteristics, those of an angel which set him apart from mankind. Twice separated from mankind, and hence twice separated from himself, Rimbaud states the ambivalence of his nature, the manifestation of beast and angel in him. In both instances, and in both works, he appears as more than a poet, as one in communication with regions lower than himself and higher than himself, both of which are forbidden regions to which he is drawn in his dual capacity of criminal and saint.

We divide the ten *illuminations* into four groups. The first contains three brief pieces on what seems to be for Rimbaud the mystical process: *Départ, Royauté, A une raison.* The second group has two poems we read as examples of mystical elevation: *Mystique* and *Veillées.* Then four poems, more loosely characterized as "exercises," on a mystical approach to the world: *Soir historique, Mouvement, Dévotion, Solde.* The final category has only one poem, *Génie,* a remarkable study of the mystical figure. Such a division may seem arbitrarily imposed. It is arbitrary, of course, and represents only one way of considering these poems.

MYSTICAL PROCESS

Départ, of only four lines, is a poem of impatience, of a great will to change direction and to change one's very being. Three past participles summarize what life has already offered: "seen" (*vu*), "had" (*eu*), "known" (*connu*). It has been the same vision always, the daily vision. What we possessed was only the noise of the city, at every time of day and night. What was known was simply the noise and the vision of the other two experiences. The change had to be a departure. The last line defines it abruptly as a departure in a new kind of affection and a new kind of noise. If we are justified in interpreting this poem as the announcement of the new mystical experience, the "affection" will be that of pure being and the "noise" will be the wings of the new power of movement.

Royauté is too brief to be called a story or a parable, but it is close to that form. It is close also to *Départ* in its rapidity and reduction. The theme, one of the most profound in *Les Illuminations,* is that of transformation. On a public square a man and a woman call out to the people. He wants her to be queen, and she wants to be queen. Their period of waiting is over. They embrace, and for a whole day they are king and queen. Tapestries hang out of the windows in the morning, and in the afternoon the two figures walk in the gardens. This is the rapid drama of transformation which, like the advent of innocency, changes and purifies. "Royalty," like the physical candor of an angel, is something that is decreed and then put on for a time.

The first characteristic of the far more complicated poem, *A une raison,* is the abundant use of the adjective "new." Three of the major substantives bear it, and one thinks of its use in *Départ* and the "new" roles of the man and woman in *Royauté.* "Reason" is personified. When she raps on the drum with her finger, a new harmony is released. When she takes one step, the new men rise up and follow her. When she turns her head away, and when she turns her head back, a new love is created. Music, creatures, and love are renewed by this goddess. The transformation theme, after its use in the call to arms of *Départ* and in the narrative of *Royauté,* continues in *A une raison,* which is more purely the poem on transformation, on the need of a spiritual change.[4] The piece continues with the children chanting a kind of prayer to heaven, a supplication to change their lot and to turn away the players. They

---

[4] Rolland de Renéville sees in *A une raison* an important mystical experience (*Rimbaud le Voyant,* p. 80). This theory is contradicted by Etiemble and Glauclère (*Rimbaud,* pp. 26–28 and 41).

beseech that she make substantial their fortunes and their prayers. The final line still concerns Reason and offers the major clue to the identification of Reason. She has come from always and will go everywhere. She is therefore characterized by her eternity and her ubiquity. She might be, from the Christian viewpoint (and the Platonic, as well) the soul, or that manifestation of the soul which Rimbaud calls "a reason." At any rate, her power is tremendous and rejuvenating. Even the children beg her for the realization of their prayers.

In one of Rimbaud's early poems, *Soleil et Chair*, he characterizes reason as that faculty that prevents us from reaching the infinite:

Notre pâle raison nous cache l'infini!

but in the prose poem it is the seat of supernatural power. It might even be one of the divine names because it is addressed almost as Christ was addressed by the sick and the suffering: "Speak only a word, Master."

A new exigency of purity animates this brief poem and attaches it sympathetically to the impatient call of *Départ* and to the miraculous change of *Royauté*. Something is in Rimbaud, and forever. He catches sight of it in a flash that is over immediately. The poem would seem to be the testimonial, imperfect and fleeting, of what by its very nature is ineffable. It would be an ancient explanation if we said that this is the kind of poem written under special dictation, but the very pale image of the goddess Reason seems to justify such an explanation.

MYSTICAL ELEVATION

Two of the poems have such a tone of mystical peace that they stand out from those that are concerned with a method and an enactment. *Mystique,* first, is a pure moment of vision which the poem transcribes successfully and in greater fulness and coherence than in others.

Each of the four versicles paints one part of the picture, all of which fuse logically and symmetrically to form the whole mystical moment. First, the angels appear on the slope. They turn, slowly perhaps, because their robes are of heavy wool. The grass on which they turn is brilliant with green and silver streaks. Their figures seemingly fill the lower center part of the picture.

Our vision then moves to the fields which spread out to the left and right of the angels and rise to the top crest of the land. These fields are covered with flames, whenever the angels are not moving. They are divided into two parts, like pictures of the Last Judgment. On the left, over the crest of land and coming down toward us, is a line of murderers and warriors. They are the sinners and they walk over the flaming prairies. To the right, in a line moving back of the top land and away from the spectator, are unnamed figures of the East and of progress.

Our eyes have been slowly rising upward toward the top of the picture. Behind the land, with its two streaks of murderers and souls in progress, is the sea or masses of figures that resemble the sea in its tumultuous upheaval, and falling over them, in an extraordinary peace, the sweetness of the heavens. The stars are so much like flowers that they seem to descend as in a basket to bedeck the land and turn it blue and to touch the very faces of the spectators.

The picture is uniquely Rimbaud's despite the reminiscences it bears of primitive pictures of the Last Judgment or of Jacob and the Angel or of the Annunciation or of children's pictures. At the opening, the angels seem to be dancing, but their movement is interrupted by the flaming fields beside them. They are forgotten in the lines of sinners and saints, and finally the entire picture is subsumed in the astonishing presence of the sky and its starflowers. The focus shifts in the picture as we look at it, and yet when placed side by side all the elements form a complete coherent picture. The title, *Mystique*, comes from the fact that all the parts are related to traditional mystical subjects, and also that the entire picture provides a vision of an enchanted world where salvation and damnation are delineated.

Veillées, as the second "elevation," is quite different in tone and structure. And yet, the elements of sweetness and peacefulness are as strong as they are in *Mystique*. The poet indicates three parts that would seem to be three kinds of "night watch." The first is the clarification of all that distinguishes watchfulness from sleep, or rather the state of attentiveness from the state of confusion. Each sentence is elliptical and profound. There is a kind of sleep that is illumination (*le repos éclairé*) and which is neither fever nor languor. There is a friend who is neither passionate nor weak. He would be the ideal friend, as the ideal lover would be neither tormentor nor tormented. A kind of life exists where the world does not have to be sought. This is the great lesson from a night watch, the pure intuition of the ideal which comes in a flash and demands no explanation.

The poet-watcher (*veilleur*) is next seen in a large room which is lighted in a theatrical way and whose walls are covered with friezes and geological signs. The banal setting seems empty save for the watcher, but he dreams of sentimental groups of beings with varied characteristics. The dream, familiar throughout *Les Illuminations* and specifically announced in the first part of *Veillées*, is almost always more closely related to rooms and cities than to human beings and inhabitants.

The objects of the room become the focus in the third part, and enlarge to enter the night and the sea outside. Here there is an even combining of tapestries from inside and lacelike undergrowth from outside; of the hearthside and the sun on the seashore.

The elements of the poem are all relative and present, but they are seen in an unusual perspective which relates them to the infinite. The limits of the world are stated in the first section, the limits of a room in the second, and the limits of the combined room and world in the third, but these very limits are made absolute by the moment in which they are seen and painted. The poem is on the subject of a vigil, when at the end of a certain period of time, time itself may be overcome by an unpredictable vision, by a suddenly deep understanding of what is seen. If the waiting is of a certain kind, anything may come from it. The zone of the marvelous (*merveilleux*) is reached through the zone of the familiar, by waiting within it until what is personal becomes impersonal or transpersonal. Poetry forces open the gates of the marvelous and discovers behind them the unknown. *Veillées,* and so many other *illuminations,* combines the daily and the marvelous in such perfectly realized proportions that one finds oneself reading a miracle without knowing that it is such, and accepting a hallucination.

MYSTICAL EXERCISES

The four "exercises," thus named, seem to be those where the elements of poetry and mysticism are more abundantly and recklessly mingled than in others, where the to-

tal effect is one of combined enchantment and disenchantment.

Soir Historique   The "historical evening" for the naïve
tourist is precisely the one when the history of the past is
confused with the surrealistic power of the present, and
when everything real becomes unreal. The poem begins
immediately, in its first paragraph, with the most radical of
transformations. The instrument which he hears the master play is a harpsichord of the meadows. He sees a card
game going on at the bottom of a lake, which is also a mirror reflecting queens and courtesans. The sun goes down,
to the accompaniment of legendary music.

Little wonder that the tourist trembles as he imagines
hunting parties and hordes rushing past him. What holds
him now is his vision, created by the talk of guides and
garden comedies. The country he is visiting, if it is Germany, builds up to the moon. All is exaggeration in this
Holy Roman Empire. Over its rocks and stairways another
flat pale world is going to be built, which will be called
Africa and the West. To travel is to confuse so many nights
and so many seas that they make an impossible sound. But
the vision is a slave to be used by the tourist. It is a chemistry, valueless and formed by the sights of reality. Wherever
the train lets him off, he experiences the adventure of
bourgeois things and magic, of the real and the unreal
worlds combining in an atmosphere of depression and re-
morse.

The final paragraph is one of violent disenchantment, of
a total destruction which the naïve tourist will know best.
The images follow one another, each larger than the rest.
The cauldron, the ravished ocean, the subterranean con-
flagration, the entire planet shooting off into space, are

biblical visions which the serious-minded alone will see and will acknowledge as far more real than legendary. The elements themselves appear caught in a revolution. Terrifying powers, held down too long, erupt at last and reveal a universe damned.

The activity of the *voyant* seems always to precede a cataclysmic effect. The card game going on at the bottom of a lake, in *Soir historique,* is the same as the example Rimbaud gives of a simple hallucination in *Une Saison (Délires II)* where he sees a parlor at the bottom of a lake. The vision of the prose poem ends in an apocalyptic vehemence, and the passage in *Délires II* ends with the celebrated reference to the disorder of the poet's mind and the farewell he addresses the world, in the *Chanson de la plus haute tour.* Tourism is the modern counterpart of the quest myth. The perils to be encountered may be too great for the pure in heart. And yet only to him, to the naïve tourist —to Galahad—will the vision be granted, even if with the vision comes an almost inevitable blacking-out. To speak the vision is equivalent to the releasing of dark powers that have been held down for a long time. The pure in heart sees, speaks what he sees, and is consequently annihilated.

Mouvement   Cast in the form of free verse, like one other *illumination* only, *Marine,* this poem involves much more than a sea picture. It is related to the theme of voyage and quest in *Soir historique* and stresses in its early phrase, *la nouveauté chimique,* a combination of "new" (already developed in *A une raison*) and "chemistry" (of *Soir historique*). The movement of the water, as seen from the boat, provides both a new kind of sensation and a new vision. The travelers are conquerors in the sense that they discover new personal traits in themselves. Their science is autodidacticism. What they see educates them, and always from the top of the boat they feel the dual experience of repose and dizziness, repose from all the usual movement of the world, and dizziness from their vision of the depths. Their study leads them into the aquatic light of the first flood. This unspeakable light (*lumières inouïes*) Rimbaud had felt in his poem on the drunken boat where lights rising to the surface of the water were compared to silent sap rising (*la circulation des sèves inouïes*). The repose and vertigo are in as strong contrast with one another as are the two lovers on the deck, isolated and immobile in their embrace, to the passing scenes of discovery.

The poem describes one of the privileged moments of life whose power and profundity set it off from the usual existence and give to the usual existence its drabbest coloration. It is the moment, mystical in its intensity and vision, which is opposed to a life of habits, security, guarantees. But in its mavelous brevity, it symbolizes the precariousness of life which is the fundamental condition of mortal man. To give and to give one's self is doctrine contrary to the teachings of the world. The privileged moments of poetic vision are like the emotions of the player who knows that he wins because of some occult power he has called upon. The deck of a boat in *Mouvement* is one more of the places elected by Rimbaud in *Les Illuminations* (streets, forests, rooms, squares) where he waits for the revelation and has it. And always it leads us into the midst of some kind of whirlwind (*trombes du val / Et du strom*) which separates the visionary innocent from the guilty world.

Dévotion This is one of the most curious of the prose poems and one of the most paradoxical, perhaps, to place among the seeming exercises on mysticism.

The entire piece is patterned on a litany of prayers and remembrances almost Villonesque in tone, because it is never without a strong element of irony. The first three "remembrances" have the same complete tripartite formula: the name of the one prayed to, an object associated with her, and those for whom the object is to work a miracle. The first two are "sisters" with comically long and foreign names. One will save the drowning man, and the mother will cure the sick. The third might well be a prostitute who is saved for "the men." Then the prayers are addressed to a variety of characters of whom no request is made: to the poet's adolescence, to an old hermit, to the spirit of the poor, to the clergy. Finally, the prayer grows more general still. It is addressed to any ceremony that will satisfy the momentary aspirations and the serious vice of the poet. It opens out into a poem, with a great magnifying power, when addressed to lofty, icy Circeto, with a courageous amber heart, whose expansion and temperature convert it into a polar chaos. No more consecutive or consequential "thens" can be spoken.

The opposition between the sacred and the profane is so evenly balanced in *Dévotion* that it ends by canceling itself out. It mounts logically to its final dispersal rather than being abruptly counteracted at the end.

Solde   Again one thinks of Villon, and more insistently this time, where the itemization of the sale is lengthy and vigorously stated. But Rimbaud is far more oblique in the details and has a tone closer to that of the prophets in their denunciations and their repetitions. What is being sold seems to be nothing less than the cosmos, and especially the personal cosmos of thought and envy.

First up for sale are those things which do not exist, or

which are not recognized (and here one remembers the Villon legacies): everything the Jews did not sell, what virtue and sin did not experience, what perverted love and mass honesty do not know, what time and science do not have to recognize, what might come from voices and senses.

The next category is the bodies up for sale. Here the list seems total. Rimbaud is selling all bodies, including his own. The bodies are like the riches of the world in their walk, diamonds that are priceless. Anarchy (for the masses), satisfaction (for amateurs), and death (for lovers) are on sale too. After the bodies themselves, Rimbaud sells the desires of the bodies, and all the lesser comforts: houses, migrations, sports, noise, action.

The list repeats itself at the end, but finds different words for its expression. The things that do not exist are now called "invisible" and "insensible," secrets for vice and gaiety for the crowd. Bodies for sale are again mentioned, and with them, for the first time, the vendors themselves, who seem to be confused with travelers. *Vendeurs* and *voyageurs* are alike in that they never come to an end. The sale is never exhausted, and the voyage is never terminated.

Under the image of the "sale," which is so absolute in its recklessness, is the poet's desire for solitude and the mystic's will to rid himself of all images of the world. The poem is a transcription of the willed effort which must precede the mystical moment when the will is suspended. The dominant feeling in the poem is the poet's (or the mystic's) growing incompatibility with the human condition. What is desired is a new domain: *élan insensé et infini*. Rimbaud holds up for exhibition and sale what he possesses and what no one else has. Superhuman in his will, he offers everything—in order to get everything—knowing that if the sale is made, he will be a thousand times richer.

The usual obstinacy of a boy and an adolescent reaches in *Solde* a high degree of will for a purpose, of a consecrated will which acts like a deep underwave upsetting all the trivial objects on the surface of the ocean. The mystical experience which this poem might be conceived of as preceding is the fact and the power of being transported and ravished, of losing all distinction between the subjective and the objective. Those in whom, as in Rimbaud, the vision of God is lost sight of and even wilfully obscured, do not necessarily lose all access to a certain kind of experience which must be called, for want of a better term, "mystical" or at least "pre-mystical."

MYSTICAL FIGURE

Surpassing all the other prose poems in protracted fervor and rhythmical animation, *Génie* subsumes the life of the poet, such as can be read in *Une Saison en enfer,* and moves more deeply into the vision of the angel-man who composed *Les Illuminations.*

The buoyancy of the lines, which is an interpreter of the spirit's enthusiasm, is a perfect representation of the remarkable understanding of human experience Rimbaud revealed. It would seem to be the total understanding of a heart communicated in a privileged comment—once only perhaps—and which we place as the culmination in self-knowledge and its poetic expression in the case of Rimbaud.

Other poems would illustrate as well as *Génie* the muscular power of Rimbaud's sentence, the strong lilt and pounding of its articulation, its ever-varied phrasing so miraculously married to breathing and to sense, but no other poem sustains this miracle of sound for so long and at so high a level as *Génie*. It stands in a full surge of enthusiasm and fervor, and never once relaxes its intensity of expression and depths of feeling (which here is the expression of understanding), until the final sentence, which even raises the high intensity of all that has preceded and unfolds in a stronger movement than ever as if it were the final, full breath of the poet in which he had to recapitulate and reconsecrate his entire life. By their form, and by their content too, the sentences of *Génie* are those which resound in contemporary French poetry, in the verse of Claudel and of St.-John Perse, and to a lesser degree, in Eluard.

Génie is the title, "genie" or "genius," but it is not mentioned by name in the poem. Only the pronoun "he" is used, over and over again, as if the name itself were too sacred to pronounce. The meaning of the word itself, *génie,* is the hardest single word to decipher in all of Rimbaud's writings. And yet the poem opens with a series of synonyms for it. It is first called "affection and the present," and then almost immediately, "affection and the future." In these two elaborate and almost pretentious phrases, Rimbaud is approaching the full definition of the word, which he reserves, however, for the second paragraph. But already, in the first paragraph, there is an initial unfolding and meaning. This power of affection prepares the poet for each season of the year. It teaches him the bewitchment of voyaging and the joy of living in one place. It is, first, the image of love which the poet can see in the sky and in all the triumphant banners.

Then, the definition becomes clearer. The second paragraph, if we take it quite simply and directly, stands as Rimbaud's most profound statement about love. The genie in him, which he first called "affection," now he calls "love" itself—love, which he sees to be the re-invented power of balance. Reason (as in *A une raison*) is unpredictable and miraculous, because it is the same as eternity, that power that has always been in him. He paraphrases it with a Greek term: a machine, loved for its fatal qualities. It is the part of him that cannot escape from itself, that is god-like (again, as in the last line of *A une raison*). This love is so intimately a part of himself that the poet has been afraid of its directing him and of his yielding to it. This kind of analysis is a full elucidation of Rimbaud's particular drama in love. His health and the free practice of his faculties have depended upon his passion for this love, since love itself loves the poet because of its everlasting life.

The guide to the reading of this difficult poem is the use of the pronouns. He (*il*) is love, a power of a god in the poet; and we (*nous*) is the poet composed of his two selves: the self that is love and the self that opposes it, or fears it, or finally accepts it. Love is able to speak to the poet, as if he were a god (*l'Adoration*) and able to separate himself from his own being. His speech is about the past which has to disappear, which has to be destroyed if love is to exist as it should, in the present and in the future.

He will not move away (since he is the poet), and he will not come down again from heaven (since he is the poet). He will not redeem others, because he is not God, he is Rimbaud.

The rest of the poem, save the final paragraph, is a series of exclamations strongly reminiscent of parts of *Une Saison en enfer,* where Rimbaud refers to himself and his life and to those particular themes he has already stressed in speaking of his life. His *voyages,* first, their literal action and their formal counterpart in the poems. His *body,* in its violence and its efforts to destroy a native grace. His *visions* and his former *kneelings* and the *punishments* he was released from. (The word "released," *relevés*, is in italics because such punishments are not usually abolished, not magically rescinded, as in the case of Rimbaud.) His *day* (*Son jour!*), the word with which the poem is going to end, and which he first defines, is the poet's day, the creation of music, the recreation of rhythm of all suffering. His *step*—again the flights of the poet which are migrations or the going home of the soul, more tremendous than ancient invasions. The poet and his *génie* (*O Lui et nous!*), which is pride, more charitable, because it is more loving, than all minor charities. The *world*, which for the poet is the song of disasters.

The final paragraph summarizes many of the landscapes of *Les Illuminations* and the winter season which has been often evoked in the work. The sentence extends throughout all the time from the winter night (*cette nuit d'hiver*) to the new daylight of the *génie: son jour,* and through all the space of the cosmos, from cape to cape, from pole to castle, from the tides to the deserts of snow. It is the time and the place of the *génie,* which is always and everywhere. The world and the time of the world try to follow his vision, his breath, his body, his day, which is his epiphany.

The poem testifies to the fullest state of euphoria and joy which Rimbaud ever tried to express. Love finds a new name in him, that of *génie,* associated with breath (*ses souffles*). It is that force which inhabits us, changes us, recreates us. It is the eternal dream of the poet and of his poetic power. When it is accepted by the poet in himself, he becomes the magician, the creator of beauty out of all that is ordinary and trivial and ugly. Nothing is useless when love dominates the personality of the poet. It exhorts the poet to ecstasy, to come out of himself, to exceed his own power, to create that element in himself he does not know. The power is love, and its characteristic is precisely the impossibility of love being resisted. Even God cannot resist the charity of his children.

Exultantly, Rimbaud lists the attributes of love: breath, flight, fecundity, body, vision, day, step. With them he defines love as that power of ceaseless innovation and renovation. It captures the world by upsetting everything real in the world. All the *illuminations* illustrate this principle. They are impulses felt by the poet, moving him toward the unknown, the extraordinary, the inaccessible. They are pictures of moments when the poet experienced something of the primal force that controls the world and all the creatures of the world. In *Génie* Rimbaud himself personifies this force.

Men who, like Rimbaud, feel the sacred in them, deeply and yet not definably in any theological sense, will always have a strong inclination to repudiate religions and what will seem to them the empty ritualism of religion. For them poetry may well replace confession, and other sacraments also, after the creation of which they can appear in the world as exorcized, and for a time at least as living in a world conceived by themselves which is opposed to the real world. The term "confession" comes to mind especially in the case of Rimbaud's poetry because throughout it he is accusing himself of failure, of seasons in hell, of winds dispersing the world, of slamming doors, of dizziness, of flights.

The poet is more conscious than most men of the two opposing worlds of the real and the imaginary. They are two powers of two weights that have to be balanced. Their unbalancing is the beginning of a race toward catastrophe.

It might be considered, in this theoretical form, a definition of tragedy or quite simply of the human condition. The poet, in the actual creation of his poetry, effects a strange and seemingly magic interruption in this flight toward catastrophe. In the poet's art the imagination and the real are no longer antithetical. They are fused together, and to such a degree that their very fusion appears mystical. In his use of words, Rimbaud is constantly alternating the processes of the decomposition and recomposition of the sacred.

6

Angelism

Pattern of Revolt (Une Saison en enfer)

IN *Les Poètes de sept ans,* Rimbaud talks of his earliest effort to change his existence. To escape from the maternal tyranny and the house itself, so completely dominated by his mother, he fled to the garden and to the farthest point in the garden, to the wall. There, crouching in the marl, he pressed his fists against his closed eyes in order to blot out the garden and the house and to create his inner visions. At such moments he could hear the wall and the fruit trees on it breathe and move. A few years later, on his way to and from school, the city of Charleville depressed him as the maternal house did. There were few signs of freedom in the drab city, so often stifled by the river fog and the smoke from the foundries. The principal buildings imposed their various disciplines and strictures: the seminary, the barracks, and the municipal court (*palais de justice*). The large church stood also in the center of

Charleville as a symbol of authority for Rimbaud. In *Les Pauvres à l'église* he derides the stubborn comical prayers of the poor, drolling their faith of mendicants:

Et tous, bavant la foi mendiante et stupide.

He is still more bitter in *Les Premières Communions* where Christ is apostrophized as the eternal thief of energy:

Christ, éternel voleur des énergies.

On the wall of the church, the boy Arthur wrote his supreme blasphemy, *Mort à Dieu,* to mark his disapproval of bigotry and narrow dogma. With the same disdain he flayed the pedants at school, and the bourgeois in the streets, parading their vanity and wickedness. Priests, teachers, and merchants he grouped together as representing the forces of constraint and oppression. From them he will take his departure, as he will from his mother and immediate family.

Mémoire possibly alludes to the first major flight, which was the first significant expression given to his revolt, when Rimbaud on August 29, 1870, left his mother and brother and sisters in the field between Charleville and Mézières, presumably to get a book at home. But he went much farther. He took the train to Paris, where he landed penniless and was put in jail. In the poem, he describes his flight as that of a thousand white angels:

Lui, comme
mille anges blancs qui se séparent sur la route,
s'éloigne par-delà la montagne!

For himself, therefore, his flight was angelic, motivated by a great thirst for purity and freedom, for a spiritual liber-

ation. Rimbaud was incapable of staying in the same city
for any length of time and in company with the same people. Like his father before him, he needed constantly to
see new places, to move freely with the changes of his spirit.
Only at the very end of his life, in a few of his letters
written from Aden and Harar, will he express a desire to
settle down in one place and found a family. Even as a
child, he was driven with a deep urgency to travel and
escape. The house, the city, the school, the church were
the first bonds he released himself from in this need for
expansion.

After the first few escapes, to Paris and Belgium, in the
fall of 1870, he discovered in the library of Charleville
another source of flight, the reading of certain books on
magic and mysticism which were to provide him with no-
tions of philosophy and aesthetics, destined to play some
part at least, although not so drastic as Rolland de Renéville believes, in the future work and life of the poet.
Colonel Godchot, Etiemble, and Renéville have provided
lists of works on occultism that were in the library when
Rimbaud consulted there, among which are Dangy's *Traité
sur la Magie, le Sortilège, les Possessions,* Massé's *De l'Abus
des Devins et Magiciens,* and especially Eliphas Lévi's
Rituel de Haute Magie.

Even in poems written in the earliest part of 1870, such
as *Soleil et chair,* Rimbaud gives evidence of seeking a
liberation in mystical values and magic. He claims, in
Soleil et chair, that man cannot know, in a metaphysical
sense, because of his human reason, which is an obstacle
to knowing the infinite. And yet there is a way, opened to
the poet especially, of feeling the universe in its multiple
"correspondences." The poet's role is to reveal the unity of
the world, and here Rimbaud uses the traditional theolog-

ical term, *C'est la Rédemption! C'est l'Amour! C'est l'Amour!*

He moved rapidly from this early nostalgic mood to violence and revolution. Only at the end of his brief career, in *Les Illuminations,* did he recapture in his writing something of the mystical strains. In February, 1871, he went again to Paris. The Commune broke out on March 18. This movement of insurrection must have corresponded to the poet's feelings, and when it was over in May, the failure inspired one of his most vituperative pieces: *Paris se repeuple* (also called *L'Orgie Parisienne*). The behavior of men is opposed to all the ideals of love, to the systems he had read about in ancient philosophies. The poet in him exploded in the sweeping doctrinal statements of his two letters to Izambard and Demeny in this same month. Poetry solicited him as a revolutionary power and as a monstrous revindication. *Le Bateau ivre* illustrated his new system and his new power, and he took it to Verlaine in September. Between September, 1871, when Rimbaud first met Verlaine, and July, 1873, when he returned alone to Roche after the Brussels drama, he lived an extraordinary adventure he tried to explain in *Une Saison en enfer.*

The world's familiarity with Rimbaud's legend grows. It recognizes more and more a universal meaning in what once seemed an extraordinarily particularized human existence and adventure. To demand what Rimbaud did of poetry and of another being is to make a pact with Satan or at least with a force representing such a delirious goal that one ceases thereby to be completely human. The role of the damned is meticulously plotted out. It is enacted with very few variations because the thirst for knowledge, for knowing what one cannot know, grows the greater, the more it is satisfied. To know, as Rimbaud wanted to know,

is equivalent to denying one's self. He did this in his re-
jections, in his fits of fury, in his "scenes" at home and in
cafés, in his assumption of the role of beast and underling.
It is equivalent to a stifling of one's self and the gradual
demonization or *abrutissement* he went through. He
learned thereby to live in primitive, unconscious zones of
his body, but he was never able to leave his body or change
his body, as he hoped. He had, finally, to accept man's
condition of being.

The story of *Une Saison en enfer* is a tragedy, or a failure, but the protagonist has in him some of the characteristics we easily ascribe, in our wonderment at such a tragic
failure, to a fallen angel. Rimbaud sets himself off against
Christianity in much the same way that Lucifer sets himself off against all the angelic hosts. On the more limited
and more purely human level, Rimbaud was an adolescent
motivated by a deep hatred for mankind, and especially
for woman, because of his resentment of maternal tyranny.

The art of *Une Saison* cannot be separated from its story.
Its outstanding characteristic is perhaps the passionate lu-
cidity with which the story is composed. Clairvoyance had
been the trait of Baudelaire before Rimbaud, of the
"prince of *voyants*." By writing, both Rimbaud and Baudelaire moved closer always to their earliest unity, to a
primordial region in them, so highly charged with mag-
netism that it was able to attract to it the world itself.
That human center which opened up under the penetrating gaze and investigation of Rimbaud and Baudelaire is
best defined as the zone of being where the temporal and
the spiritual merge. It permits such poets as Rimbaud and
Baudelaire to enact dramatically and passionately whatever is real to them. Their poetry reflects this merger of
the temporal and the spiritual, and especially the harmoni-

zation and the balance of the two. Their song is inner and deeply personal because of this center site from which it rises. There the real and the surreal are equally apprehended. What is seen directly and what is provoked by hallucination merge in the miraculous unity of the poem. As a social being, Rimbaud rejected all of the usual compromises, and as a poet, he scorned the usual modes of knowledge. With a blind determination, possessed by very few categories of human beings—adolescents, saints, heroes —he moved rapidly toward a seizure of the supernatural. The sole power he cultivated was the practice of hallucination, the creation of images generated by the torrent of immediate thought. It was the cultivation of a frenetic disorder of images, out of which could be born the kind of poem which *Les Illuminations* represents: the poem where reality and dreams are perfectly fused, where visions appear prophetic in their unaccustomed relationships with one another, and in their dazzling transpositions.

The drama of revolt and despair, as it unfolds in *Une Saison,* describes an adolescent who would have to choose between absolutes, between a kind of heroism which would unquestionably develop into holiness, and a life of the unconscious which would lead him back to childhood and to the kind of madness which has recently been ascribed to surrealism. It was the latter choice he made.

Pattern of Poetry (Les Illuminations)

Poetry is one of the principal methods of preparation by which man tries to change his being into an angelic being. It represents a deep temptation to do something that cannot be done. Pure song would be the accomplishment of pure spirit. But even the attempting of such an achievement has about it a revolutionary purity. Great poets are insurgents. They are in revolt against the limitations of reason and logic. If they appear often to be the opponents of established social order and conventions, that is because of a far deeper and more metaphysical revolt, waged against all the daily insufficiencies of human reason. Sade, Baudelaire, Rimbaud, and Lautréamont are alike in this respect. Each, with his own speech and poetic creation, waged a relentless war against human intelligence in its limited aspects of reason, logic, consciousness. Their writings appear to us now as heroic attempts to understand the world and to efface the frontiers of the real world by means of a metaphorical intelligence, which in its very nature is limitless. They are diametrically opposed to the rationalistic tradition of the seventeenth and eighteenth centuries, and take their place beside the gnostic writers and the masters of the occult tradition, of all those who tried to break down the rigid framework of logic in order to reach the darker world of dreams and the more luminous world of visions, of what the Middle Ages called *le merveilleux*. This represents the action of the poet in his more supernatural and subversive role. The poetry of Baudelaire and Rimbaud, and the prose writings of Sade and Lautréamont, form a body of literature which in its deepest meaning is non-literary. It transcends literature by its "sacred" character, by its penetration into the hidden recesses of the mind and the memory of man, by the pure power of rhythm and sound and image it reveals, by the communication it establishes between the supernatural forces of nature and man.

Between the end of the Middle Ages and the time of the Marquis de Sade in the eighteenth century, and especially Baudelaire in the nineteenth, there is almost no example of a poet believing in the occult power of language.

Maurice Scève, of Lyon, in the sixteenth century, would be the most prominent exception during this long period of an artist maintaining his faith in the incantatory magic of words. Charles Baudelaire was the first poet-aesthetician in France to analyze in his doctrine on analogy and correspondences the relationship between the creation and God. In his essay on Théophile Gautier (1859), Baudelaire provided a definition of poetry which has had an extraordinary success for almost one hundred years, and which categorically states that to write as a poet is to practice a kind of witchcraft with the sound of words. *Manier savamment une langue, c'est pratiquer une espèce de sorcellerie évocatoire.* The poet is the decipherer of the universe and the translator of the supernatural.

About thirty years after Baudelaire's essay, Stéphane Mallarmé, in his essay, *Crise du vers,* continues this lesson on the metaphysics of language and carries it as far as it is possible to go. Mallarmé is concerned with the magical concept of the Work, with the "pure" Work which implies the poet's disappearance, who thereby yields the initiative to the words themselves: *L'œuvre pure implique la disparition élocutoire du poëte, qui cède l'initiative aux mots, par le heurt de leur inégalité mobilisée.* When the poet says, "a flower!" the one absent from all bouquets rises up in its musical form. This is Mallarmé's most startling illustration of the very principle of poetry in its incantatory effect. *Je dis: une fleur! et . . . musicalement se lève, idée même et suave, l'absente de tous bouquets.* The final paragraph of the essay describes the line of poetry, *le vers,* as creating a new word, foreign to ordinary language, and achieving an isolation of the word.

Almost midway between these two essays on poetic theory by Baudelaire and Mallarmé, Rimbaud's *Lettre du voyant* (1871) stresses the Promethean tendency of the poet. In his role of fire-stealer and self-knower, his consciousness is bound up inextricably with the universal consciousness. The poet is the supreme *savant,* because poetry is beyond all other literary genres. It is really beyond literature. We are far from having exhausted all the implications and meanings of Rimbaud's theory, especially in its relationship to Baudelaire and to Mallarmé, but at least it stands out clearly as a revolt, as a position with regard to poetry which will be continued by André Breton and the surrealists. The overpowering ambition of surrealism was to translate the secret associations which relate the inner world of a man to the exterior world containing him. An entire lineage of poets, culminating with the surrealists, has been struck with the relatedness between personal experience and traditional esoteric. Nerval's experience in poetry is related to the cabala, Baudelaire's to Swedenborg, Mallarmé's to the witchcraft of evocation, Rimbaud's to his angelic temptation and his theft of celestial fire.

In his Promethean role, Rimbaud eradicated from his poetry almost all trace of sentiment, and achieved in its stead a poetry of sensation, strong because it is so totally devoid of sentimentality. But whatever is Promethean in man is destined by its very nature to catastrophe of tremendous proportions. The halo of lightning we associate with Prometheus fell over Rimbaud also and caused in him a tragic extinction of poetic utterance.

The tension of the images and the rapidity of the movement in *Les Illuminations* announce their collapse. After the literal revolt, discernible in *Une Saison,* which was a reaction against society, arises the revolt against literature and the usual poetic language, which in *Les Illuminations* is a great demand for purity of speech. But the two reactions, against society and literature, are related. Rimbaud's search for the transformation of lyric language is a subtle gauge for the measurement of modern sensibility. Belief in magic had somehow survived up to the modern period and continued in its weakest form of chance. But not until the writings of Balzac and Baudelaire was there much belief that the sacred, in its magical manifestations, existed in the world and had the power of changing the destiny of men and places. *Les Illuminations,* in its series of physical, highly tensed impressions, transforms the most familiar sites into strange, distant places. The prose poems are like fetishes, endowed with the power of charging inert objects with remarkable meanings, of animating distant beings and lands. With the example of Rimbaud's work, modern poetry is bent upon giving an image to that which has no image: *Je notais l'inexprimable (Délires II).* In the very disorder of his mind, Rimbaud found his way back to the sacred: *Je finis par trouver sacré le désordre de mon esprit (Délires II).* The silences and the nights which Rimbaud studied and wrote of, and the rages and the vertigoes too—*J'écrivais des silences, des nuits. Je fixais des vertiges (Délires II)*—are the very signs of modern poetry, the images contemplated by Novalis and Hölderlin, by Poe and Baudelaire, by Mallarmé, Lautréamont, Nietzsche.

Under the revived spell of the supernatural and of magic, the modern poet has become again the man astonished at everything. He is the man who questions every object, slowly and meticulously in the case of Mallarmé, rapidly and flashingly in the case of Rimbaud. Before his very eyes, and even as he asks his question, the sacred is decomposed and recomposed. His deepest need is to accept the full definition of religion and he can only turn his back on the forms of religion as he finds them. Rimbaud's "alchemy of the word" is based upon a belief that what he sees in front of him each day is not all. What is necessary for him to secure as a poet is a disposition with which he sees a perspective, a miraculous freedom. In Rimbaud's particular vocabulary and imagery, this freedom is associated with flight and escape. It occurs imaginatively at the end of *Les Poètes de sept ans;* it is in the flight of the white angels in *Mémoire;* it is the entire theme of *Le Bateau ivre;* it is more subtly present in *Les Illuminations.* Finally, it is the poet's need and principal activity protected by sleep. To wake up is to end the flight and to face the tragic consequences of the escape in sleep. The poetry of Rimbaud and the images occurring in sleep contain the same fusion of the real world and a world created by the poet. When the sleep ended and the poetry was therefore cut off, the tragedy was so rapid and so total for Rimbaud that it has always been difficult for other men to call it a tragedy. No poet was ever so vulnerable as Rimbaud. No poet was ever able to cease being a poet as quickly as Rimbaud. After being the master of the world he had created, Rimbaud ceased being a master in any sense when he could no longer behold that world.

Throughout *Les Illuminations* Rimbaud remains the image of the man loved when there is no more love. He testifies to the deepest nostalgia of romanticism, man's desire to become as God, the deifying activity of the poet. Over and over again, he names objects only to say in the next sentence that he did not really mean them. Each *illumination* might be considered as transpiring within an instant of time, during which a question is asked and an answer given. To the metaphysical questions, What is? What is real? is given the reply: Existence is. The poem, in its form of sensation, rises up from the coinciding of this question and this answer.

Like the soothsayers of antiquity and the Hebrew prophets, Rimbaud received, briefly but without any shadow of doubt, the word as a vocation. For as long as he was faithful to this concept of the word as a gift, he remained the creator of sacred plans and designs, thereby merging time with eternity. The power of the word is precisely this reconciliation it is able to bring about between the eternal and that which is limited by duration. The word is a divine gift to man and it is also the means by which man reaches back to God. It is the bond uniting Creator and created. It is the means by which the created becomes in his turn creator.

In each of the principal themes of *Les Illuminations* Rimbaud appears in roles of creature and creator, of man tempted to turn pure spirit. The child in *Après le Déluge* is not a contemplative, but a questioner, who cherishes his memories of violence and blood on the one hand, and of tenderness on the other. His purest moments of contentment are followed by yearnings for the renewal of violence and destruction. The experience of childhood combines the activity and pursuit (as in *Aube*) which ends in the ecstasy of knowledge, and the retreat away from the world, the refuge of the white room underground, described in *Jeunesse*.

The poet, too, is a dual being, both prince and genie in *Conte,* both boy and girl in *H,* the self-perpetuating god in *Parade,* and the son of Pan in *Antique.* He is both Rimbaud and Verlaine, both poetry and death, in *Vagabonds.* He is the one who affirms his method and who at the same time announces the advent of the assassins (*Matinée d'ivresse*).

The cities of *Les Illuminations* are composed of vast constructions which disintegrate in a flash. The length and expansiveness of their avenues are expressed by pure assonance at one moment in *Métropolitain* (*Damas damnant de longueur*). Babel is the archetype for Rimbaud's cities which collapse before they pierce the heavens with their speech.

There is great solitude in the poems on childhood and the life of the poet, and there are few inhabitants of the cities. This poet is a kind of mystic constitutionally incapable of coming close to mankind. He resembles the Reason he evokes in *A une raison,* who disposes of ideas like a divinity, who is able to liberate the pure idea of love (in *Conte*), and who detaches himself from the sensible world (at the end of *Matinée d'ivresse*). The autobiography of the angel-man in *Génie* is narrated in terms of his breath, his step, his day. The present and the future are one. They are equalized in his assumption of love which is the power beyond his real power, the genie that permits him to exceed himself. *Je est un autre.*

Ambition and Failure of the Voyant

The author of the celebrated May letter could hardly have realized the profundities he was formulating when he wrote out his pages on poetic history and poetic belief for Paul Demeny. By May, 1871, he had achieved for himself something of the *voyant*'s temperament he defines in the letter. The writing of the letter must have helped confirm and strengthen all the tendencies of his nature which were forming and which characterize the poet of the next three years.

The *voyant* is the man who wills to see the world in a special way, and who ended by seeing it, in Rimbaud's

case, with the example of *Les Illuminations* before us, as
a world rich in forms and colors, a universe designed with
clear lines, highlighted with glaring rays or subdued in
dark shadows. Baudelaire was the great example for the
adolescent of Charleville. He had been the first *voyant,* the
king of poets, and a real god by his recreating of the world.
Far from being merely the receptive poet, Baudelaire had
made himself into the visionary whose words were hallucinated in the power of evocation they contained.

Rimbaud became an adolescent Baudelaire, possessed of
an even more indomitable will. Adolescence is always the
period of search for a duty, for a reality which is usually
indefinable. Rimbaud defines his duty as the will to turn
voyant, and he remained a poet during the length of time
that will was triumphant. In the practice of his will power,
he perceived, as Baudelaire had perceived before him, a
strange and remarkable energy which was able to join and
unite all the disparate forces in the world. He would even
reach some knowledge of love by this method, not by
identifying himself with any of the objects in the world,
but by moving beyond the objects, beyond the point in
time when he perceived them as joined harmoniously, in
"correspondence." The poet-rhetorician stays with the objects he sees and describes, but the visionary moves beyond
them and liberates himself from them. The "invention"
Rimbaud's poetry represents is of a mystical order. He
qualifies it in the most exalted terms when he claims to
have found in it something like the key of love. The passage occurs in the second part of *Vies: Je suis un inventeur
bien autrement méritant que tous ceux qui m'ont pré-
cédé; un musicien même, qui ai trouvé quelque chose
comme la clef de l'amour.* He was as deeply concerned
with the outcome and success of this method, as other ado-

lescents are concerned with the development of their ath-
letic capacities, with the breaking of past records where
they would be alone and pure and heroic. Such ambition,
both poetic and physical, does not exist without a large degree of torment, of *Angoisse,* as Rimbaud calls it in his
prose poem, where he acknowledges that with the moment
of success there will be also an awareness of some inherent
flaw, some fatal limitation, a sense of shame over his lack
of skill.

The ambition was delirious, but Rimbaud knew deeply,
and was soon to experience even more deeply, the dangerous narcissism of adolescence which comes always in the
wake of the very sensibility that makes the writing of poetry possible. When the sensibility is excessive, it is unable
to fix and channel the richness it discovers. It lives more
in the realm of ambition than of poetic achievement
through an unwillingness to be diminished or humbled.
The narcissism of adolescence, by its characteristic of end-
lessness, provides a lesson, by analogy, on the infinite. It
continues in the making of lyric poets who are eternal
adolescents, eternally unadaptable, forever incapable of fixing themselves into a pattern of life. The essentially romantic trait of narcissism is its inevitable obsession with
the indefinite and the unlimited. This may well be a form
of angelism, at least a latent angelism, expressed in flight
or instability or a turning away from major conflicts of
existence. The great ambition of the lyric poet is to pass
beyond or obliterate all the obstacles which might impair
his principal ambition: the song of the world's original
purity.

Rimbaud was convinced of being the heir of all the
great lyric voices before him. His is the most recent poet's
existence, but it is not unique and not separated from

other existences. In *Mauvais Sang* he remembers former roles he lived in distant periods: that of a peasant, a soldier, a crusader. In *Vies* he remembers the Holy Land and a Brahman teacher. As he watches the flames of a hearth-side fire separate and divide in a gust of wind, the past is revealed to him: armies, storms, cities (*Nocturne vulgaire*). The contemplation of a wall, in *Veillées,* is sufficient to call up hallucinating and rapidly moving forms. When, in *Phrases,* one of the richest evocations of former existences, the poet throws himself on his bed and closes his eyes, he sees the figures of his imagination, ideas, and dreams, in the form of queens and girls.

In 1872, when Rimbaud was fully involved in his career as a poet, Friedrich Nietzsche published his *The Birth of Tragedy*. The lives of the two men present many striking parallels. Each had a sister who created and fostered a false legend about the brother. Each looked upon Christianity as a destroyer of energy. A strong tone of prophecy is in both works, especially in Nietzsche's, and an apocalyptic sense of dreadful things to come. Specifically in Nietzsche, and implicitly in Rimbaud, is the belief that traditional morality is moribund and that civilization, in its essential strength, is dangerously threatened. Nietzsche's use of the word "decadence," and especially as it applies to the literature of his day, might serve to describe certain aspects of Rimbaud's style and method of writing. He points out that contemporary writing does not possess the sustained grandeur of the *Iliad,* of Shakespeare, of Goethe, and that the single word dominates the sentence, as the sentence clouds the meaning of the full page, and that the single page is remembered rather than the book as a whole. Even the example of Wagner in Nietzsche's life bears some analogy with the role of Verlaine in Rimbaud's.

Especially in the celebrated definition of the origin of art, as combining Apollonian and Dionysian elements, does the philosophy of Nietzsche recall the poetic theory and practice of Rimbaud. The measured, luminous construction of so many of the *illuminations* testifies to the Apollonian power to create harmonious beauty, which Nietzsche illustrates with the example of Greek sculpture. The rapid, fulgurant collapse of the landscapes, cities, and dreams in *Les Illuminations* has in it something of the drunken Dionysian frenzy threatening all forms and all codes. The ceaseless striving of Rimbaud as poet to defy all limitations is also Dionysian. The spirit of Apollo creates illusions, and the spirit of Dionysus suggests the activity of blind will. (It is true that the Dionysian, in the later writings of Nietzsche, becomes synonymous with passion controlled.) In *The Birth of Tragedy,* Nietzsche emphasizes the Dionysian as the negative and necessary dialectical element in tragedy.

The philosopher and the poet, in the exceptional attention that has been paid to them during a half-century (there are more than 1,000 books on Nietzsche and more than 500 on Rimbaud), testify to the deep ambivalence in the creation of any major art, to the strange combination of opposites required by the work, whether it be called Apollo-Dionysus or *spleen-idéal*. Nietzsche believed that an artistic creation is prompted by something which the artist lacks. Homer, for example, would have created no Achilles if he had been an Achilles. Taken separately, *Une Saison en enfer* appears largely Dionysian, and *Les Illuminations* largely Apollonian. But combined, they illustrate Nietzsche's doctrine that art is both a response to suffering and a celebration of life.

Cocteau, in his letter to Maritain, explains that instinc-

tively he goes against the law. This is why he was impelled
to translate Antigone.[1] God, he says, accepts no tepidness.
He exacts either silence or revolution. Here, again, Rimbaud would admirably illustrate the newer formula. And
Maritain, in his answer to Cocteau, corroborates much of
the doctrine on Rimbaud's angelism when he says that the
poet is joined with the secret powers operating in the universe (*Le Poète est connaturalisé aux puissances secrètes
qui se jouent dans l'univers*).[2]

The very ambivalence of the poet's nature contains the
clue to his final dissatisfaction with poetry, to his final
flight and silence. The vocational and geographical changes
in Rimbaud's life are well known: the poet, at twenty, renounced poetry and became in the space of a few years a
colonial merchant. He stopped writing, but did not stop

---

[1] "Or l'instinct me pousse toujours contre la loi. C'est la
raison secrète pour laquelle j'ai traduit *Antigone*" (*Lettre à
Jacques Maritain*, p. 45). The theme of angelism recurs frequently in Cocteau's *Rappel à l'ordre*, especially in the essay,
Le Secret professionnel: "Jusqu'à nouvel ordre, Arthur Rimbaud reste le type de l'ange sur terre." Cocteau refers in the
passage to other "angels," Verlaine, Satie, Mallarmé, and concludes with the statement: "Je ne dresserai pas ici une liste des
angéliques. Mais seuls ils comptent pour moi; seuls ils me
touchent, et si je reconnais la valeur chez d'autres, ceux-là
seuls sont pour moi dignes du nom de poètes" (p. 204).

[2] *Réponse à Jean Cocteau*, p. 25. The entire passage, and
indeed the entire letter, treats deeply and movingly the poet's
inspiration. As there are several meanings in Holy Scripture,
there are many meanings in things created by God. The saint
completes the work of the Passion, and the poet completes the
work of Creation. "Comme le saint achève en soi l'oeuvre de la
Passion, le poète, lui, achève l'oeuvre de la Création."

existing, and it is wrong to judge the latter part of his life on the sole documents available: the letters he wrote home and his business letters. In those pages, it is true, there is no trace of the poet he had been. The style of the letters is flat and commonplace. Their contents are, on the whole, utilitarian, limited, practical. Yet it seems foolhardy to accuse him of a literary betrayal and of a failure in a poet's career. The very silence, so absolute, about all that had been central to him for five years was sufficient proof that he had willed to pass into some other region of thought, some other spiritual domain about which we can never hope to learn anything. Whatever major events he passed through were not communicable, and the events he did translate earlier into his poetic work were barely communicable. The written words of Rimbaud testify to a fundamental tragedy of such a nature that it would not be possible to continue translating it. In the eyes of the world, a divorce took place between the poetic character he had once been and the very different character he became in Aden and Harar, and that is all we know and can know.

The last ten years of Rimbaud's life, culminating in his prolonged agony, paralleled the year or two of his life as poet spent with Verlaine. The two experiences consumed him, each in its own way. The first brought to a close his poetic ambition and at the same time provided him with its fullest expression. The second diminished him physically and finally assassinated him. The two experiences with poetry and Africa have the common characteristic of flight, of ceaselessly moving about. This basic motivation of Rimbaud is most lucidly explained in *Vagabonds*. There it appears in a fairly autobiographical state, in its full complexity of cruelty imposed by Rimbaud, of suffering incurred by him, of idealism and his will to create out of Verlaine a great poet. In it he appears in his dual function of Prometheus as fire-stealer, submitting to the angelic temptation, and as chained sufferer and victim of the eagle. The text is remarkable for its double analysis of the poets, for the understanding of both cruelty and pity. He is the poet bringing to Verlaine both bad luck (*guignon*) and a state of innocency which was never understood. He was made into a poet by Verlaine, and then, in his new state, jeered at his alchemist creator (*ce satanique docteur*). The legend of Faust and of all willed metamorphoses is deeply a part of Rimbaud's life.

All of Rimbaud's ambivalences are expressed in *Vagabonds*. He is both savage and innocent, a Manichaean unable to choose between good and evil, a friend who sincerely wants to recover for Verlaine a primitive, godlike state, and at the same time a poet in his own right, eager "to find the place and the formula." After the motif of restitution, that of poetic ambition is the most tenacious in the early years. To look for the "place" is the role of vagabond. To find the "formula" is the vocation of the lyric magician. If the hallucination (or trick) succeeds, the metaphor-formula should coincide with the poem-creation. The "formula" we take to be the unity of the creative word.

The position of Rimbaud, by his personal inhumanity and cruelty, by his flights and need for independence, is the most solitary in all the history of French literature. His literary silence is as ironic as the loss of his leg at the end of his life, which tragically interrupted all possible flights over mountains, deserts, rivers, and seas. The most passionate believer in the pure magic of speech ended in silence, and the most passionate vagabond of French poetry ended his existence as a legless cripple, a *cul-de-jatte,*

as he calls himself in a letter to his sister, of July, 1891:
je ne suis plus qu'un tronçon immobile.

From the beginning of the tremendous experiment,
Rimbaud never ceased having premonitions of failure. But
these very glimpses of collapse threw into higher focus the
poetic ecstasies he reached. Almost as if he had become a
chronic victim of dazzling blindness, his most brilliantly
colored perceptions in the prose poems enlarged so rapidly
that they tended always to end in the pure whiteness the
mystics speak of. Rimbaud is one of the modern poets who
are deeply aware of the abyss opening out at their feet.
Hölderlin, Baudelaire, Antonin Artaud were as concerned
with the always possible failure of their mental powers
as Rimbaud with the possible failure of his artistic attempt.
The entire chapter, *L'Impossible,* in *Une Saison,* is on the
agonizing theme of failure: in childhood, religion, philosophy. What he lacked is almost beyond analysis, but it is
stated in poetic summary, as the last line of *Conte,* where
the poet's desire exists alone without the music capable of
transforming it. Even more lucidly still, the failure is exposed in *Adieu,* as the conclusion of the infernal season,
where the poet confesses he once thought he had acquired
supernatural powers, and where he announces a return to
the earth, to a peasant's life and its daily contact with the
real world.

The Poet and the Angel

In his fundamental poetic drive, Rimbaud is opposed to
the efforts of the intellectual whose main function is the
reduction of the unusual and the supernatural. If the intellectual's regime is prolonged, it converts religion, for example, into morality, or hygiene. One of the conditions
necessary for the rebirth or the return of the sacred in the

world is an experience, like Rimbaud's, of familiarity with the unpredictable and the fantastic. His poetic experience, however brief, was a divorce from the predictable, by which the mechanics of habit were abolished. The unusual presupposes the usual or the normal which it contradicts. The real world exists in the writings of Rimbaud, but somewhat obscured in the shadows cast by the extraordinary world created by his imagination.

The peril of such a construction lies in its necessarily monotonous narcissism. Most men, at first, will turn away from a work, such as Rimbaud's in poetry and Proust's in prose, where the subject matter is so profoundly and poignantly self-centered. They are supreme examples of a work where man is monstrously caught in himself. The success of such an analysis comes from the resolution of opposites. Rimbaud's system of figuration first severs all contact with the universe of recognizable phenomena, and then reforms it. The vision of the exterior world and the artist's vision of his inner world recognize one another, in the work, each by its own metaphysical imperfections, each by its own insufficiency and need of the other. The real has to be pierced and fructified by the imagination. This would be one way of explaining the poetic work of Nerval, Baudelaire, Rimbaud, and Mallarmé. In this process of violation and unification, *Les Illuminations* offers the most extreme examples of objects being removed from their natural settings and of unusual sensations being provoked so that both objects and sensations become productive of metamorphoses and migrations. By losing its way in the universe of *Les Illuminations,* an object finds its place in the miraculous world of fiction. It moves out of the universe we perceive in order to descend through the substrata of worlds that are imaginatively or mentally represented in us. This is at-

tached, of course, to the making of all art, which is interpretation, transfiguration, volatilization. Rimbaud creates,
at the end of his process, a total kind of animism. Nothing
remains fixed in his pictures, which are all Heraclitean
concepts of the real world, and here again he recalls the
world of Proust, so dominated by Time, a world whose
only permanence is change.

An image in Rimbaud, therefore, is a power provoking
surprise because it appears out of context, outside of its
customary décor. It is convincing because it disturbs. It is a
kind of catalyst, precipitating unpredictable combinations.
The *Illuminations* are minor volcanoes whose lava, once
cooled, leaves unrecognizable figurations. They are fire
images principally, abolishing any notion of distance, because they are so volatile, supple, spontaneous. They perform the fundamental function of the metaphor, by joining and reconciling opposites. These opposites, in their
fundamental sense, are always the psyche of the poet and
the exterior world. The operation of the metaphor is a
magical combination in that it fixes once and for all the
thought of a man which is in constant flux. Here, again, the
example of Proust comes to mind, in the ultimate goal of
art, which he so closely defines in *Le Temps retrouvé,* as
that creation of man which opposes the flux of time and of
thought.

When the poet translates his vision of his poet's universe,
he disturbs our vision of the world. The reader is disorientated when he sees the mobile landscapes of Rimbaud in
place of the stationary landscapes of his own world. But this
effect of dizziness and disorientation the poet willed to create. In Rimbaud's particular case, his eagerness for voyaging and the acquisition of languages is reflected in *Les
Illuminations* where he demonstrates an overpowering

drive for conquest and freedom. By making of poetry a language capable of translating the visions of his metaphorical genius, Rimbaud helped to create his character of an angel, of a man able and willing to renounce his habits and native atmosphere for another atmosphere and another perspective consecrated to the most total kind of solitude.

The purely theological *données* which might help to elucidate Rimbaud's angelism are few but highly significant. Between the spiritual world and the world there are no real barriers or walls. Angels were created at the same time as man. They are pure spirits functioning as intermediaries between God and the world and they are able to exert influence on men. Angels are more perfect than men. They have a more highly developed conscience and know immediately the principle of things. The relationship between these two beings is so close that man is constantly striving to develop the angelic part of his nature and to surpass his human condition. This is what might be called the angelic pretense in man whereby he tries to dilate his self and reach a knowledge that will be more intuitive and innate than his human intelligence.[3]

The prose poems of Rimbaud often appear exercises or strategems by which the poet is attempting to break down or efface the material world in order to reach the supernatural. In this aspect of his work, Rimbaud has no resemblance to Proust, but takes his place beside Plato and Plotinus and St. John of the Cross. To know the full poten-

---

[3] The best philosophical study of angels is by J. D. Collins, *The Thomistic Philosophy of the Angels* (Catholic University, 1947). The vast literature pertaining to the Manichaean heresy would be useful for this study. Manichaeism in love is treated in *L'Amour et l'Occident,* by Denis de Rougemont, and by C. S. Lewis, in *Allegory of Love.*

tiality, the full greatness of man, and especially to know more than his full greatness, brings with it a grave peril. The temptation of knowledge is closely related to sin. In Rimbaud's deep nostalgia for a world beyond the world, he remains aware of its danger and conscious of the dizziness of a possible great fall. Concomitant with his attraction toward heaven is a pulling downward. In Rimbaud is Prometheus the fire-stealer as well as Icarus, the one who fell after having risen high and close to suprasensible realities.

Despite the fact that angelism always involves the risk of the sin of pride, the poet's mission and the angel's have so intimate a resemblance that they often appear identical: that of putting men in some kind of relationship with a limitless world. The history of modern poetry in France since the beginning of the nineteenth century reflects a tendency toward angelism by its progressive spiritualization. Angelism explains more fully than any other single concept both the achievements and the failures, the conquests and the dangers, of modern poetry. Gérard de Nerval's angelism was his fervent approach to the abyss of the world and to his final defeat in madness. Baudelaire's angelism was quite evenly shared with his diabolism. The angel in him was always rising out of a knowledge of sin, out of a scene of debauchery. *Aube spirituelle* traces this metamorphosis of man turning angel as a reaction against excessive evil. But the lyric, *Les Plaintes d'un Icare,* is the fullest development of this spiritual adventure, so dangerous that it is fated to failure:

> *mes yeux consumés ne voient*
> *Que des souvenirs de soleils.*

Baudelaire resurrects all aspects of the myth in order to describe his spiritual aspiration and its collapse: his sunstruck eyes, his hope of finding the end of space, the burning from his love of the beautiful, the breaking of his wing, and his tombless death in the sea.

Jacques Maritain's definition of the angelic suicide as being the result of a forgetting of matter (*Suicide angéliste par oubli de la matière* [*Frontières de la Poésie*, p. 12]) applies more directly to Mallarmé than to Baudelaire or Rimbaud.[4] In the sonnet on Poe, Mallarmé ascribes to the poet the traits of an angel, and the entire piece describes the tomb as a stone fallen from the sky. Throughout all of Mallarmé's work the poet progressively moves closer to silence and absence. In *Les Fenêtres,* one of the early pieces, his angelism appears almost identifiable with narcissism:

Je me mire et me vois ange!

The protagonist is a dying man in a hospital who experiences a great revulsion against his dying and the world in which he is dying. His whole being protests against the drama of matter in which he is caught. He drags himself to the window and looks through it into a magnificent dream picture of a golden galley ship. His will is to break with his origin in sin and matter, and to recover a primordial innocency and purity of nature. In the vision he has of nature itself (and here the poem is reminiscent of *Les Illumina-*

---

[4] For Maritain, the function of Baudelaire and Rimbaud is that of having urged modern art to move beyond the frontiers of the spirit. But this is a region of extreme danger. Picasso he describes as one who is constantly approaching the sin of angelism. See p. 29: "Le rôle capital de Baudelaire et de Rimbaud c'est d'avoir fait passer à l'art moderne les frontières de l'esprit. Mais ces régions sont celles des suprêmes périls, les plus lourds problèmes métaphysiques y tombent sur la poésie, c'est là que se livrent combat les bons et les mauvais anges, et ceux-ci se déguisent en messagers de lumière."

tions), he sees an attempt at creation and rejuvenation similar to his own personal attempt. But the drama of *Igitur*, and what Claudel is to call "the catastrophe" of *Igitur*, is the tragic conclusion of this superhuman effort to escape from concrete reality.[5] Whereas the hallucinations of Rimbaud have the prestige of color and movement and pageantry, those of Mallarmé are the fear of impotency and defeat, the poems themselves on absence and non-being.

Rimbaud is so totally impregnated with angelism that one almost forgets to specify it. Angels, it is true, appear very rarely in his text (they figure notably in *Mémoire* and *Mystique*). But the *chasse spirituelle* of Rimbaud, the title of his lost manuscript which applies so admirably to all his work, is a form of angelic temptation. Certain brief, elliptical sentences, such as *La vraie vie est absente,* which corroborate an angel's outlook, resound higher than all others. The will to become magus or angel (*moi qui me suis dit mage ou ange,* in *Adieu*) and to enter into competition with the creation is the will of the man-angel, described by Verlaine in *Crimen amoris,* when he has Rimbaud exclaim that he will create God Himself!

> *Oh! je serai celui-là qui créera Dieu!*

---

[5] Claudel's essay is now reprinted in his first volume of *Positions et Propositions,* pp. 195–207. The Hamlet theme in the nineteenth century, or man's complacency with disaster and night, he relates to the work of Poe, Baudelaire, and especially Mallarmé. "Il s'est trouvé au 19e siècle une lignée parfaitement déterminée de trois poètes, dont la grande nuit métaphysique, qui est non pas le néant mais le silence de la lumière (Dante), était pour ainsi dire le climat spirituel, elle formait la condition même de leur parole et de leur œuvre, le fond nécessaire à leur apparition" (p. 198).

Impressively, the list of quotations where Rimbaud claims an exit from the world could lengthen: *Décidément, nous sommes hors du monde (Nuit de l'enfer)*; *je suis réellement d'outre-tombe (Vies I)*; a change of the familiar self into a more real self: *car Je est un autre (Lettre du voyant)*; a knowledge of the spirit's battle: *le combat spirituel est aussi brutal que la bataille d'hommes (Adieu)*.

It was a long evolution to experience, from his Gallic ancestors with their sense of sacrilege and lust, which Rimbaud felt to be an important part of his heritage, to the secret need of redemption in the angelic models ahead of him. *Une Saison en enfer* narrates his consciousness of the pull both ways: backward, first, toward the obscure people of his origins whom he sensed in his threatened health and his remembrance of terror: *Ma santé fut menacée. La terreur venait (Délires II)*; and then ahead, to the premonitions of a reality existing beyond that translated in *Les Illuminations*. What we know of the biography itself is a cruel contradiction of this premonition, which was replaced by eighteen years of long expiation, eighteen years of commerce with the harshest kind of reality.

On first view, *Les Illuminations* does not seem to be made up of poems of unhappiness, but rather it seems remarkably estranged from the familiar themes of pain and suffering in the earlier poems. Yet, in deeper readings of the prose poems, the poet's passion does appear purely destructive, and directed against the entire world. They are experiments with destruction, with a dazzling effacement of all appearances and all forms of the world. But this fundamental force of destruction creates the fragmentary, elusive beauty which characterizes *Les Illuminations*. Before the extinction of light, a fairy-like wonder world of glittering brilliance explodes: *Les brasiers, pleuvant aux rafales de givre* ("the embers raining gusts of frost"; *Barbare*); *les herbages d'acier and des prés de flammes* ("pastures of steel" and "meadows of flames"; *Mystique*); *des anges de flamme et de glace* ("angels of flame and ice"; *Matinée d'ivresse*); etc. The experience is always taking place on the frontiers of the known world. And within the poems themselves the explosion of the real fires is always being converted into ice and cold. To freeze a fire would be to fix and stabilize the ephemeral, to effect a purification.

To reach such a point, beyond the vulnerable world of explosions, would be the attainment to a self-sufficiency. *Les Illuminations* is one work in the evolution of a century during which poetry was constantly striving to know a self-sufficiency. It was seeking its sources more and more deeply within the self of the poet, within his bottomless secrets. One whole aspect of modern poetry has been a metaphysical sounding of the poet's self. To this search *Une Saison en enfer* has made a rich contribution. Another aspect of modern poetry, and one that is closely allied with the metaphysical investigation, is an effort to dissolve the real world, to bring about a disintegration of the concrete physical world, by means of language. *Les Illuminations* is the outstanding work of this nature. Great poetry has always demonstrated a turning-away from what is "real" in the world. It may become an object of poetry if it is incorporated emotionally by the poet. This is the attempt to render eternal something which by its nature is sensational and hence fleeting. The despair of never being able to reach the absolute lies immediately beyond every poem. In this sense, every poem is certain of failure and predicts the poet's silence. Even more than *Une Saison, Les Illuminations* predicts and explains Rimbaud's silence. Rimbaud attempted what he knew was impossible and therefore produced a poetry of latent catastrophe. He was even more victimized by his angelic ambition than Baudelaire, who was more firmly held prisoner by his dreams and demons and the ever-widening abyss at his feet.

Behind the will to destroy, which Rimbaud illustrates in his role of angel of vengeance, exist his knowledge and use of a freedom of the spirit which, again, we usually associate with angels. The godlike myth of Prometheus and the angelic myth of Icarus, as they appear in Rimbaud, renew the vigor of ancient symbols, those closely connected with the destiny of man in its highest spiritual power. Rimbaud's mythology seeks to create a very concrete angelic love and poetry in which the concepts of freedom and revolution will liberate the human spirit. When he considers his past, he beholds a series of metamorphoses, a spirit seeking an emancipation from some form of enslavement or limitation. When he considers his future, he sees the emancipated spirit in a recovered state of innocency and limpidness.

Rimbaud was old enough, ironically, in his late adolescence to have lived through most of the dreams of humanity. After remembering or even experiencing directly many kinds of mortal liberties, he looked forward to absolute liberty, to that liberty which André Breton, many years after Rimbaud, will define as the final exaltation of man: *Le seul mot de liberté est tout ce qui m'exalte encore* (*Premier Manifeste du Surréalisme*, 1924). The angel's liberty is total dedication of love. The angel would be the original model for all the idols which succeeding centuries of humanity have covered with gold or bronze or patina. The poet Rimbaud tried to remove these layers of metal and color, and in doing so appeared more of an iconoclast than the purifier he was.

Génie, more than any other single poem, paints the poet in his traits of a supernatural envoy and even of a god who manifests himself in the guise of a human without ever relinquishing his supernatural prerogatives. The angel and the poet are here called "genie," who is spoken of in the third person (*Il est l'affection et le présent*), even as the self was spoken of in the *Lettre du voyant: car Je est au autre.* He is the unity containing all forms, all perfections, all achievements. He is especially characterized by the flight of the spirit over all the earth, touching and joining all opposites. *Génie* is in itself a *chasse spirituelle* where the soul possesses angelic knowledge and an extraordinary power of detachment from the real world. The legend of the poem seems to be the genie's power to destroy the real world in order to reach what lies beyond the real. It is the apprenticeship of ecstasy where the poet, turned angel, seeks to know the ideas which lie beyond their derived philosophies.

But such an experience is fated to end in failure in terms of the angel-poet. The poet in his work wills to explain what he has seen and learned, whereas the angel gives no thought to self-expression, no thought to communicating his experience of immanency. The poet is multiple in that one part of him experiences and another part tries to write of the experience. The temptation of silence is always the sign of the poet turning mystic. *Je voudrais me taire,* Rimbaud wrote in *Une Saison;* and also, *je ne sais plus parler!* (*Matin*). The human spirit, as such, seems incapable of self-conquest.

Rimbaud marks a central stage of development in the history of modern French poetry, between Nerval and Claudel, which is best described as a re-sanctification or re-spiritualization of human speech. His work, abruptly and dramatically interrupted when it seemed compelled by a mystical silence, was succeeded by certain writings of Mallarmé which have given a more serene confirmation to the inevitable poetic failure. The intolerance of the adolescent rebel was followed by the longer vigilance of Mallarmé, with his incomparable mastery of poetic form, but the older poet waged a similar battle, that of his being against the void. The single proposition of his final work, *Un coup de dés jamais n'abolira le hasard,* states the central struggle of a human will engaged in an effort to defeat chance, and condemned to failure. Mallarmé, no less than Rimbaud, is the plaything or the victim of the rapid, seemingly disconnected images that rise up from his own unconscious, and which in the poem rise up from the sea, an ever-changing world of chance. The will of the poet, like the will of the pilot in the shipwreck scene of *Un coup de dés,* tries to rescue some of the surging, restless images by capturing them at their very source and finding suitable words that will espouse their form and vigor. But science is illusory for both poet and pilot. They are both caught in a world of becoming in which every moment will be different from all others, and they too will be different no matter how strong and controlled and directed by instinctive powers the will of the poet may be, and no matter how vast the scientific knowledge of the pilot, since the ocean is subject to unpredictable and all-powerful forces. A storm at sea, such as that figured in *Un coup de dés,* is comparable to the intimate obsessions and anxieties of such a poet as Rimbaud. Chance cannot be abolished from the art of navigation, and it cannot be abolished from the development of a single thought. Before a thought (or a poem) reaches its complete expression, it releases unpredictable emotions and sensations that are going to participate in the completing of its form.

Rimbaud tried to make of poetry a magic means of seizing and articulating what is ineffable, and therefore to make of the poet a kind of medium, as receptive to poetic speech as an angel's will is receptive to God's. He tried to make of the poetic word an instrument of discovery, a new language which is not so much an expression in the usual sense as it is a sign of his spirit. His temperament unquestionably had traces of auto-divinization. *Car Je est un autre* might well mean that he is a potential god. *Mage ou ange?* he queries. His tremendous effort to establish a relationship between the lowest and the highest in him, by means of his celebrated derangement (*dérèglement*), is another version of the Apollonian-Dionysian union, a will to escape from his purely human condition.

The weakness of language is its vagueness, its character of approximation, which Rimbaud tried to suppress by finding a closer identification between a thing and its verbal expression. By the pure use of language, Rimbaud created for himself a method of knowledge, or at least what can be called his knowledge of the universe, his relationship with the universe and his power over it. The so-called philosophical attitudes which may be derived from his work were never solutions for him. They were temptations or ways of escape. He tried one after the other as a child might: flight from the world (*Le Bateau ivre*), a merging of himself with the elemental forces of nature (*Génie*), and a repudiation of the world sullied by sin (*Nuit de l'enfer*).

He willed to make himself free as a man and as a poet, only to find that this freedom resulted in an extraordinary solitude, such as only an angel could bear. Childhood wounded him and made him a poet, when he began roving through cities and countries and crossing seas. His human ill-success taught him a rapture so pure that he was able to live in the deserts of the heart. He changed a world. And today he is not so much a poet as he is the world he invented, the climate he created.

In *Une Saison en enfer* he came to grips with the most dangerous passions, those which expose a man and which reveal him consecrated to suffering and to death. There he was the tragic hero because he had cut himself off from the laws, the constraints, and the habits which civilization interposes between man and his passions or his fate. There he belongs to the small group of tragic people eternally separated from mankind, and perpetuating the image of an implacable catastrophe. But in *Les Illuminations* his actions and flights resound strangely in a universal harmony. There the moments he describes are fabulous, and his beauty is ineffable, like that of the genie of *Conte* who dies with the prince because he *is* the prince. There, poetry is immanence for the genie who covers the entire universe in his flights and knows the principle of things in the fecundity of his spirit.

Appendix

Rimbaud in the Sorbonne

THE ORAL doctoral examination in an American university has little resemblance to the *soutenance de thèse* for the "state doctorate" which is the highest degree the Sorbonne offers. The ceremony in Paris is open to the public. It occurs quite frequently and in most cases is a tiresome procedure. The duty of the jury, usually composed of five professors, is to point out the inadequacies, weaknesses, and omissions of the theses, both the main thesis and the complementary one. On January 12, 1952, in the Salle Liard, the *soutenance* of M. René Etiemble, on the *Myth of Rimbaud,* was, on the contrary, one of the main events of the season. The large hall was crowded with students, professors, writers, and notables from Paris society.

The jury was composed of Professors Levaillant, Carré, Bruneau (who presided), Jasinski, and Dédeyan. Each in turn complimented M. Etiemble on the giganticism of his task and spoke on some aspect of the two theses. Levaillant, first, praised the indefatigable scholar. Etiemble had been working on his investigation for twenty years. His subject

259

was accepted by the Sorbonne in 1937. Since that time he had lived in the United States (where he taught at the University of Chicago), in Central America, in Egypt. He had accumulated 16,000 *fiches* or items on the myth of Rimbaud—a prodigious documentation, even for a *thèse de doctorat* at the Sorbonne. He had read in many foreign languages and discovered practically everything published about Rimbaud between 1869 and 1950. Between the school of symbolism and the most recent movement of "lettrism," Etiemble studied every attempt to make of Rimbaud what he calls a myth or a fable disproving or controverting the truth. To his first novels (*Un Enfant de chœur* and *Peau de Couleuvre*) and to his explosive critical writing in *Les Temps modernes,* Etiemble added a long work of meticulous scholarship. The theses had been read only by the jurymen, and they indicated often during the examination that Etiemble had not altered, for the writing of his *Mythe de Rimbaud,* his polemical style. Levaillant pleaded with Etiemble to soften some of his attacks. When Dédeyan stated that Etiemble risked being excommunicated from all churches, the candidate replied under his breath that such was his hope.

Etiemble explained that at the beginning the object of his research was purely bibliographical. But as time went on, he became aware of a forceful "influence" on literature, of scandalous interpretations of Rimbaud which constitute the "myth."

The thesis bears not on the works of Rimbaud, but on his commentators, who are legion. M. Etiemble calls the genre he is attacking "mythistory." What characterizes the literary myths of Rimbaud is the fact that each is based on some error of interpretation of a very limited number of texts. For the symbolists it was particularly *Le Bateau ivre.*

For the surrealists it was the prose work, *Un Cœur sous une soutane*. The Catholic myth of Rimbaud's deathbed conversion was promulgated by his sister Isabelle, but Etiemble points out that another witness, Riès, claims the poet died with blasphemy on his lips. More important than these contradictory stories is the entire myth of Rimbaud which Etiemble sees as a completely organized religion, with its forms of worship, its ceremonies, its sacred books, its sacred interpretations. The use of the scholastic term *aseity,* meaning the quality of belonging to what is by itself (God), in a poem on Rimbaud by Louis de Gonzague-Frick, is a convincing proof to Etiemble that a new religion has been formed around Rimbaud. He calls the eyewitnesses of the poet's life the "evangelists": Verlaine, Isabelle the sister, her husband Peterne Berrichon, a school friend Ernest Delahaye. They were responsible for the first exaggerations, for the method by which each school in turn has appropriated Rimbaud: symbolists, surrealists, Fascists, Communists, existentialists.

The interpretations of the "sacred" texts have played an important part in the development of such myths—the meaning of the word *illumination,* for example, and of the phrase *Je est un autre.* Finally, when Rimbaud has been treated as demon, angel, magician, prophet, nothing human remains. Rimbaud is a god. This is the result, for Etiemble, of the curious combination of hagiography and scandal characterizing the works of Rimbaud. He insists that a new religion has been born which is one manifestation of the mysticism impairing the intelligence of our period, and which equates the name of Rimbaud with Hitler, Stalin, Father Divine. Etiemble's inquisition spares no one. He disapproves especially of the Catholic interpretation, the writings of such men as Daniel-Rops and Claudel.

On the whole, the members of the jury manifested a profound respect for Etiemble and for the extent of his knowledge, for his powers of destruction. At one moment, M. Levaillant, realizing the candidate's passion for truth, quoted, *Amicus Plato, sed magis amica veritas.* M. Dédeyan, the Sorbonne professor of comparative literature, reminded Etiemble that he had claimed the birth today of other literary myths—Lorca, T. E. Lawrence, Genet, Artaud—and asked whether Lautréamont should not be added to the list. Etiemble replied that in a recent stock-taking, Rimbaud surpassed Lautréamont and Mallarmé combined, and that he feared the Artaud myth promulgated by the *Revue K,* where the name Artaud was considered to be a mysterious contraction of *Art*(hur Rimb)*aud.*

During the second half of the *soutenance,* Professor Carré, in his praise of Etiemble's work, called it the most extensive investigation on a quasi-contemporary writer. He even confessed that he himself had added to the myth of Rimbaud as Christian, and approved of Etiemble's castigating himself for contributing to the myth of Rimbaud as *communard.* M. Jasinski, the last of the jury to speak, was the most critical, the most adverse to the idea of the thesis and especially to the spirit in which it had been written. He even suggested that Etiemble does not like Rimbaud and is perpetrating in his thesis some kind of vengeance on the poet who must have harmed him when he was young! In describing the thesis as a whole, he used the word *canular,* from the language of the Ecole Normale Supérieure, which designates an elaborate trick of mystification.

Despite this severe stricture, the decision of the jury was unanimous in granting M. Etiemble the degree of *doctorat d'état, mention très honorable, à l'unanimité.*

The word *canular* must have struck the imagination of

Etiemble who, from Montpellier where he resumed his teaching in the university (today his professorship is at the Sorbonne), sent to the weekly newspaper *Arts* a letter on the question of whether the myth of Rimbaud is a *canular*. At the time of the *soutenance,* the word had amused him. He knew the rules of the game demanded that the jury inflict some degree of torture on the candidate-victim. But with the report that the sociologist Roger Caillois had also considered exaggerated the use of "myth" or "religion" when it was only a question of verbal inflation, Etiemble began wondering if he himself were the real creator of the myth and whether he had been deceiving himself during the twenty years' labor. He reread his 2,000 pages without having his convictions altered. In applying the word myth to the first part of his *Structure du Mythe*—the various characterizations of Rimbaud as surrealist, existentialist, Communist, *voyou,* atheist, Catholic, etc.—he is using the term in its loosest connotation of error, collective lie, illusion. But in the second part of the main thesis, he uses the word in its fuller sense of legend in its relationship with the supernatural and involving some kind of rite. The fact that twenty authors have spoken of Rimbaud as the myth of Satan, and that André Breton in the surrealist exhibition of 1947 erected an altar to Léonie Aubois d'Ashby, the mysterious heroine of one of the *Illuminations,* has helped to justify Etiemble's second use of myth in the central part of his thesis. He claims that the statement by Pierre Debray is not at all exceptional: "Since God exempted Rimbaud from the ordinary condition of man, his immaculate conception . . ." A decalcomania has been created in which every episode in Rimbaud's life corresponds to an episode in the life of Christ: the birth at Bethlehem, the debate with the doctors, the forty days in the desert, the way of the cross, the death, resurrection, transfiguration. The sacrament of suicide has been initiated by Vaché, Rigaud, Hart Crane, in the name of Rimbaud.

The sentence of Roger Caillois, whispered to a neighbor at the *soutenance:* "Ils appellent ça religion, ce n'est que de l'inflation verbale," was quoted by Etiemble in his letter to *Arts* and provoked a reply from Caillois himself the following week. Caillois first emphasized that the "they" of his sentences refers to everyone: the critics of Rimbaud who consider him a god, and the professors of the Sorbonne jury inasmuch as they agree with the investigation. Etiemble's article in *Arts* had clearly defined the two uses of myth. Caillois has no quarrel with the first general meaning of falsification. It is the second, sociological meaning of the term, as used by Etiemble, that Caillois questions. Both aspects are based upon words, expressions, metaphors. The vocabulary is religious, but Caillois considers that the writers who used it were not religious. The fact that they said Rimbaud was a god does not necessarily imply that they believed it. The altar erected by Breton was a poetic gesture and the word *aseity,* used by Louis de Gonzague-Frick, may have been borrowed from Apollinaire's *Le Larron.* Breton's altar had no piety attached to it, and the word *aseity* had no connection with dogma. Caillois wonders whether the recent postage stamps bearing the face of Rimbaud (from the Fantin-Latour portrait) have greatly affected the idolaters. Between such phenomena and religion in its pure sense there are many intermediaries. A suicide, for example, is neither a rite nor a sacrament unless it be performed in some kind of ceremony and fulfil some theological function. Otherwise it is simply a gesture of revolt or despair, far more philosophical than religious. To substantiate his viewpoint, Caillois recalled the activities of the bobby-soxers in relationship to Frank Sinatra. There were societies formed, insignia, faintings, collective manifestations. Articles in the *New Yorker* revealed that a religious vocabulary was used and a degree of ecstasy reached in some of the manifestations which seemed liturgical. If the fanatical disciples of Rimbaud have created out of his life a decalcomania of the life of Jesus, it is important to remember that a decalcomania of a religion is not a religion.

The writer Joseph Delteil, who has lived for some years near Montpellier, participated once in the debate in a letter sent to *Arts*. Rimbaud is not a god (Delteil thanks heaven for that!) but he is not an ordinary poet. For Delteil the question of Rimbaud's humanity comes first. On the day Rimbaud chose Harar rather than the Académie Française or the island of Guernsey, he instilled in every artist an uneasy conscience. The fact that Rimbaud turned to hard manual labor after writing such a work as *Une Saison en enfer* marks the outstanding logic of the poet's life.

Each week in Paris the critical debate grew more complicated. It is a usual thing for a critic to write about a poet. Etiemble's thesis is more unusual: a man writes on the men who wrote on a poet. Then Caillois wrote on Etiemble, and in *Arts* Arthur Adamov wrote on Caillois and on Etiemble's article. In reading the latter article, Adamov grew angry because he could find nowhere Etiemble's personal view of Rimbaud. He developed Etiemble's notion of myth by claiming the existence of a myth whenever there exists an identification between a few men and a single man who takes on for them a character symbolic of what they would like to be. Each creative artist whose work transcribes the particular torment of its age becomes an idealized picture whose formation and success are indeed worthy subjects of study. Adamov feared that Etiemble had not gone beyond the stage of pure documentation, the establishment of a gigantic card index. Adamov's criticism joined that of others in finding an irritated, impassioned style in Etiemble's writing which impaired the pure objectivity of his research. The difficulty is in the differentiation among the various cults of Rimbaud: the Catholic apologists, André Breton's fetishistic attitude, and the narratives of personal recollection. Perhaps more from Etiemble's style than from the "evidence" he has accumulated, one feels he is put out by any kind of attention given to Rimbaud.

On the one hand are the facts of Rimbaud's life: his precociousness as a poet at fourteen; the revolt he waged against his family, his city, and all bourgeois standards; his study of the occult sciences; his flair for shocking; his vagabond life with Verlaine; his denunciation of rationalism; his poetic work with its important innovations in the art of the prose poem; his flight from Europe and existence as a merchant-adventurer in Africa; his agonized return to France and death in the Marseilles hospital. It would be difficult to find a poet's life more susceptible than Rimbaud's of varying interpretations, more capable of engendering an entire body of legend. The contribution of Etiemble to Rimbaud scholarship is to confirm what already seems truthful concerning Rimbaud and to complete, as far as possible, the work of extirpating the false from the true. Already, for example, the precociousness of Rimbaud as poet had been confirmed, but the originality of the early poems had been seriously questioned. The struggle he waged with his mother and immediate surroundings is certainly a fact, but there is nothing so vastly extraordinary about his revolt. Most boys would have behaved in the same way, given the same conditions. The insistence upon the extent of his readings in occultism was radically modified once the list of books in the public library of Charleville was established. His sullenness and unbearable behavior in literary groups in Paris might easily have masked the typical timidity and gaucherie of a young fellow from the provinces. The only real documents existing on Rimbaud's life with Verlaine are the writings of the two poets themselves. What remains of Rimbaud after all the errors have been rectified and the disguises removed is the poet-creator of a new work and the twenty-year-old poet who renounced all literary activity and who held to his word to the end.

M. Etiemble knows the writings of Rimbaud as well as any living critic. The value of his thesis is not so much the denunciation of the errors concerning Rimbaud as the study of the genesis of those errors and the particular ways in which they were propagated. At the poet's death, his sister and brother-in-law were largely instrumental in disseminating an account of Rimbaud's death and of his conversion *in extremis.* The symbolists named Rimbaud a forerunner of their school and the type of *poète maudit,* but they knew very few of his poems and praised them excessively, according to Etiemble who has little respect for such a poem as *Le Bateau ivre.* Rimbaud's myth, in its religious sense, developed in the period of surrealism, between the years 1920 and 1935. Those were the ten years when, according to Etiemble, men began living by the rules of Rimbaud, and derived from his work suicidal doctrines.

One of the members of the Sorbonne jury believed that M. Etiemble's thesis will instigate a new chapter in literary history. Other similar myths have existed and continue to exist, and literary scholarship during the past fifty or sixty years has been concerned with contradictory, well-established errors—the myth, for example, of Chateaubriand's trip to America and the extent of his travels there, and the myth of Molière's life and character. Certain contemporary writers have themselves tried to counteract their myths as they were in the process of developing. Jean-Paul Sartre, for example, has helped to diminish his Saint-Germain-des-Prés legend, and André Gide, in his posthumously published *Et nunc manet in te,* gave to his own portrait a pathetically human explanation.

Selected Bibliography

EDITIONS OF RIMBAUD

Œuvres Complètes. Texte établi et annoté par Rolland de Renéville et Jules Mouquet, "Bibliothèque de la Pléiade," Gallimard, 1946. Nouvelle édition revue, 1954.

Poésies. Edition critique. Introduction et notes par H. de Bouillane de Lacoste. Mercure de France, 1939.

Une Saison en enfer. Edition critique. Introduction et notes par H. de Bouillane de Lacoste. Mercure de France, 1941.

Les Illuminations. Edition critique. Introduction et notes par H. de Bouillane de Lacoste. Mercure de France, 1949.

Œuvres. Introduction, notices et notes par Suzanne Bernard. Classiques Garnier, 1960.

BOOKS ON RIMBAUD

Arnoult, Pierre, *Rimbaud*. Albin Michel, 1943; nouvelle édition, 1955.

Bouillane de Lacoste, Henry de, *Rimbaud et le problème des Illuminations*. Mercure de France, 1949.

Breton, André, *Flagrant Délit*. Thésée, 1949.

Carré, Jean-Marie, *La Vie aventureuse de Rimbaud*. Plon, 1926; réédition augmentée, 1949.

Cassou, Jean, *Pour la Poésie*. Corréa, 1935.

Chadwick, C., *Etudes sur Rimbaud*. Nizet, 1960.

Coulon, Marcel, *Le Problème de Rimbaud: poète maudit*. Gomès, Nîmes, 1923.

Coulon, Marcel, *La Vie de Rimbaud et de son œuvre*. Mercure de France, 1929.

Daniel-Rops, *Rimbaud, le drame spirituel*. Plon, 1936.

Debray, Pierre, *Rimbaud, le magicien désabusé*. Julliard, 1948.

Delahaye, Ernest, *La Part de Verlaine et Rimbaud dans le sentiment religieux contemporain*. Messein, 1935.

Delahaye, Ernest, *Souvenirs familiers à propos de Rimbaud, Verlaine, Germain Nouveau*. Messein, 1925.

Etiemble et Gauclère, *Rimbaud*. Gallimard, 1950.

Etiemble, René, *Le Mythe de Rimbaud*, t. 1: *genèse du mythe*. Gallimard, 1954; t. 2: *structure du mythe*. Gallimard, 1952. Nouvelle édition, 1961.

Fondane, Benjamin, *Rimbaud le voyou*. Denoël et Steele, 1933.

Fowlie, Wallace, *Rimbaud*. New Directions, 1946. Dennis Dobson, London, 1947.

Fowlie, Wallace, *The Clown's Grail*. Dobson, London, 1948 (chapter on Rimbaud and Crane).

Fowlie, Wallace, *Rimbaud's Illuminations*. Grove Press, 1953, and Harvill Press, London, 1953.

Frétet, Jean, *L'Aliénation poétique*. Janin, 1946.

Frohock, W. M., *Rimbaud's Poetic Practice*. Harvard University Press, 1963.

Gengoux, Jacques, *La Symbolique de Rimbaud*. La Colombe, 1947.

Godchot, Colonel, *Arthur Rimbaud ne varietur*. Chez l'auteur, Nice, 1936.

Goffin, Robert, *Rimbaud vivant*. Avant-propos de Jean Cassou. Corréa, 1937.

Graaf, Daniel de, *Arthur Rimbaud*. Van Gorcum, Assen, 1948.

Hackett, C. A., *Rimbaud l'enfant*. Préface de G. Bachelard. Corti, 1948.

Hackett, C. A., *Rimbaud*. Bowes and Bowes, 1957.

Houston, J. P., *The Design of Rimbaud's Poetry*. Yale University Press, 1963.

Izambard, Georges, *Rimbaud tel que je l'ai connu*. Mercure de France, 1946.

Losseau, Léon, *La Légende de la destruction par Rimbaud de l'édition princeps de Une Saison en Enfer*. Bruxelles, 1916.

Magny, Claude-Edmonde, *Arthur Rimbaud*. Pierre Seghers, 1949.

Mallarmé, Stéphane, *Œuvres Complètes*. Gallimard, "Pléiade," 1945.

Matarasso, Henri, et Petitfils, Pierre, *Vie d'Arthur Rimbaud*. Hachette, 1962.

Méléra, M.-Y. *Résonances autour de Rimbaud*. Editions du Myrte, 1946.

Miller, Henry, *The Time of the Assassins*. New Directions, 1956.

Mondor, Henri, *Rimbaud ou le génie impatient*. Gallimard, 1955.

Renéville, Rolland de, *Rimbaud le voyant*. La Colombe, 1947.

Rimbaud: documents iconographiques. Préface et notes par F. Ruchon. Genève, 1946.

Rivière, Jacques, *Rimbaud*. Kra, 1930.

Ruchon, F., *Jean-Arthur Rimbaud. Sa vie, son œuvre, son influence*. Champion, 1929.

Silvain, René, *Rimbaud le précurseur*. Boivin, 1945.

Starkie, Enid, *Arthur Rimbaud*. Faber, 1938. New Edition, Hamish Hamilton, London, 1947. W. W. Norton, New York, 1947. New Directions, 1961.

Tzara, Tristan, Introduction, *Œuvres Complètes de Rimbaud*. Editions du grand chêne. Lausanne, n.d.

Verlaine, *Les Poètes maudits*. Messein, 1920.

ARTICLES ON RIMBAUD

Blanchot, Maurice, "Le Sommeil de Rimbaud," *Critique*, No. 10, 1947.

Bousquet, Joë, "Rimbaud et Swedenborg," *Critique*, No. 35, 1949.

Claudel, Paul, Préface aux *Œuvres de Rimbaud*. Mercure de France, 1912. (Reprinted in *Positions et Propositions*.)

Etiemble, "Le Mythe de Rimbaud," *Revue de Littérature Comparée*, January, 1939, pp. 172–77.

Etiemble, "De Rimbaud à Rimbaud," *Les Temps Modernes*, October, 1949.

Etiemble, "Le Sonnet des voyelles," *Revue de Littérature Comparée*, April, 1939, pp. 235–61.

Fowlie, Wallace, "Rimbaud in 1949," *Poetry* (Chicago), December, 1949.

Fowlie, Wallace, "Rimbaud in the Sorbonne," *Partisan Review*, November, 1952.

Mackworth, Cecily, "Arthur Rimbaud," *Horizon*, vol. IX. No. 51, London, 1944.

Mespoulet, Marguerite, "Des Natchez au bateau ivre," *Revue de Littérature Comparée*, XIII (1933), 299–316.

R. F., "A-t-on lu Rimbaud?" *Bizarre*, Nos. 21, 22, 1961.

Weinberg, Bernard, "Le Bateau ivre or the limits of symbolism," *PMLA*, LXII (1959), 165–93.

Zabel, Morton Dauwen, "Rimbaud: Life and Legend," *Partisan Review*, July–August, 1940, pp. 268–82.

OTHER BOOKS USED IN THIS STUDY

Breton, André, *Manifeste du surréalisme*. Kra, 1924.

Claudel, Paul, *Positions et propositions*. Gallimard, 1928.

Cocteau, Jean, *Lettre à Jacques Maritain*. Stock, 1926.

Cocteau, Jean, *Le Rappel à l'ordre*. Stock, 1926.

Coléno, Alice, *Les Portes d'ivoire*. Plon, 1948.

Collins, J. D., *The Thomistic Philosophy of the Angels*. Catholic University, 1947.

Friche, Ernest, *Etudes claudéliennes*. Editions des Portes de France, Porrentruy, 1943.

Maritain, Jacques, *Frontières de la poésie*. Plon, 1927.

Maritain, Jacques, *Réponse à Jean Cocteau*. Stock, 1926.

Monnerot, Jules, *La Poésie moderne et le sacré*. Gallimard, 1945.

Raymond, Marcel, *De Baudelaire au surréalisme*. Corréa, 1947.

Wilson, Edmund, *Axel's Castle*. Scribner's, 1931.

Index of Names

Index of Titles

278